D1596493

Autonomy at Work

Gerald I. Susman
foreword by
Eric Trist

The Praeger Special Studies program—utilizing the most modern and efficient book production techniques and a selective worldwide distribution network—makes available to the academic, government, and business communities significant, timely research in U.S. and international economic, social, and political development.

Autonomy at Work

A Sociotechnical Analysis of Participative Management

PRAEGER SPECIAL STUDIES IN U.S. ECONOMIC, SOCIAL, AND POLITICAL ISSUES

Praeger Publishers New York Washington London

Library of Congress Cataloging in Publication Data

Susman, Gerald I
Autonomy at work.

(Praeger special studies in U.S. economic, social, and political issues)
Bibliography: p.
Includes indexes.
1. Industrial organization. 2. Work design. 3. Psychology, Industrial. I. Title.
HD31.S767 658.4 75-23997
ISBN 0-275-56140-2

PRAEGER PUBLISHERS
111 Fourth Avenue, New York, N.Y. 10003, U.S.A.

Published in the United States of America in 1976
by Praeger Publishers, Inc.

Printed in the United States of America

To my wife, Liz

FOREWORD

Eric L. Trist

This book by Gerald Susman is a welcome addition to the growing literature concerned with the quality of life in the work place as a central component of the quality of life as a whole. This literature is searching for an alternative to the bureaucratic form of organization, one that will be democratic and variety increasing rather than authoritarian and variety decreasing and one where personal fulfillment is a value conjoint with operational effectiveness. So far, this literature has lacked an overall conceptual account that brings together the basic ideas that have influenced its development. Susman's book fills this gap.

The basic ideas involved have a greater historical depth and a wider theoretical range than many people today realize. They depend on a recognition of the critical importance of the principle of self-regulation, or self-organization. The foundations of this theoretical tradition were laid before World War I in the classic experiments of the Gestalt psychologists, which demonstrated the importance of wholes in organizing the world of the perceiving and thinking human subject. In the interwar period Kurt Lewin extended this work into the areas of intention and will and in order to do so developed a field theory of human action. During his Berlin period, he carried out a series of major experiments on individual-task relations. Later, on coming to the United States, he extended these studies to the level of the group, founding at the end of World War II the discipline of Group Dynamics. Once it was demonstrated that the group had holistic properties that could vary between different configurations, as in experimentally created group climates, the group could become a field of empirical psychological inquiry.

Without the legacy of these studies we should be in a poor position today to tackle the problems involved either in the design of new forms of work organization or in the redesign of existing forms, many of which are showing signs of increasing dysfunction. The critical importance of wholeness of task, meaningfulness, relatedness, autonomy, discretion, learning, and participation were all adumbrated in this early work. Susman has steeped himself in the original sources. His book richly benefits thereby.

Another tradition on which he draws is that part of psychoanalytic theory that emphasizes object relations—that is, the relations, unconscious as well as conscious, between the individual and both his fantasized and real others and their interplay. This tradition was developed by a number of British psychoanalysts from the 1930s onwards—not only Melanie Klein (1932, 1948) but such writers as Fairbairn (1952) and Winnicott (1958). At first sight, this may seem a far cry from the worker and the work place, but Susman uses the object relations idea to extend Chein's (1972) concept of directed action, which he makes the basis for the theory of motivation he develops. This putting together of a psychoanalytic concept with one deriving from the Lewinian tradition is a significant step forward. The future-oriented force field created by the linked sets of objects with which the individual aspires to complete a relationship produces the process that may be called work. "Hic labor, hic opus est" as Virgil once said. If one may translate "labor" as effort, one might perhaps in a modern idiom translate "opus" as project and infer that in the nature of the project lies the meaning of the effort. But effort is necessary to attain meaning, since the objects with which one must relate in order to accomplish human purposes, whether belonging to one's internal world or one's external environment, are not completely under one's control. In order to succeed, one has actively to use one's adaptive capacities and to be able to learn from experience. The reduction of the concept of work to that of a commodity, a certain amount of which one sells in the marketplace (only too often to perform machinelike tasks), is a trivialization of a basic human activity that has pervaded industrial society. The coming of a postindustrial order may restore the concept of work to its full human dimension.

During the years immediately following World War II the object-relations idea was transposed from the level of the individual to the level of the group. Bion (1947-51) in a series of remarkable papers added a depth dimension to group dynamics, distinguishing the "work group" carrying out a purpose involving a task in the real world from the "basic group" operating on unconscious and unlearned assumptions. At the Tavistock Institute where Bion was working, these ideas became fused with those of the Lewinian tradition and were carried into organizational studies based on an action-research approach concerned with improving organizational performance and the quality of work experience.

At first these studies focused on organizations exclusively as social systems (Jaques 1953), but it soon became apparent that the technology had also to be included as a critical presence in what Lewin had called "the hull of non-psychological facts" in the life space of the group. As part of the culture of the work group in Bion's sense, technology could be used both as an instrument and as a defense. Moreover, the way technology was used in contemporary organizations embodied an ideology, the value system of production engineering, based on a mechanical world view that provided the design principle on which was built the social no less than the technical side of organizations. Herein lay a contradiction, for man and the groups he forms are based not on mechanical but organismic principles. Many years later Emery (1967) was to formulate this difference as a choice in design principles between the redundancy of parts and the redundancy of functions.

Susman has used this idea as the starting point for much of his thinking about job design, and indeed it is a concept that may be said to have changed the field at the highest level or generalization.

At this earlier time, realization of the importance of the distinction came about through action-research studies that the Tavistock Institute was invited to undertake in the British coal-mining industry, where nationalization had done nothing to ameliorate bad labor relations or low productivity. These, it was found, stemmed in large measure from the mechanical way (involving far-reaching job breakdown into one-man/one-task units) in which work was organized at the coal face. Unless this was changed, little improvement could be expected. An alternative was available in "composite working," which had evolved from certain traditions belonging to the less mechanized days of the industry in which autonomous groups undertook the whole work of the production cycle, flexibly interchanging tasks and shifts among themselves. Composite was superior to conventional working as regards both performance and work satisfaction. A piece of good fortune that befell me at this time was to have carried out the initial studies in this program in association with a colleague, K. W. Bamforth, who had been a miner (Trist and Bamforth 1951). Otherwise the significance of what was encountered would not have been grasped with intuitive certainty as distinct from occasioning conceptual excitement.

That these principles were not specific to mining was demonstrated not only in another industry but in another culture in Rice's (1953) work in the textile industry in India. That they could be extended into the service sector was shown by Pollock's (1954) work in retailing and by Menzies' (1960) work in a large teaching hospital in London. This study, building on a paper of Jaques (1953), advanced the idea of organizational structure as psycho-social defense and showed how changes in medical technology strained traditional concepts of nurse training and rendered dysfunctional conventional patterns of ward organization.

These studies led to the introduction of a new unit of analysis—the sociotechnical system—and to the beginnings of a new theory, namely, that organizational and work design should endeavor to optimize for the socio-technical system as a whole rather than for either the social or technical systems taken separately. Scientific management had concentrated on the technical to the exclusion of the social, while the human-relations school had reversed this direction of unilateral emphasis. The sociotechnical task was to increase "the goodness of fit" between the two, to discover "the best match." In a later language, which had the advantage of Somerhoff's concept of directive correlation, Emery (1963) reformulated this correspondence as the joint optimization of coupled but independently based systems.

The systems concept was not widely used in the social sciences in the early 1950s, but it influences the sociotechnical approach from the beginning in the form of Von Bertalanffy's (1950) ideas on open as distinct from closed systems. To advance to these was but a short step from Lewinian field theory, and the idea of the organization as an open sociotechnical system that had begun to develop was articulated by Emery (1959) in a comprehensive monograph for all levels of the organization in relation to the environment. As regards the primary work group, Herbst (1962) developed a mathematical model of autonomous group functioning.

Meanwhile, the Tavistock workers found that colleagues in other countries had encountered similar phenomena and were proposing a similar direction for the reorganization of work: Westerlund (1952) in Sweden regarding the Stockholm telephone exchange; van Beinum (1963) in Holland in telecommunications; and Davis (1955, 1957) in the United States in the electrical appliance and chemical industries. In the United States also, the beginning of the 1950s ushered in the movement toward job enlargement and job rotation while by the end of the decade this had broadened to include the idea of job enrichment (Herzberg et al. 1959). These latter approaches were based on the individual rather than the work group but constituted evidence that the process of extreme job breakdown had reached its limit and that a countervailing trend was setting in in the most advanced industrial society (which had most confidently pursued the mechanistic model).

That the concerns of sociotechnical inquiry might be related to quite fundamental value changes emerging in Western societies as forerunners of the transition from an industrial to a postindustrial order was not realized until what has become known as the Norwegian Industrial Democracy Project got under way in the early 1960s. This project arose out of a crisis in Norwegian industry concerning participation; it redirected an exclusive preoccupation with representation on boards of management to an interest in extending workers' decision-making powers over work at their own level. The Norwegian Confederation of Employers and Trade Unions took the unprecedented step of seeking the assistance of social scientists on an issue likely to explode with political dynamite. The Norwegian Institutes of Work Research, led by Einar Thorsrud, drew in the Tavistock group. Fortunately, enough progress had been made in sociotechnical studies to permit a positive response to this major challenge from the societal level. There resulted not only a considerable extension of sociotechnical theory and practical experience but also the beginnings of an international network among social scientists in this field, which extended from Europe to the United States. At an international conference on the Quality of Working Life held at Arden House in 1972, the extensiveness and relevance of this network became apparent (Davis and Cherns 1975).

The first phase of the Norwegian Industrial Democracy project was concerned with showing the limitations of workers' representation on boards of management (Thorsrud and Emery 1964), the second with conducting a series of sociotechnical field experiments in different industries (Thorsrud and Emery 1969). The technologies involved became progressively more sophisticated and the units progressively larger till whole plants were included. As the experiments went on, many vicissitudes were encountered, and the complexity of the issues became better understood. The first steps were taken in formulating a theory of sociotechnical change as a continuous learning process. A search began for criteria and measures to evaluate what had been attempted. Not surprisingly, these have not been easy to establish.

Nevertheless, the results obtained in Norway were convincing enough to industrial leaders in Sweden for them to take up the sociotechnical approach in a far-reaching manner and to involve the trade unions. A new generation of better-educated Swedes was not content to be restricted to monotonous repetitive jobs, and the importation of foreign workers failed to solve the problem. The phenomenon of work alienation became recognized in all the major European countries and in the United States. Movements countervailing work alienation by redesigning work organization have now arisen everywhere in the industrial world, though their strength and scope vary widely. The decision of Volvo and Saab-Scania to move away from the assembly line toward methods in which quasiautonomous groups assume responsibility for identifiable productive subsystems has been commonly taken as a symbol of a shift to a new paradigm.

These massive developments turned the attention of sociotechnical scientists to macrosocial phenomena, and Emery and Trist (1965), on the background of Tolman and Brunswick's (1935) paper, itself predicated on Lewinian ideas, introduced the concept of the causal texture of organizational environments. The rate of change associated with the advent of the information technologies (often thought of as constituting a second industrial revolution) has raised the environment of advanced industrial countries to new levels of complexity, interdependence, and uncertainty (with major effects elsewhere in the world). This phase change has produced characteristics of environmental turbulence that cannot be met adaptively by bureaucratic organizations, however expert in scientific management. Their response capability is too slow and too limited to meet the pace and variety of environmental demands. Turbulence control cannot be effected by organizations operating on the design principle of the redundancy of parts. The alternative design principle, the redundancy of functions, can, however, endow them with the hoped-for flexibility and rate of learning in the face of the novel. But this alternative design requires in the first place the greatest possible degree of self-regulation being built into the basic units of which the organizations are composed. This brings us back to the primary work group and the dimensions and degrees of its autonomy, which constitute the theme of Susman's book.

Surprisingly, until his book, we have not been provided with a systematic analysis of the dimensions and degrees of autonomy. Susman, building on an earlier paper of Gulowsen (1972), approaches this question by distinguishing three classes of decision: those concerning independence, those concerning self-governance, and those concerning types of self-regulatory activity. He separates boundary-transaction uncertainty from conversion uncertainty. He proceeds to introduce categories of technically required cooperation, type of interdependence, and type of coordination. A final question relates to the degree of separability of coordination from regulated activities. This set of concepts provides a framework for the analysis of autonomy, which makes a systematic and rigorous treatment of it at last more easily possible both for the research worker and the designer.

In approaching design, he not only seeks to secure a balance of attention between the technical and social aspects but also considers the latter from a phenomenological point of view. In this, he reinherits the original Gestalt tradition and reestablishes the experiencing human subject as an active contributor to his own future. Until very recently, the social sciences have avoided the teleological question. But work such as that of Ackoff and Emery (1972) on purposeful systems (building as it does on the earlier work of Singer and Sommerhoff) has made the encounter with choice and value a more manageable affair for the working social scientist than it has hitherto been.

In sociotechnical studies, this encounter cannot be avoided, for these studies are becoming increasingly design oriented (Herbst 1974). Design oriented they must be, if the future of work organizations, especially those employing the newer technologies, is not to be mortgaged to the past. Design inherently involves choice, and choice inherently involves values in the process that Vickers (1965) has called appreciation.

It is pertinent that in facing these issues, Susman should have reached out not only into the wider organization theory that writers such as Selznick (1957), Parsons (1960), and Thompson (1967) have made available but also into planning theory of the kind developed by Ozbekhan (1971), Ackoff (1969), and Jantsch (1975). Organization theory must relate itself to planning if it is to become future oriented and capable of addressing the questions of choice and value inescapable in sociotechnical studies concerned with improving the survival chances of man.

Parsons has made distinctions between the institutional, managerial, and technical levels of organizational life. Susman has related these to the normative, strategic, and operational levels of planning as put forward by Ozbekhan. The establishment of this set of correlations has great power, especially as, in addition, Susman shows that these three aspects are present in some degree at all organizational levels and indeed enter the field of the primary work group. If this were not so, hierarchies would be separate rather than interconnected, and the below could not affect the above in any essential way. There would be no hope for a concept of democracy.

In view of what began to happen in Norway in the 1960s and what has begun during the 1970s to spread to some extent throughout the whole of the Western industrial world, the question of autonomy at work has become linked to the wider question of industrial democracy. This term has three connotations. It would seem possible to link them to the three levels of organization and planning that have been discussed. The representation of workers on boards of management, which may be called representative democracy, may be postulated as a function of the institutional level of the organization and the normative level of planning, which are both concerned with relating the ends of the organization to those of the wider society. Historically evolved systems of collective bargaining, which may be called interest group democracy, may be regarded as a function of the managerial level of the organization and strategic planning, concerned as these are with conflict resolution among parties competing for shares in the same resources and seeking agreement concerning which means are to be accepted as legitimate. By contrast, the establishment of higher degrees of participation and autonomy may be called work-linked democracy and related to the technical level of organization and to operational planning, which are concerned with what happens in the work place itself.

Change efforts that seek to move organizations away from the bureaucratic and toward a transbureaucratic paradigm, from a design principle based on the redundancy of parts to a design principle based on the redundancy of functions—and able therefore to contend with environmental turbulence—are scarcely likely to succeed, it may be argued, unless they proceed at each of these three levels of organization and planning and in all three aspects of industrial democracy. To develop an art and science for the management of organizational change is among the most critical needs of our time, if we are to succeed in establishing a greater degree of control over our changing world. A book such as Susman's advances this capability by showing that a fuller understanding of the meaning and importance of autonomy at work is basic to this end.

PREFACE

This book is concerned with the quality of working life in advanced industrial societies. This is a subject in which businessmen, government officials, and researchers in public and private institutions are increasingly expressing an interest. These representatives of society, though perhaps not motivated by the same considerations, are beginning to recognize the hidden costs to individuals, organizations, and society of meaningless and repetitive work. Although the area of the quality of work has been ignored in the United States for many years, evidence is accumulating that it affects, among other things, productivity, mental and physical health, adjustment to leisure and retirement, and the ability to retrain for new jobs. In addition to awareness of hidden costs, the role of work in the life of the individual is being reassessed by psychiatrists, social scientists, clergy, and concerned laymen. Also, the idea that work should be a challenging, integral part of an individual's life is capturing the imagination of the public through the mass media. *Fortune, Time,* and *Newsweek* magazines have carried feature articles, as have such newspapers as the New York *Times* and the Washington *Post.* The quality of work has recently been the subject of several television documentaries as well as popular books. It is now a common theme of management training seminars and national conferences. Presently, there is legislation in the United States Congress concerning the quality of work as well as increased disbursement of funds from public and private agencies to study this subject. In short, the quality of working life in advanced industrial societies is an idea whose time has come.

This book presents an analysis of current conditions and the forces for improving the quality of work in advanced industrial societies as well as a framework for designing new work forms to improve the quality of work. It is a book for serious students of this subject—those who wish to understand the forces for change as well as those who wish to design and implement new work forms. The book assumes that the reader is acquainted with basic psychological and sociological concepts related to work and motivation, organizations, and industrial society. It is assumed the reader has little familiarity with general systems concepts; thus, these concepts are explained as they are introduced.

The book is intended for advanced undergraduate and graduate students in industrial psychology, sociology, organizational behavior, and industrial engineering. It is also intended for members of managerial and technical staff in public and private organizations who are concerned with the problems of quality of work and wish to redesign the work places of their employees so as to improve productivity and create more meaningful work experiences.

There are three main parts to the book. Part I discusses the reasons for developing a new framework for the design of work and introduces a model of motivation that assumes that human behavior is purposeful and future oriented. Part II presents a framework for understanding work groups as systems in dynamic interaction with their environment. It is proposed that work groups be designed as autonomous, self-regulating systems. Such work groups permit "pockets of discretion" within the larger organization and are the best means to increase decision making at the work place for rank-and-file workers. Part III discusses principles of sociotechnical design that are based on achieving a "best match" between a social and a technical system. When such a match is achieved, the resources of both the social and technical systems are optimally utilized in achieving outcomes that are desired by work-group members. Work-group members perform best when achievement of desired outcomes leads them to experience self-enhancement. Design principles that facilitate the likelihood of such experiences are discussed in both Chapters 7 and 8. Chapter 9 summarizes the approach to design developed in this book, considering it to be a contributor as well as consequence of the transition of advanced industrial societies to post industrialism.

ACKNOWLEDGMENTS

This book has many intellectual forebears. In particular, I am indebted to the pioneering work of Kurt Lewin, who was one of the first social scientists to formally conceptualize human behavior as purposeful. Lewin's work provided a foundation for the intellectual tradition that developed at the Tavistock Institute of Human Relations in the 1950s and 1960s. It was out of this tradition that the first sociotechnical concepts were formulated and utilized in field research. One of the individuals most instrumental in developing these concepts was Professor Eric L. Trist, who now chairs the Management and Behavioral Science Center at the University of Pennsylvania, to whom I owe a great personal and intellectual debt. Since first meeting him in 1966 I have admired and respected his wide-ranging intellect and vast research experience. More recently, as co-collaborator with him in field research, I have come to appreciate him as a warm human being and friend. I express my gratitude to him for reading early drafts of the manuscript and offering constructive criticism. I also extend to him my deepest appreciation for writing the Foreword to this book.

I would also like to express my gratitude to my colleague Roger D. Evered for reading and commenting on the manuscript. Also I wish to thank the many students who offered comments and criticism when the manuscript was used in a graduate seminar, Spring 1975—notably Melvin Blumberg, James B. Thurman, and L. R. Scheewe. I am indebted to my wife, Liz, not only for tolerating the many evenings and weekends that I spent at my desk working on the manuscript but also for being a sounding board for my ideas. Several times she brought useful books and articles related to her own specialty, child development, to my attention. Finally, I would like to express my appreciation to the secretaries in my university department, Marie M. Straka, Ildiko M. Takacs, Sharalyn Bowersox, and Nancy Hillard, each of whom typed one or more revisions of parts of the manuscript.

CONTENTS

Chapter | Page

Chapter Page

LIST OF TABLES

LIST OF FIGURES

Figure		Page
6.5	Distribution of Regulatory Decisions Under Varying Conditions Faced by Groups Within Cells 5 through 8	144
7.1	Strategic and Tactical Decisions in Sociotechnical Design	159
7.2	Directive Correlation Between a Social and Technical System	162
8.1	The Work Group Composed of Job-Holders or System Contributors	188

PART I

CHANGING CONDITIONS, ASSUMPTIONS, AND MODELS

INTRODUCTION TO PART I

Part I outlines the conditions calling for changes in traditional approaches to the design of work at the operative level of organizations. Chapter 1 is concerned with the nature of work in an advanced industrial society and such a society's changing structural and cultural conditions, which make traditional work arrangements no longer acceptable to an increasing percentage of blue-collar and white-collar workers. Chapter 2 is concerned with the costs to society, its constituent institutions, and the individual resulting from traditional work arrangements. This chapter is also concerned with the criteria by which value judgments are made for ignoring costs or for giving priority to reducing costs in one societal sector at the expense of another. Chapter 3 discusses the underlying assumptions of many current models of motivation and their implications for design at the work place. An alternative model is developed that assumes that man is purposeful and that his behavior is future-oriented. Man performs best when his work provides him with opportunities for experiencing self-enhancement through goal achievement.

CHAPTER 1
JOBS AND WORKERS IN AN ADVANCED INDUSTRIAL SOCIETY

FOCUS OF THE BOOK

This book is concerned with the nature of the work performed by the majority of workers in an advanced industrial society and the consequences of that work for the physical and psychological well-being of those who perform it. Evidence will be presented that, under present socioeconomic conditions, the undesirable consequences to the individual, the organization, and society of much of the work as presently designed and performed is no longer justifiable on economic, psychological, or humanist grounds. This book is concerned with the work that actually produces the goods and services necessary or desired in an advanced industrial society; it is not concerned with the work of those whose primary responsibility is to coordinate the work of others or plan what goods and services to produce or how to organize the resources to produce and distribute them. This latter exclusion doesn't mean that the jobs of middle and upper managers are so well designed that they don't merit our consideration. There is much evidence to the contrary (see Ritti 1971 and Herzberg et al. 1959, for example). It is, however, at the primary production level that the greatest dissatisfaction is usually felt (Argyris 1964). Those who hold jobs at this level generally have the least discretion and fewer alternatives than others to escape through seeking a new job or through enriched leisure. Also, it will be suggested later that many negative aspects of supervisory and middle-manager jobs may result from the basic organizational and job design assumptions underlying primary production jobs.

The concern with work that actually produces goods and services as distinct from the work that involves primarily coordination and planning doesn't imply that a separation between the two is natural and always necessary. One of the premises of this book is that such a separation is artificial and will produce increasing dissatisfaction among those whose work is limited to production only, with no opportunity to plan or coordinate their work. As will be discussed later, there are technological factors that limit the ability of a single worker or work group from planning and coordinating all the work they perform. There are also, however, historical, cultural, and sociopolitical factors as well as economic ones that have produced a separation of planning and coordination from doing and have produced a subdivision of doing into fractionalized, meaningless components (see Marglin 1971). Chapter 2 will discuss some of the factors that have produced the present-day organization of work. It is clear that such an organization of work has required a set of assumptions among those who participate in such an arrangement and a set of conditions in the society to sustain those who must perform the work. It is the objective of this chapter to outline what these assumptions and conditions are and to demonstrate that the assumptions and conditions that have permitted the traditional organization of work to function reasonably well in the past are changing rapidly, so that both those who produce and those who plan and coordinate increasingly find these arrangements unacceptable.

Those who actually produce the goods and services in our economy no longer consider boredom, alienation, and lack of dignity as integral and necessary to their working lives. The worker's increased concern for his dignity and self-respect as well as the right to make decisions that immediately affect him will result in more emphasis in collective bargaining on issues affecting the quality of working life and governance of the work place. Management will, of course, respond in negotiations to the challenge posed to its prerogatives. But it will also be taking steps on its own initiative to reduce the absenteeism, turnover, and sabotage resulting from increased worker dissatisfaction with their jobs. Pressures from foreign and domestic competitors will lead management to seek solutions to sagging productivity. Once management recognizes that applying more of the same old techniques will not solve these problems but actually exacerbate them, it will seek solutions through the redesign of jobs and work groups as well as through greater participation in decision making. While these actions will be motivated primarily by economic considerations rather than humanistic ones, the results will change the worker's relationship to his work and to supervision. It is the solutions and programs that both management and labor can and are likely to use and their consequences that will be the major focus of this book.

THE JOBS: WHO PERFORMS THEM?

The main focus of this analysis is on the work performed by (1) blue-collar operatives, (2) laborers, (3) white-collar clerical workers, and (4) service workers, excluding private household domestics. These four categories of workers are among those used by the Bureau of the Census, U.S. Department of Commerce for analyzing population and social trends. Workers from these four categories totaled half the employed population of the United States in 1969 (see Table 1.1, below). Operatives make up the largest category of blue-collar workers. They are semiskilled and typically work on factory assembly lines or in related jobs such as inspectors and material-movers. Nonfarm laborers make up the smallest category of blue-collar workers and are unskilled. Listed also as operatives, but of less concern for our purposes, are bus, cab, and truck drivers. White-collar clerical workers are employed mainly as secretaries, stenographers, typists, receptionists, office machine operators, bank tellers, telephone operators, and shipping and receiving clerks. Finally, nondomestic service workers are employed in hospitals as custodians and attendants, in restaurants and hotels, barber and beauty shops, and in plants and office buildings as guards and cleaning personnel.

Although this book is concerned with the work of all those involved in the actual production of goods and services, most of the discussion will be on the blue-collar worker and the organization of his work. The nature of the work performed by occupants of other occupational categories will be discussed where the topic under consideration is clearly applicable, and relevant problems and examples are known to the author. This emphasis reflects the fact that conceptualization of the problems associated with the design of manufacturing work is more developed than with other work categories. One of the objectives of this book is to develop a framework based on what is now known, but with enough generality to evaluate and redesign work sites that have received little analysis in the past.

IS AUTOMATION A SOLUTION?

One might suggest that little concern should be given to restructuring many of the jobs in the above four categories because the very fact that they are so routinized means that they are ripe candidates for automation in the near future. This will in fact happen to many of the jobs held by blue-collar operatives and laborers as well as white-collar clerical workers, but it is not even plausible for many of the service occupations mentioned above. Also, there is no assurance that many of the new jobs that automation creates will be any more challenging or meaningful than the ones they replace. Workers who hold such white-collar clerical jobs as key-puncher, card-sorter, and dispatcher express a high degree of alienation from work (Shepard 1971), as do blue-collar operatives on automated transfer lines producing engine blocks (Faunce 1958). Also, there is little reason to expect that automation, in the relatively near future, will substantially replace the jobs now performed by operatives. The economic incentives based on the relative substitution of machines for men does not automatically favor the former, and even if there were an all-out commitment to automate all jobs with the present potential to do so, the costs would be prohibitive for even the most advanced industrial society.*

Automation will continue to replace many of the jobs of blue-collar operatives and laborers in manufacturing industries and reduce their percentage of the total number of jobs held by employed individuals. However, this reduction will be due mostly to the rapid increase of workers in other categories such as professionals and clerical and service workers. The actual number of blue-collar operatives will increase from 17.5 million workers in 1968 to 19 million workers in 1980 (Bell 1972). These data and the considerations mentioned above suggest that the jobs in these four categories will be occupied by a significant segment of the employed population for many years to come and are ample justification for concern with restructuring them.

STRUCTURAL AND CULTURAL CHANGES: THE PAST 20 YEARS

In order to observe the structural and cultural changes affecting attitudes toward work, a useful reference period is 20 years. A 20-year period represents a generation and is sufficient time for enough new workers to enter the labor force with initial work experiences that differ from those employed in or around 1950. While such structural and cultural changes in

---

*Professor Yale Brozen of the University of Chicago claims that to automate as completely as possible the manufacturing sector of the American economy alone would require an investment exceeding $2.5 trillion, and this assumes that output would remain constant. At current investment levels of approximately $15 billion annually it would require two centuries to accomplish this. It would take longer if expanding population were also taken into account (see Blumberg 1969).

this 20-year period are assumed to affect the attitudes of those whose working lives have coincided with these changes, the effects are not expected to be as dramatic as for those whose working lives have begun more recently. Recent data suggest that the most dramatic changes in attitudes have occurred in the last five years (Herrick and Maccoby 1972). Understanding these attitudinal changes requires looking back over at least a 20-year period and in some cases longer to determine the factors that are now producing the accelerated pace. Four basic factors are considered below as contributors to the increased job dissatisfaction among workers. These are changes in the nature of (1) work and the work place, (2) the work ethic, (3) the patterns of consumption and motivation, and (4) authority.

The Changing Nature of Work and the Work Place

As Table 1.1 shows, although other occupational categories had been growing more rapidly since 1900, blue-collar occupations represented the largest percentage of the employed population in 1947. In that year, they represented an all-time high of 41 percent; operatives and laborers made up 21 percent and 6 percent respectively. Both white-collar and service workers had been dramatically increasing since 1900 and represented 35 percent of the employed population in 1947; clerical workers represented 12 percent. Service workers, excluding household domestics, represented 7 percent of the employed population.

By 1969, blue-collar occupations represented only 36 percent of the employed population, operatives and laborers making up 18 percent and 5 percent, respectively. By 1980, this occupational group is expected to decrease to 33 percent, operatives and laborers representing 16 percent and 4 percent, respectively. By 1969, white-collar workers grew to become the largest percentage of the labor force, 47 percent, clerical workers making up 17 percent of this figure. White-collar workers are expected to increase to 51 percent of the employed population by 1980. Service workers had increased to 11 percent of the employed population by 1969 and are expected to grow to 14 percent by 1980.

Also shown in Table 1.1, the fastest-growing occupational category within the white-collar sector is composed of professionals. In 1947, 7 percent of the employed population was in this category, by 1969 this figure had increased to 14 percent, and it is projected to increase to 16 percent by 1980. Within this category, teachers were the largest group in 1969; the second largest group was professional health workers, followed by scientists and engineers and, finally, engineering and science technicians (Bell 1972).

TABLE 1.1

Occupational Distribution of Employed Population (in percent)

Major Occupational Group	1900	1947	1969	1980
White-Collar	18	35	47	51
Professional workers	4	7	14	16
Proprietors, managers, officials	6	10	10	10
Clerical workers	3	12	17	18
Sales workers	5	6	6	6
Blue-Collar	36	41	36	33
Craftsmen	10	14	13	13
Operatives	13	21	18	16
Laborers	13	6	5	4
Service	9	10	12	14
Private household workers	5	3	2	*
Other service workers	4	7	10	*
Farm	37	14	5	3
Farmers and farm managers	20	9	3	*
Farm laborers and foremen	17	5	2	*

*Data not computed in source.

Sources: For data 1900-69, Wolfbein 1971, p. 46; for projected data to 1980, Bell 1972, pp. 163-89.

TABLE 1.2

Sector Distribution Of Employment By Goods and Services Projected to 1980 (distribution by percentages)

	1947	1968	1980
Goods Producing	51	35.9	31.7
Agriculture, forestry, and fisheries	15	5.1	3.2
Mining	2.1	0.8	0.6
Construction	3.9	5.0	5.5
Manufacturing	30.0	24.9	22.4
Durable	16.0	14.7	13.3
Nondurable	14.0	10.2	9.1
Service Producing	49	64.1	68.4
Transportation and utilities	8.0	5.6	5.0
Trade (wholesale and retail)	17.0	20.6	20.6
Finance, insurance, and real estate	3.0	4.6	4.7
Services (personal, professional, business)	10.0	18.7	21.2
Government	11.0	14.7	16.9
Federal	3.5	3.4	3.0
State and local	7.5	11.7	13.9

Source: Bell 1972, p. 169.

As Table 1.2 shows, during the first half of the twentieth century, the majority of workers were employed in goods-producing industries. By 1968, six out of ten workers were employed in service-producing industries, and this ratio is expected to increase to seven out of ten by 1980. The fastest growth area in employment since 1947 has been in state and local government. The major reason is the growth of educational services, which accounted for 50 percent of state and local government activities in 1968 (Bell 1972). General services were the second fastest growth area for employment between 1947 and 1968. The spread of services has been both in white-collar occupations, such as trade, finance, education, health, and government, and in blue-collar occupations, such as transportation and auto repair.

The data in Tables 1.1 and 1.2 show clearly that the predominant mode of production in the U.S. economy has shifted from manufacturing to services and the major form of employment from blue-collar to white-collar and service occupations.

The changing distribution of occupations has been accompanied by changes in the nature of work and the organizational structure of the work place. Within the goods-producing sector of the economy, growth has been occurring for products whose production requires less bureaucratized forms of organization and less routinized work performance. Bell (1972) points out that the major growth in the goods-producing sector will occur in construction (Table 1.2), where seasonal employment and deployment of resources to temporary sites demand a less structured work organization (Stinchecombe 1959).

In manufacturing,which is still the largest single source of employment in the economy (Table 1.2), growth will occur for products such as computers and electrical components, which require a custom-crafted rather than mass-produced mode of production. In the factory itself, production has changed from being labor intensive, where the worker's direct contribution to the product is coordinated with the flow of orders and materials, to being capital intensive, where mechanization and automation shift workers from direct to indirect production jobs such as inspector and maintenance man.

In the service-producing industries, many of those who provide services do so directly to or in consultation with those who receive them. Except where the service is of such a narrow scope and the relationship highly formalized, the demands for initiative and judgment are generally greater for those working with people rather than inanimate objects.

These changes in the nature and organization of work are in the minority, but they are important not only because they will increase in number but also because many of these jobs are strategically placed in the organization and permit those who hold them to win from employers concessions that may serve as models for others. Many of these jobs also have a science and/or craft base, which reinforces the claims for professionalism among job-holders. Professionals demand autonomy based on their possession of exclusive knowledge and adhere to peer rather than organizational norms (Etzioni 1964). Finally, those social groups whose prestige and authority are based on possessing or carrying out the basic values of society provide models for the conduct of others and exert great influence on the formulation of societal attitudes and opinions. Just as the secularization of theological doctrine formed the basis for the prestige of entrepreneurs for most of the industrial era, so science forms the basis for the prestige of professionals and technicians in the approaching postindustrial era. Today, it is the professionals and technicians who make a major contribution through their prestige and authority to the formation of opinions about what should be demanded from work and what code of conduct is appropriate for such work as well as whose working lives and problems are most frequently depicted in the mass media. As the code of conduct and demands of this group become more widely accepted, there will be increasing frustration for those whose work remains organized for routine performance and submission to schedule. They will be asked to perform activities that they and others no longer consider important to improving one's self-worth.

The Changing Work Ethic

It has been suggested that the predominant mode of production in a society influences the internalized ethic of work performance of its producing members (Bendix 1956). There are other socioeconomic factors not totally independent of the mode of production that are also hypothesized to influence a work ethic, such as economic hardship and abundance, which will be discussed in the next section. In England, prior to the Industrial Revolution, an internalized work ethic developed out of the combined legacies of craftsmanship, the Puritan ethic, and the rising ideology of individual striving and success. These legacies included, among others, a belief in the preordained coincidence between virtue and success and a personalized burden for substandard work. The main impact of such beliefs was the impetus it gave to the development of entrepreneurial activity, but it was not inconsistent with promoting the qualities of work and conduct that were suited for factory production. As Bendix (1956) says, the depravity that was assumed to characterize the laboring poor in England was rarely mentioned without reference to the good qualities that every self-respecting man can develop, and the demands for submission, unequivocally demanded by the higher classes and government, were couched in terms that made submission synonymous with the ideal qualities of work and conduct.

The importance of these qualities for the management of an enterprise became more acute as production moved from separate households to the factory, and goods were no longer produced by handicraft methods but by machines and mass-production methods. Quoting Bendix (1956 p. 204):

> Under the conditions of factory production . . . workers must be willing to do the work assigned with a degree of steady intensity. They must have a positive interest in accuracy and exercise reasonable care in the treatment of tools and machinery. And they must be willing to comply with general rules as well as with specific orders in a manner which strikes some reasonable balance between the extremes of blind obedience and capricious unpredictability.

If Bendix is correct about the relationship between a society's predominant mode of production and the work ethic of its members, then the code of conduct he describes above is well suited to the regularized intensity of performance required for factory production. However, the statistics cited above on changing occupational patterns suggest that the factory and its inherent rhythm of production is declining in importance as the basic work archetype of the society. While it is true that mechanization of material and information handling has proceeded at a rapid pace to reduce much of the distinction between factory and office work, there has been a more rapid increase in forms of work requiring not regularized intensity but the deployment of cognitive and manual skills at irregular intervals and in unprogramable combinations and that requires greater interdependence among those who contribute these skills. Such work requires not submission to a predetermined schedule but self-direction and commitment to generalized goals and, especially in the case of providing services, to an emphasis on communication and social skills.

The unprogramability of many of these new work forms prevents the organization from specifying rules and regulations for all contingent conditions, and therefore it must increasingly rely on internalization of goals among job-holders that are consistent with its overall objectives. Professionalism, as discussed above, leads to the internalization of work-related norms. However, this is only a partial substitute for rules and regulations, as these norms are not always consistent with organizational objectives. Because of this and because not all unprogramable jobs are amenable to the development of related professional norms, organizations will increasingly rely on participative forms of decision making to accomplish their goals. It is becoming accepted in industry that participation in decision making leads to greater commitment in carrying out decisions (Lewin 1947). The practice of participation will increase first in those jobs where the nature of work requires it, but as it cannot be carried out in isolation from other workers and its limitation to certain workers cannot be justified on the exclusiveness of these situations, there will be demands for its spread to other parts of the organization.

Changing Patterns of Consumption and Motivation

The basic fact of life facing most industrial workers during the first half of the twentieth century was the existence of economic hardship and job insecurity. Wages were low and what purchasing power the worker possessed went for basic necessities; luxury and leisure items were few and well beyond the income or time available to most workers to consume them. Unions had little power compared to employers until the 1930s, so workers had little or no protection against any indiscriminate or profit-oriented actions of companies that might leave them unemployed. Facing such conditions, the worker was usually cautious and complacent on his job and found little time to be concerned with activities other than maintaining an income that was sufficient to provide food and moderate comfort for his family. The need to earn a livelihood was supplemented by a system of beliefs and social and cultural supports that justified and encouraged the motivation to work. In a work-oriented society, adult males are expected to work; they aren't considered responsible individuals unless they do. The kind of job the worker holds helps determine his self-image and status in society, and work is an important regulator of the time and place of social relationships. However, a Puritan or Protestant work ethic need not be posited to explain such behavior and was hardly the daily motivating force of the mass of workers who migrated to this country from Southern and Eastern Europe after 1890. With survival even more precarious in the city and towns of industrial America than on a patch of land in their agrarian homelands, there were no "fruits" of labor other than continued sustenance. It was survival, not salvation, that dominated the thoughts of most workers during these times, as frivolous or wasteful consumption could lead to disastrous consequences for the worker and his family.

Growth in Income

There has been, of course, phenomenal growth in the American economy since 1900, and this growth rate has accelerated since 1950. The American worker has shared in this growth. As Table 1.3 shows, the total

TABLE 1.3

Median Family Income and Percentage Change for Years 1950 and 1970 of Occupation of Job Held Longest by Family Head

	1950[a]	1950[b]	1970	Percent Change (in 1970 dollars)
Total	$3,319	$5,385	$10,803	101[c]
Occupation				
White-collar				
Professional, technical, and kindred workers	5,029	8,159	14,417	77
Managers, officials, proprietors	4,591	7,449	14,048	89
Clerical and kindred	3,833	6,219	10,203	64
Sales	4,149	6,732	11,951	78
Blue-collar				
Craftsmen, foremen, and kindred	3,925	6,368	11,185	77
Operatives	3,407	5,528	9,343	69
Laborers	2,524	4,095	7,806	91
Service workers				
Excl. household	2,976	4,828	8,318	72
Household	1,170	1,898	3,063	61
Farm workers				
Managers	2,000	3,245	5,991	85
Laborers	1,576	2,557	4,284	68

[a] In 1950 dollars.
[b] In 1970 dollars.
[c] Total includes occupations not shown below.

Sources: 1950 data from U.S. Department of Commerce 1952, p. 60; 1970 data from U.S. Department of Commerce 1971, p. 60.

median income among American families has grown from $3,319 in 1950 to $10,803 in 1970, an increase of 101 percent, when adjusted for price inflation. Median income among families whose heads were operatives increased 69 percent during the same period; that of laborers increased 91 percent. Median income among families whose heads were clerical workers increased 64 percent; that of nonhousehold service workers increased 72 percent. With fringe benefits available to help cover expenses associated with retirement and hospital and life insurance, many workers are now in a position to buy more than minimal necessities, and the income is used to buy an array of consumer goods. The extension of consumer installment credit to finance purchases for as long as 36 and 48 months augments the worker's ability to "buy now" and brings many luxury goods within the range of family monthly income.

Legislation

During the 1930s and 1940s, the activities of labor unions and the legislation of the federal government did much to reduce the inordinate power that employers held over workers. The Depression had sparked a resurgence in the growth of labor unions that was consolidated and further stimulated by the National Labor Relations Act, popularly called the Wagner Act, of 1935. This act authorized the National Labor Relations Board to oversee and help resolve industrial disputes and specifically contained provisions that guaranteed workers the right to form or join labor organizations and bargain collectively. It also prohibited employers, under legal sanction, from engaging in such practices as "dominating over, interference with or assistance to any employee organization; discharge or discrimination in hiring or conditions of employment to encourage or discourage membership in a labor organization; discrimination because an employee filed charges or gave testimony under the act and refusal to bargain in good faith" (Derber 1970, p. 304). During and in the decade following World War II, the National War Labor Board protected the worker's right to dissent and extended due process by widening the scope of the grievance-handling procedure to cover all issues of the contract agreement and extending it to industries where it had never been used previously.

Several federal legislative acts during and since the 1930s have contributed to reducing the worker's economic insecurity. The Social Security Act of 1935 provided for federal old age benefits, state unemployment compensation, and a variety of benefits and security provisions for dependent and crippled children, economically deprived mothers, and the blind. It also supported vocational rehabilitation and public health service. The Employment Act of 1946 committed the United States to a high-production, high-employment policy, which contributed significantly to economic growth and lowered the probability of repeating a 1930-like unemployment situation. Since 1935, social security benefits have increased frequently, and various adjustments have been made to bring more people under the coverage of retirement programs. In 1965, the Medicare program was adopted, giving hospitalization and medical benefits to persons over the age of 65.

Economic Security

The entrepreneur and engineer have brought prosperity to the United States and the American worker has shared in it; organized labor and federal government have provided the American worker with the security of not being deprived of that prosperity by the capricious actions of either employers or fate. As important as these achievements are, they have led to another achievement not immediately apparent or anticipated by those who either facilitated or obstructed the change in the worker's basic condition. It is now easier than before for the worker to react to mindless jobs and demeaning supervision. Psychological withdrawal and overt compliance were possible reactions to such conditions always, but the worker can now react with absenteeism, turnover, strikes, or grievances with less economic peril for himself and his family. As long as his take-home pay remains sufficient to fulfill basic necessities, some discretion remains to escape dreariness by being absent or between jobs. This is a more likely explanation for the upsurge in these reactions than that a Puritan work ethic has sustained these workers until now at jobs that, in many cases, cannot hold the attention of individuals of normal intelligence.

Unfortunately, absenteeism and psychological withdrawal are not adequate in themselves as methods to cope with continual affronts to one's personal dignity, and the continuation of such conditions is likely to lead to unconscious or conscious guilt and anger. These reactions are likely to increase as professionals and other more glamorous occupations are depicted by the society as models of worthwhile work and conveyors of self-respect.

If the worker is able to win a longer vacation time or a shorter work week, he may escape his job. While the evidence is inconclusive, it does suggest that people do not adequately compensate for unchallenging work through leisure activities (Parker 1971). If this is so, there are humanist grounds for changing the nature of jobs and supervision. However, on economic grounds alone, the increased economic and job security that permits the worker to choose to escape an unpleasant situation challenges the employer to reduce the costs of absenteeism, turnover, and shoddy workmanship by reattracting (or, more accurately, finally attracting) the worker to the work place. More money and benefits, while desired by workers, will not provide a long-run solution to the problem unless the nature of the work itself and supervision are also changed. More money and benefits will not eliminate psychological withdrawal and a minimalist orientation on the part of workers in reaction to organizations that shape such behavior through the assumptions made about employees (Argyris 1964).

Economic security, in addition to permitting the worker the freedom to escape from a boring job, leads to the development of what Maslow (1943) calls "higher-order needs." Maslow proposed a model of motivation based on a hierarchy of needs that begins with physiological safety, social, and ego needs and ends with the highest need: self-actualization, which is concerned with developing one's unique talents and abilities and exercising self-expression. According to Maslow, unless the individual is neurotically fixated at lower-level needs, self-actualization becomes dominant as lower-level needs are satisfied; the individual then seeks out situations where self-actualization can be realized. Although the present and past circumstances of many people's lives do not permit the creative use of their free time, leisure can compete very well with typical rank-and-file jobs for the worker's allegiance and involvement.

Galbraith (1967) has pointed out in *The New Industrial State* that humans make inflexible demands for the satisfaction of basic survival needs and are indifferent to the manner in which these needs are satisfied. However, higher-level needs, being less basic to survival, can be satisfied in a variety of ways, and the greater the person's choice of means, the more he may be subject to manipulation by social influence. Large corporations through the mass media try to persuade the worker-consumer to spend and use his increased income and free time for goods and services that no longer constitute basic necessities. There are negative appeals based on anxiety of rejection, such as in ads for toothpaste, mouthwash, and deodorant. There are appeals based on the vicarious improvement of social status as in ads for automobiles, appliances, and vacations. There are also appeals to use the worker's increased free time for consuming the goods and services of the leisure industry, such as in ads for hobbies, recreation, vacation homes, and travel. In the latter case, the appeal is to adventure, fun, and excitement, but as Charles Reich (1970) tells us in *The Greening of America,* there is no longer in America any appeal to a viable concept of work; herein lies a fundamental contradiction for a system that requires both diligent workers and diligent consumers (p. 193):

> ...the overly persuaded consumer may no longer be a willing worker. To have consumers for its constantly increasing flow of products, the Corporate State must have individuals who live for

> hedonistic pleasures, constant change, and expanding freedom. To have workers for its system of production, the State must have individuals who are ever more denying, self-disciplined, and narrowly confined. In theory, they are supposed to accept the discipline of their work in order to enjoy the pleasures of consumption. But the theory is all wrong. For some people it is wrong in fact, because hard work does not leave time or energy for outside enjoyment. For some people, it is wrong in principle, because if they are persuaded to believe in the principle of hedonism, they find it hard to hold on to the principle of service. And for a very large group of people, it is simply impossible on a personal level; they are psychologically unable to go back and forth between self-denial and pleasure.

The domination of the individual's awareness by higher-level needs obviously doesn't mean that he and his fellow workers will put down their tools and leave the work place in droves for ski resorts and secluded mountain cabins. There are economic as well as psychological reasons that compel him to remain. It is not easy to abandon the role of family breadwinner; work is where his friends are, and the society offers few viable alternatives in the near future for self-definition. Although workers may withdraw psychologically in droves, as present evidence suggests they do, work still offers the best potential for the satisfaction of higher-level needs. Leisure, which appeals to status and ersatz adventure, is fleeting and ultimately unsatisfying since it substitutes for status enhancement rather than actually altering one's social status. Creative free-lance work is limited to only a few people by opportunity and temperament and even the most engrossing hobbies are part-time activities for most. Work within a large organization is the only significant means available for the majority to satisfy their higher-level needs. Thus, the opportunity and challenge exist for employers and workers to make the modern organization the place where these needs can be satisfied. Whether this is accomplished by the actions of employers or organized labor or the actions of both jointly, alteration in the nature of traditional work offers the best opportunity to solve the problems created by new societal conditions.

Changing Patterns Of Authority

Increased job and economic security offer a partial explanation for changes in the workers' attitudes and behavior toward managerial directives. Security reduces the necessity for what Herbert Kelman (1961) calls "compliance," which is overt conformance to the directives of another, regardless of attitudes privately held. It is now less necessary than previously for the worker to offer compliance to directives with which he disagrees or which adversely affect his interests. If he is in a unionized company, he is protected from arbitrary dismissal through grievance and arbitration procedures, and, whether he is protected or not, he may choose to seek another job without suffering such catastrophic economic consequences as was once likely to be the case. However, increased job and economic security do not explain why workers are less willing to submit to decisions made by others even if the consequences of those decisions do not adversely or may favorably affect them. What is involved is not refusal of compliance but a denial of authority, a suspension of what Chester Barnard (1938) referred to as the "zone of indifference" that workers had previously allowed management. Conferring authority upon management includes a suspension of the worker's critical judgment of management's right to make decisions that affect him and suspension of examination of the premises of those decisions. The processes leading to erosion of authority are complex but involve changes in the composition of the work force and the conditions facing it as well as in justifications drawn upon by management for the right to make decisions.

Managerial Bases of Authority

At the turn of the century, the prestige of the entrepreneur was high, and his superiority was ordained by an American ideology that considered as evidence of election to such status his success in the competitive struggle with nature and against men who must, because he rose above them, be of lesser virtue and intellectual ability. This prestige was buttressed by status differences between those who occupied the ranks of management and the ranks of labor. Entrepreneurs who had succeeded in developing large enterprises in the nineteenth century were predominantly of Anglo-Protestant backgrounds and recruited managers with similar attributes. The labor force drew its membership from the great migration wave after 1890, which brought people to America mainly from the countries of Central, Southern, and Eastern Europe. Most of these countries were agrarian or in the early stages of industrialization. Social relationships in such countries were traditional, being based on historical and cultural factors that led to emphasizing attributes of birth rather than achievement. Traditional authority meant unquestioning obedience to the representatives of such institutions as the church, royalty, and the head of the family. The new immigrant arriving in this country related to hierarchy as he had learned to relate in the past. The transfer of obedience from the traditional hierarchies of Europe to the hierarchies of American management was made easier as the latter had already adopted ceremony and insignia to reinforce its distinctiveness and right to privilege.

As corporations grew in size and complexity, their day-to-day administration required less of the risk-taking and independence of the entrepreneur and more of the technical and scientific skills of the professional manager and technician. The worker saw less of the entrepreneur whose personal authority rested on his proven superior judgment and more of the professional manager and engineer who substituted judgment with technique. Bendix (1956) has written that Taylor's (1911) scientific management and similar techniques did much to undermine the personal authority upon which early entrepreneurs and managers relied. The scientific method, upon which engineers claimed their techniques relied,* replaces virtuous living and superior judgment with "impartial inquiry" as a basis for authority to manage. Management initially opposed many of the tenets of scientific management, which, in theory, would make them as subject to rules and discipline as the workers. However, the growing prestige of science as well as its promise of accomplishment led management to incorporate into its ideology the social philosophy if not the methods of science. This included unswerving faith not only in what science could do to improve productivity and the efficiency of the enterprise but also that conflict between management and labor could be eliminated by following "objective" procedures. What management might not have immediately realized is that scientific methods and techniques are not the monopoly of management and that scientists and engineers could be hired by labor unions to challenge managerial directives on its own terms.

Education Level of the Worker

Several changes in the composition of the labor force have contributed to the reduction in the worker's uncritical acceptance of managerial directives. To begin with, social distance has diminished between workers and managers, which reduces the degree to which social status reinforces managerial authority. By 1960 only 26 percent of the blue-collar labor force (skilled, semiskilled, and unskilled) were either foreign-born or of foreign or mixed parentage compared to 34 percent for this figure in 1950 (Bell 1972). Not only are the majority of workers now born and raised in the

---

*These claims more often represented appeals to the prestige of science than reflected practice of its methods. See Ellul (1964) and Mumford (1970) for discussion of differences between technique and scientific method.

TABLE 1.4

Median Years of School Completed by Labor Force 18-64 Years of Age

	Total	Males	Females
1940	9.1	7.7	11.0
1952	11.1	10.6	12.0
1959	12.0	11.7	12.2
1962	12.1	12.0	12.3
1968	12.3	12.3	12.4

Source: Wolfbein 1971, p. 58.

United States, where high value is placed on democratic and equalitarian principles, but there has been a remarkable increase in the level of educational attainment. As Table 1.4 shows, the median years of school completed has increased dramatically for males, from 7.7 years in 1940 to 12.3 years in 1968. The median years of school completed increased for females from 11 in 1940 to 12.4 years in 1968. Back in 1940, one out of every ten men who worked was "functionally illiterate"—that is, had not gone beyond the fourth grade—more than half (54 percent) never went beyond elementary school (Wolfbein 1971). The percentage of Americans with a high school diploma has almost doubled from 38 percent in 1940 to 75 percent in 1970. In the same 30-year period, the percentage of Americans with college degrees has gone from 6 percent to 16 percent; the proportion of those with one or more years of college has gone from 13 percent to 31 percent (Maccoby 1972).

As Michael Maccoby (1972) has pointed out, blue-collar workers as well as other Americans now find that their local schools and colleges are generally more stimulating and democratic than either their home or work place. Contemporary education increasingly stresses initiative and achievement as well as how to interact with others in a democratic and fair manner. When the educated worker compares the routinization and submissiveness required of the work place with the values he has embraced and the experiences he has had at school, he is likely to react with anger and frustration. Berg (1971) and Sheppard and Herrick (1972) provide data to support a negative relationship between level of educational attainment and satisfaction with routinized jobs.

CHAPTER

2

THE ORIGINS AND CONSEQUENCES OF TRADITIONAL JOB DESIGN

In the earliest days of the Industrial Revolution, entrepreneurs contracting with independent workmen for the production of goods and services were little concerned with how work was organized and performed. The entrepreneur's investment in production was limited to the raw materials he supplied to workmen, and he exercised control commensurate with his risk by paying a piece rate for the number of products produced and refusing to accept products he judged to be of substandard quality. The workman claimed the right to produce the product as he saw fit for he too invested in the production process by contributing the skills he had acquired and the tools he made or purchased; he could enforce this claim by withholding these skills and tools as his interests dictated. This balance of rights was quickly overturned in the latter half of the eighteenth century when the enormous productive capacity derivable from linking machines to inanimate energy sources was harnessed to produce the goods and services for newly created and expanding markets. Only wealthy entrepreneurs could provide capital of sufficient magnitude to purchase these machines and the facilities to house them, thereby excluding the worker as a significant investor in the production process.

To assure that workers would not interfere with maximizing the return on the entrepreneur's investment by deciding the conditions under which work would be performed, entrepreneurs sought to extend their control to include the work process itself. This was accomplished by establishing managerial prerogatives over what occurs inside the factory through appeal to values concerning property rights and by extending the division of labor to such lengths as to eliminate the skills that independent craftsmen could offer or withhold in bargaining for wage rates.

It was natural under values sanctioning an owner's right to dispose of his property as he saw fit for the entrepreneur to extend his property claims to cover the organization and regulation of activities that influence how his investments were utilized. In an age of independent farmers and small proprietors, liberty and property rights were inextricably intertwined, and the exercise of these rights was in little overt conflict with other rights—for example, human rights—for the actions each owner took on behalf of his property had little effect on the health, safety, or general welfare of others. Consistent with such times and values, the entrepreneur claimed that no individuals or governments should interfere with his actions to maximize the return on his investment. He claimed that in a developing economy the accumulation of capital was of primary importance for improving the standard of living enjoyed by all; this was best accomplished by permitting each entrepreneur to pursue independently his maximum return on capital. Such claims were respected in court cases and in laws passed by legislatures. Apparently, no inconsistency was acknowledged by these civil bodies when entrepreneurs made simultaneous appeals for government intervention to enact tariffs to protect their markets from excessive competition and uncertainty.

The mechanization of production contributed to the rise of the factory system—that is, the concentration of labor and capital at specific sites. Machines were bulky, arrangements between machines were inflexible, and it was necessary that machines be close to their power source—for example, to rivers to produce hydroelectric energy. While mechanization contributed to the rise of the factory system, it was not the sole explanation for its existence or for the extreme division of labor that accompanied it. Specialization was proceeding at a rapid pace in the manufacture of products where little or no mechanization existed or was required. Adam Smith's (1937) well-known passage in *The Wealth of Nations* on the benefits of specialization refers to the manufacture of pins, for which mechanization was virtually nonexistent.

Although entrepreneurs and their managers were aware that specialization of labor could lead to increased productivity if tasks were divided along specific dimensions, no rational procedure existed for determining what these dimensions were. This did not prevent the application of division of labor to factory production. Other than the belief that more of the same would lead to increased productivity, ad infinitum, the only other plausible explanation for extending the division of labor to the point of creating minute fractions of tasks was the entrepreneur's desire to control the wages and conditions under which labor was employed. The division of labor into fractions of tasks reduced the entrepreneur's dependence on skilled workers who could disrupt factory production if they were to choose when and under what conditions they would work. Such a division of labor also reduced the wages the entrepreneur had to pay to workers. With such highly fractionated tasks, workers had little or no skills to offer employers; they had to compete with an abundant supply of workers for the available jobs and could be easily replaced if they refused to accept or tolerate the conditions offered (see Braverman 1974).

The division of labor into minute tasks also permitted entrepreneurs to control the work process itself. The greater the division of labor, the greater the need for integrating the tasks that workers were assigned, the latter being a responsibility the entrepreneur or his appointed managers readily assumed. If workers rather than entrepreneurs had assumed these responsibilities, which was a technically feasible alternative, the latter could be subject to the workers' threats to control or withhold their production as a unit.

The division of labor fosters the development of managerial hierarchies to coordinate and control the activities of workers. Since each manager's span of control is limited to a small percentage of the total factory labor force, the greater the division of labor, the more the levels in the hierarchy. In addition to coordination and control, managers plan for what and how tasks are to be performed, creating in the process new departments and a new contributor to the production process: the technician. It can be expected that as the division of labor increases, the worker's discretion over how his work is to be performed decreases. In Daniel Bell's words (1961, p. 235) the hierarchical structure "draws in all possible brain work away from the shop, everything is centered in the planning, schedule and design departments."

MECHANICAL AND ORGANIC WORLD-VIEWS

The desire of entrepreneurs to create and maintain low wages for factory workers contributed, along with other factors, to a division of labor of fractionalized tasks. However, the division of labor as a principle for the organization of productive activity preceded the factory system, and, for that matter, the mechanization of production. Adam Smith (1937) observed that "the invention of all those machines by which labor is so much facilitated and abridged seems to be originally *owing* to the division of labor" (p. 9). He suggested that concentration by men on a single object or operation leads to the discovery of "easier and readier methods of performing their own particular work" (p. 9). In *The Wealth of Nations,* many examples of the benefits of division of labor refer to trades such as carpentry, baking, and blacksmithing, where each tradesman produces and exchanges a complete product with other tradesmen. By specializing in the production of a single product, each produces more than he can consume and benefits by exchanging his surplus production with those who can provide him with the products he desires. All the tradesmen benefit from this arrangement, according to Smith, because more and cheaper products are available than if each tradesman produced everything he needed by himself (see pp. 5-6).

While ostensibly discussing the same unit of analysis, Smith gives his most famous example of the division of labor, the manufacturing of pins; however, he is discussing no longer the trades associated with the production of a single product, but the specific activities required to produce a single product. The obvious question is whether implications drawn from the former are applicable to the latter. The fact that in the latter a worker offers unskilled labor for wages rather than a product for a price would suggest that the benefits and disadvantages in the two cases are quite different. However, the important point to be drawn from the discussion of the specific activities required to produce a product is that operations are being discussed by Smith as proper units of analysis in their own right.

By discussing human activities as being independent of the human mind that guides them, Smith was reflecting an emerging mechanical world-view that was developing prior to the time of his writing and that predominates in the design of work to the present day. The mechanical world-view is in sharp contrast with the world-view that existed prior to the publication of Smith's *The Wealth of Nations.* It would be inconsistent with the objectives of this book to offer other than a brief sketch of the differences between a mechanical world-view and the world-view that Lewis Mumford (1970) calls organic.

A mechanical world-view is characterized by faith in applying rational methods to the betterment of the human condition. Each successful application of rationality builds on previous achievements, resulting in a process called historical progress. It is also characterized by belief in an objective world that exists independently of any human observer, a world that consists of a finite set of parts ordered in such a fashion that proper analytical methods can discover the manner in which these parts are related to each other, and a world in which knowledge about the operation of each of these parts is summative, leading to an explanation of the whole.

In contrast, in the organic world-view, harmony and equilibrium, not progress, are the primary ends of human activity. History is to be understood as a series of events that are recurrent and eternal rather than successively leading to a progressively better future. In the organic world-view, knowledge is gained through contemplation and revelation to the end of better understanding the relationship of man to the eternal and divine. God, or a similar concept, is considered the source of all knowledge. Events in the world and of its parts cannot be understood independently of the deity's relationship to the world, and thus the understanding of parts independent of their relationship to the whole is precluded.

Mumford (1970) has eloquently traced the intellectual developments leading from the organic world-view predominating in the middle ages to the mechanical world-view that emerged in the sixteenth and seventeenth centuries. Three intellectual contributors to the mechanical world-view discussed by Mumford who are relevant to our discussion are Galileo Galilei, Isaac Newton, and Rene Descartes.

Galileo, in pursuing his experiments with gravity, challenged the scholastic doctrine of the church by asserting that to understand the actions of gravity on physical objects, one need not deal with causes other than those immediately impinging on a given situation, thus obviating the search for primary or divine causes. Underlying Newton's mathematical equations predicting the motions of heavenly bodies was the assumption that the universe consisted of a finite number of elements whose actions can be explained by a finite number of causes. Descartes, in his philosophical treatises, promoted the view of the independent existence of the mind and body, each of which can be understood in its own right. This view encouraged treating the human body as an object of investigation and, no doubt, hastened the anatomical and physiological discoveries of scientists such as William Harvey and Andreas Vesalius. Such a view of man also contributed to current job-design practices, the discussion of which will follow in this and the next chapter.

Mumford and others, including Marshall McLuhan (1964), have described technological and intellectual developments that suggest that a mechanical world-view is on the wane and an organic world-view is reemerging. The new organic world view would differ from the earlier one in being conveyed upon the cultural symbols and objects of the present, with contemporary conceptions of the supernatural and divine as well as of the harmonious and balanced.

VALUES OF CRAFTSMANSHIP

An analysis of productive activities in their own right, as represented in Adam Smith's pin-manufacturing example, would have been inconceivable within the context of the handicraft values that were institutionalized in the guilds that dominated for centuries prior to Smith's writing. As was the Catholic Church, guilds were promoted and sustained in the Middle Ages by an organic world-view. The ideals of craftsmanship as carried in a guild organization from master to journeyman and apprentice were to produce objects that reflected both the manual and artistic skills of the producer.

Both were creatively blended in the producer's mental imagery of the future product, which, in turn, guided the craftsman's activities toward the product's realization. These ideals of craftsmanship inextricably bound action with the human mind that produced the action, thus making analysis of action by itself inconceivable.

It was immaterial to the realization of craft ideals whether or not what was produced had utilitarian value. Even when mechanization was becoming of great interest to French and Italian craftsmen in the sixteenth and seventeenth centuries, as exemplified by the miniaturization of clocks and the creation of lifelike motions in mechanical automatons, the creative impulse was for the "miraculous"—to use S. Giedion's term—rather than the utilitarian (see Giedion 1948; Mumford 1970). That such remarkable achievements in mechanization and miniaturization were not applied to economic activity is due, in part, to the lack of interest in such application in strongly Catholic Italy and France, where values of the organic world-view dominated.

Efficiency is also immaterial to the realization of craft ideals. Though not irrelevant in productive endeavors, there is little interest in efficiency beyond procuring essential materials, thus providing only boundary conditions within which skill and artistic ability can be demonstrated. In eighteenth-century England and Scotland, where Catholicism was weak and rationalistic, utilitarian values were strong, it was natural in such a setting for a marriage to take place between mechanization and economic efficiency. This marriage manifested itself in mechanical inventions such as power-driven textile looms and the application of rational techniques to the analysis of human action.

PURPOSEFUL VERSUS MECHANISTIC BEHAVIOR

The analysis of human activities and their arrangement in accordance with objectives determined by an agent other than the activities' originator represents a historcal break with the period preceding the industrial era. Freed from such considerations as salvation, piety, or artistic appreciation, which may have previously concerned the originator of activities, the external agent arranges activities to suit his own objectives, which, in the setting being discussed, are economic. Whatever the variety of objectives set by the external agent, such as profit or organizational growth, the common denominator underlying the arrangement of activities to accomplish these objectives is efficiency. Efficiency, unlike the objectives that concerned medieval man, is open ended, and the external agent's faith in progress through scientific analysis leads him to efforts to push back continually the limits to efficiency.

Unlike the craftsman of the preindustrial era, the worker whose activities are determined and directed by an external agent does not engage in purposeful behavior. Purposeful behavior is guided by objectives to which goals and activities are subordinate; goals and activities change as the conditions that facilitate or inhibit the pursuit of objectives change.

Ackoff and Emery (1972, pp. 240-41) define a "purposeful" system as one that "can choose courses of action with respect to an . . . objective. . . . if a purposeful system fails to achieve a goal in one situation it may change its goal in order to better pursue the same objective." Regardless of whether the worker has set his own objectives, his behavior is purposeful as long as he chooses the goals and activities needed to accomplish the objectives. According to Ackoff and Emery, an objective is a desired outcome that is not obtainable in the time period being considered, but progress toward it is possible during that time period and is obtainable at a later time. Progress toward an objective can be achieved, however, by the pursuit of goals that, according to Ackoff and Emery, are obtainable in the time period considered (these concepts are relative, of course; they depend on the time frame). Job designers can program activities to meet goals, and conceivably these goals could lead to achievement of objectives only if the conditions under which goals are formulated do not change. If conditions do, in fact, change, new goals by which to reprogram activities have to be formulated to assure that the original objective is attained. If the worker's goals and activities are predetermined, then his behavior ceases to be purposeful, and he becomes an instrument of the external agent who programs him. Those whose activities are predetermined are not guided by objectives but by programed instructions, as is the case for machines.

Although the factory system developed in conjunction with the rise of capitalism, its most important consequence for behavior at the work place is not the manner in which profits are distributed but the fact that work is divided into those who plan it and those who perform it. Those who plan work in the factory, managers and technicians, decide what activities workers are to perform. The former may be said to engage in purposeful behavior because they continually determine and modify (the worker's) goals and activities in pursuit of objectives. Only if the worker selects his own goals for guiding his actions in pursuit of objectives is his behavior purposeful.

Consistent with its desire to maintain power over the process of production and with complete faith in economic progress through scientific analysis, management reduced the image of proud craftsman to a homunculus having all limbs and no brain. The brain, of course, was to be supplied by management, which would make decisions as to the best placement of the worker's body and extremities. The limbs were to be coordinated in imitation of the era's archetype of efficiency, the machine. By imitating the machine, miraculously and endlessly producing thousands of identical products without fatigue, human activity could be arranged to produce similar results. Such faith reached its logical extension in the writings of Frederick W. Taylor (1911) and Frank Gilbreth (1911). Both studies the human body to discover how it could best be transformed into a mechanism, to discover its limits, and to eliminate, for the sake of efficiency, superfluous and "irrational" movements. Gilbreth studied human motion in its own right. To him, all forms of movement were entities with independent laws. By studying the similarities in all human activities, Gilbreth believed he could provide the building blocks for a new science of time and motion.

The analysis of human productive activity into micro-motions undoubtedly contributed to further development of mechanization, for just as the machine could become a guide for designing how workers should perform their activities, technicians could study human motion and mental processes and design facsimiles to free man from some of the most repetitive aspects of production. Along with many other factors, automation of production has contributed to an emerging postindustrial economy, in which manufacturing, particularly its most repetitive forms, is declining as a significant source of employment. Those classified as operatives who actually produce the goods and services in our economy are faced with new roles that differ from those of the industrial era. However, the prevailing world-view of the industrial era, which led to the material progress now enjoyed, still guides the design of work. No new model of work has arisen to replace the one most representative of the industrial era, the one developed by Taylor, Gilbreth, and their disciples. Like the history of media, which McLuhan (1964) discusses, new technological developments are not usally used to their potential at first. To exploit their potential, the sociocultural framework out of which the new development arose must be transformed from one that was actually more appropriate to the new development's antecedents.

The postindustrial era has created many new jobs that have no relationship to mechanical production or its demands, but yet the rhythm and ethos of the industrial era continues in the way in which jobs of the postindustrial era are designed. Jobs are designed for repetitive action whether job occupants deal with clients or inanimate objects, with diagnosis rather than record-keeping, with applied research rather than production. Even with such transformations in the nature of work taking place, the organization is still assumed by managers and technicians to be a static system—if not in regards to their own work at least in regards to what operatives do—a system that can be designed once and for all and instructions passed to operatives on the one best way to perform their activities. Repetition is numbing to the brain as well as the body, and both are ill-fitted for work that demands unvarying action without pause. Human beings, unlike machines, are dynamic systems based on growth and change, a process that repetition of action denies.

PURPOSEFUL BEHAVIOR AND JOB DESIGN

The conception of man created by the mechanical world–view and supported by those whose interests it has previously served is increasingly an unsatisfactory basis for designing jobs in the postindustrial era. The rising expectations of the work force and its changing relationship to the production process will result in making work based on mechanical-world-view assumptions less economically acceptable to management. Assumptions based on the mechanical world-view with direct implications for job design include what motivates behavior and the gains to be expected from programing activities.

Programing activities in the same manner that motions are engineered into machines denies purposeful behavior to human beings. It results in severing the intimate tie between action and intent that is so characteristic of human behavior in settings other than the traditionally designed work site. Consistent with designing activities as extensions of the machine, human motivation is introduced in traditional job design in a manner analogous to how power is supplied to machines—that is, like a neutral power source that indiscriminately energizes all activities to which it is applied. Like electrical current applied to a motor, such a conception of motivation assumes that increases of rewards will cause workers to perform predetermined and preset activities more rapidly. Unlike such assumptions arising from treating man as a machine, the next chapter introduces concepts and provides examples demonstrating that motivation of workers cannot be understood apart from the context in which their work is performed or from the meaning that workers attribute to their tasks.

Although workers can be made to behave superficially like a machine, this does not mean that behaving like a machine will result in the greatest productivity for the tasks to which workers are assigned. Besides the fact that it may be cheaper to hire human labor than to design a machine to perform a particular task, humans are assigned to tasks that machines cannot be designed to do as well or at all. This may be due to the task's requirements for flexibility or variability of response but also because objectives assigned to humans may be nonoperational—that is, a means-end chain cannot be traced backwards from the objective to the means to accomplish it—for example applied research, development, and so on. In the latter case, intermediate goals may have to be set and sacrificed to assure that the objective is accomplished. While machines can be programed to provide responses to anticipated conditions (environment), it cannot be programed to produce responses to conditions that were not considered at the time of programing. Man is superior to the machine in being able to respond to unanticipated conditions, for, unlike the machine, man is free of his immediate environment to create responses to an environment that has not yet been formulated or completely understood. When unanticipated conditions arise in organizations, as may increasingly occur in the postindustrial era, the job designer must rely on commitment, not programing, to achieve objectives. Commitment and similar concepts are discussed in Part III of this book.

TRADITIONAL DESIGN OF JOBS

Consideration of the human contribution to the production process does not generally begin until after decisions have been made concerning product design and plant and equipment layout. Such decisions involve commitments of capital that are not easily alterable in the short run. Once management invests in plant and equipment, it is reluctant to incur "sunk" costs to accommodate workers. The result is that the worker's greatest virtue, his adaptability and behavorial plasticity, becomes a liability for him when the production process is planned, for the worker offers the fewest immediately apparent constraints to those who design the production process. Once the overall production process has been determined, it is divided into the basic operations required to produce the desired product or service. These operations consist of major components or processes of production. Methods engineers usually become active at this stage to determine what human activities are required to complete an operation, and they decide what activities are the most efficient for workers to use. The word "activities" subsumes what are called micro-motions and elements in the field of operations management. The following definitions are in general use by job designers (Chase and Aquilano 1973, p. 414):

1. *Micro-motion:* The smallest work activities, involving such elementary movements as reaching, grasping, positioning, or releasing an object.

2. *Element:* An aggregation of two or more micro-motions, usually thought of as a more or less complete entity, such as picking up, transporting, and positioning an item.

3. *Task:* An aggregation of two or more elements into a complete activity, such as wiring a circuit board, sweeping a floor, cutting a tree.

4. *Job:* The set of all tasks which must be performed by a given worker. A job may consist of several tasks, such as typing, filing, and taking dictation, as in secretarial work; or it may consist of a single task, such as attaching a wheel to a car, as in automobile assembly.

After decisions are made as to what activities are "best" for production, the process of job design begins. Job design concerns how activities are to be combined into tasks and how tasks are combined into jobs. Davis, Canter, and Hoffman (1955) divide the job-design process into three parts: (1) specification of the content of individual tasks; (2) the specification of the method of performing each task; and (3) the combination of individual tasks into specific jobs. The first and third parts are concerned with determining the content of a job, while the second indicates how the job is to be performed. For consistency, Davis, Canter, and Hoffman refer to the process of designing job content as job design and the process of determining methods of performing each task as methods design.

Davis, Canter, and Hoffman (1955) have also pointed out that no one department or group of technical specialists has sole responsibility for determining job content. Job design appears to evolve from decisions made by line foremen and various engineering departments and sometimes, though seldom, involves the personnel department in an advisory capacity. One can surmise from this that job design is the domain of those whose outlook concerns the analysis of activities. Little systematic attention is given by them to the effect of job content on the motivation or attitudes of workers.

One can see the extent to which mechanical-world-view assumptions enter into job design by observing the criteria that job designers use to determine job content. Like other decisions based on assumptions rather than knowledge, the criteria used are unsystematic, but are all generally consistent with the mechanical-world-view conception of man as an all-limb/no-brain homunculus. From this conception, the human contribution to production (body and extremity movements) is, like the machine, a cost of production that should be minimized by lowering its initial cost (minimize wages and training time through specialization) and then dividing this cost over as many units of production as possible. The latter is accomplished by minimizing unit operation time, which job designers achieve by dividing tasks among workers so as to provide each with a full workload and as little idle time as possible. Management is the brain to supplement the activities of the homunculus and makes as many decisions as possible prior to actual production. Those decisions that arise after production begins are assumed to involve corrections of deviations from plans to assure that quality is being maintained.

Since minimizing the direct cost of production is the primary criterion used by those who design jobs, no consideration is given to costs that may accrue indirectly from production such as increased supervisory costs or that may be unnoticed because consideration of such costs is inconsistent with the mechanical world-view of man. Both types of costs will be discussed in the following section.

COSTS OF TRADITIONAL JOB DESIGN

In order to transcend the consequences of the mechanical world-view and develop a new model for job design, the costs of traditional job design must be acknowledged. A thorough analysis of the costs of traditional job design must determine what a cost is and to whom it accrues. Costs are embedded in value judgments concerning what is good and desirable and what is bad and undesirable. Like the consequences of any implemented decision, a job design that is actualized has consequences that may be judged as good or bad depending upon the scope of the consequences one wants to consider (for example, social, political, economic, or moral consequences) and upon value judgments concerning what is a good or bad consequence. Neither of these two considerations is independent of the other, and, in fact, the scope of consequences is affected by value judgments concerning those consequences and vice versa. More will be said about this in a later section in which Vickers's (1965) concept of appreciation is discussed.

A cost resulting from traditional job design is acknowledged not only by its negative consequences for some social entity but also by what positive consequences have been forgone or not been actualized as a result of traditional job design. The social entities for which costs are considered are the individual, organization, and society.

Figure 2.1 shows four circles, each of which represents a social entity that is affected by the design of jobs. The circle in the middle of the figure represents the effects of job design on performance of the job itself. This is generally measured in terms of productivity, quality, direct costs of production, delivery time, and so on. The circle at the bottom of the figure represents the individual worker; the circle at the upper right represents the organization that employs the worker; the circle at the upper left represents the wider social system. The arrows with solid lines in Figure 2.1 suggest

FIGURE 2.1

Effects of Job Design on Society and Its Constituent Parts

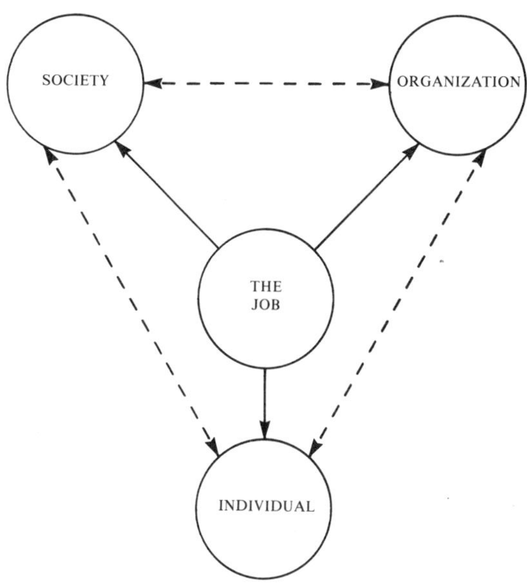

Source: Compiled by the author

that the job, through its design, affects each of the three social entities directly and independently. However, many effects are mediated through one social entity to another; individuals are members of organizations, and both individuals and organizations are constituent parts of the larger society. When the effects of job design on a particular social entity are discussed below, it will be assumed that many such effects are mediated through other social entities. However, what these other entities are and the process by which mediation occurs may not be stated explicitly. The arrows with broken lines in Figure 2.1 represent these likely mediations.

What Is Traditional Job Design?

Before proceeding with an analysis of the costs of traditional job design, it would be useful to be more precise about what is meant by the term "traditional job design." In terms of job content, traditionally designed jobs are those with high specialization, repetitive tasks, short cycle times, low variety and low discretion, and possibly, but not necessarily, mechanical pacing. In terms of "job context," or what Herzberg et al. (1959) call "hygiene factors," traditionally designed jobs are supervised in an authoritarian or nonparticipative manner by supervisors who hold assumptions that workers are not to be trusted to perform their work without constant surveillance. Other hygiene factors such as pay, safety, and working conditions may be inadequate in traditionally designed jobs, but improvements in these factors without concern for those mentioned above are not of immediate concern to this discussion.

What Is Job Redesign?

The results of studies reporting changes in job content and/or job context are difficult to compare because changes do not start from the same initial conditions. Also, since researchers mean different things by job redesign, the changes undertaken are not always the same. For the sake of consistency, the following terms are used in this chapter when it is necessary to distinguish between different design efforts: "job enlargement" refers to changes such as job rotation, decreased specialization, and increased cycle times. These changes are sometimes called horizontal changes because they do not include increased decision making for workers. "Job enrichment" refers to adding discretion to workers' jobs that once resided elsewhere in the organization such as quality control, maintenance, and so on. The term "autonomy" is used interchangeably with job enrichment, although the former term is more often associated with work groups than with individual jobs. "Participation" refers to consultation between supervisors and workers concerning decisions that supervisors ultimately make. In this case, decision making has not shifted to the workers, but supervisors are open to the workers' influence attempts and the process occurs before a decision is formally made. Phrases such as "considerate, human relations" or "people-oriented supervision" refer to a supervisory style. While changes that move in the directon of such supervisory styles are desirable, they are not considered examples of job redesign and will not be discussed here.

Costs on the Job

Job performance is generally measured by productivity—for example, physical output per worker, and/or by quality, errors, scrappage rates, and so on. Studies of work groups are not easy to compare with those of individual jobs. In the former case, composite measures are frequently used because task interdependence makes it difficult to isolate individual productivity.

Improved performance on redesigned jobs is theorized to result from either or both of two sources. One source is increased motivation or improved attitudes toward work. Redesigned jobs are theorized to provide a greater sense of accomplishment and responsibility, reduced boredom, greater meaning in work, and a feeling that the work has social value and significance (Herzberg 1968). The other source of improved performance is a design that is more appropriate to the job than existed previously. For example, redesigned jobs may reduce materials handlings and space requirements and offer the worker more freedom to set his own pace and greater flexibility to react to unplanned events. Most likely, improved performance in job-redesign studies, when it occurs, results from a combination of these two sources. The perspective developed in this book is that a job-redesign effort must evaluate both the social and technical aspects

TABLE 2.1

Summary of Selected Studies on Job Redesign

Research Study	Results
Rice (1958)	Higher productivity and quality
Davis and Werling (1960)	Higher quality
Kilbridge (1960)	Higher quality
Biganne and Stewart (1963)	Higher product quality
Trist et al. (1963)	Higher productivity
Conant and Kilbridge (1965)	Higher quality
David and Valfer (1965)	Higher quality
Paul et al. (1969)	Higher productivity
Huse and Beer (1971)	Higher productivity and quality
Hill (1971) (Shell U.K. Ltd.)	Higher productivity
Burden (1975) (Shell U.K. Ltd.)	Higher productivity and quality
Emery and Thorsrud (1975)	
Christiana Spigerverk	Temporary productivity increase
Hunsfos Mill	Higher productivity and quality
NOBO Factories	Higher productivity
Norsk Hydro	Higher productivity and quality
Hill (1972) (Motorola Co.)	Higher productivity and quality

Source: Compiled by the author.

of a contemplated change in order to achieve a "best match" between both (Emery and Trist 1960).

Table 2.1 shows the results of selected job-redesign studies in terms of both productivity and quality. While the results for productivity are mixed, it is important to point out that in no case was there a decrease in productivity. The conclusion from this selection of studies concurs with that drawn by the Task Force Report to the Secretary of Health, Education and Welfare entitled *Work in America* (1972), which states (p. 112), "In no instance of which we have evidence has a *major* effort to increase employee participation resulted in a long-term decline in productivity." The failure to show productivity increases in some job redesign studies may be due to scheduling and technological constraints in surrounding departments. However, it is impossible to know if this was considered in such studies without more detailed data than were presented. Productivity increases in a particular department may be restricted also if the wages reeived in that department increase relative to other departments (Whyte 1955; Emery and Thorsrud 1974). Improves quality is also a frequent finding in many redesign studies. It can be speculated that on enlarged jobs, workers are better able to assess the results of their actions and correct their errors. Responsibility for a larger role in the production process may increase the worker's motivation to improve quality, as it is easier for him to identify his contribution to the product or service he produces.

Costs to the Organization

A number of studies have shown that job-redesign efforts result in cost reduction to the organization. Studies of work-group autonomy show reductions in administrative overhead by assigning decisions to workers that supervisors and inspectors made previously (Melman 1958). Supervisors have subsequently been used more efficiently to schedule supplies and support services to workers (Rice 1958; Trist et al. 1963). A study of participation showed reduced production-scheduling costs through a reduction in absenteeism (Marrow, Bowers, and Seashore 1967). Also when jobs are enlarged so that workers are responsible for producing a complete product, flexibility of scheduling is increased because production can be raised or lowered proportionately without concern for redistributing workloads (Butera 1975). A study of job enrichment showed reduced training costs through reductions in turnover (Ford 1969; Weed 1971). Redesign studies suggest an overall improvement in labor-management relations (reduced grievance rates) resulting from job enlargement (Ford 1969) as well as from worker participation in decision making (Whyte 1955).

Costs to the Individual

We will switch at this point from reviewing studies showing costs forgone because of traditionally designed jobs to reviewing studies that show costs incurred by individual workers. The evidence is impressive that workers on redesigned jobs have increased job satisfaction and reduced alienation (Biganne and Stewart 1963; Paul et al. 1969; Hackman and Lawler 1971). Aside from whether these attitudes positively affect job performance and organizational effectiveness, one can consider positive attitudes toward work as a desirable social objective. However, there is much evidence to suggest that work attitudes affect the worker's physical and mental health as well.

A 15-year study (Palmore 1969) concluded that work satisfaction was the strongest predictor of longevity, after controlling for such variables as tobacco use, genetic inheritance, and physical health ratings by physicians. Significant factors associated with heart disease, which accounts for about one-half the deaths in the United States, include job dissatisfaction, represented by tedious work, lack of recognition, poor relations with coworkers, and poor working conditions (Jenkins 1971); low self-esteem (Cobb and Kasl 1970); occupational stress, components of which include extraordinary workloads (French et al. 1965); and conflict or ambiguity in occupational roles (Pepitone 1967). In addition to heart disease, peptic ulcers (Susser 1967) and rheumatoid arthritis (King and Cobb 1958) have been found to be associated with occupational stress.

Mental health has also been shown to be associated with work. A variety of mental health problems have been found related to job satisfaction, including psychosomatic illnesses, low self-esteem, anxiety, tension, and impairment of interpersonal relations (Kornhauser 1965).

Alienation is a widely used and frequently misunderstood concept, and the objectives of this book do not permit adequate space for clarifying its origins and various uses (but see Israel 1971 and Schacht 1970 for excellent analyses of the concept). Sheppard and Herrick (1972) developed an index of alienation based on the extent of agreement or disagreement with the following three questions: (1) "These days a person doesn't really know who he can count on"; (2) "In spite of what some people say, the lot of the average man is getting better, not worse"; and (3) "It's hardly fair to bring children into the world with the way things look for the future." A high alienation score suggests estrangement from society, a sense of powerlessness, and fatalism. Sheppard and Herrick found their index of alienation inversely related to job ratings for discretion and variety as well as for pay level and job security, and positively related to authoritarian attitudes and lack of a sense of political efficacy and achievement. Sheppard and Herrick also found high alienation scores correlated with votes for extremist candidates in the 1968 presidential election. Susman (1973) presents data also showing an inverse relationship between job ratings for discretion and variety, and indices based on Seeman's (1959) definitions of alienation (including self-estrangement). Sennett and Cobb (1972) present poignant data based on psychoanalytically oriented in-depth interviews of workers showing what the authors call "the hidden injuries of class"—self-guilt and lack of self-esteem resulting from feelings of personal responsibility for failure.

Costs to Society

Every society, whether one is speaking of the nation-state or some similarly identifiable unit, is a system whose parts (its organizations, groups, and individuals) are shaped by the structure and values of the society as a whole. The constituent parts, in turn, shape the structure and values of the society. However, when one or more parts change more rapidly than the others, severe strain is placed on the society as a whole to accommodate to such change. The greater the incongruity between the structure and values of the parts and the whole, the greater the strain. Some recent changes associated with the socioeconomic institutions of advanced industrial countries may be producing strains of this sort. Such changes include shorter work weeks, longer vacations, earlier retirement increasing demands among minority groups for participation, and acceleration of change in the things, places, and people to which individuals relate (Toffler 1970).

One might easily expect that an individual's work, at which so much of his waking time is spent, would have ramifications far beyond the immediate work place. As less time is spent at the work place and more free time is available to individuals, problems of adjustment will increase. Individuals who have spent their lives at routine tasks that have provided no opportunities for discretion or social interaction will find themselves ill prepared to engage in purposeful activities when they are not at work. Margolis and Kroes (1974) cite a case study of an elderly man whose mental and physical health deteriorated rapidly after retiring at age 65. He recovered his health rapidly when, due to a manpower shortage, he was called back to work by his former employer. Meissner (1971) presents data showing that workers on jobs with low variety and discretion were more likely to engage in passive free-time activities, such as watching television and spectator sports, than were workers on jobs with high variety and discretion. Workers on the latter jobs engaged in directed or active free-time activities such as hobbies, evening education courses, participation in community affairs, and so on.

Dealing with free time constructively—to ensure the psychological and physical health of a society's citizens as well as to provide them with resources for living in complexity—is a difficult problem for a society to solve. Solutions may run from providing more people with part-time but challenging work to planning facilities where constructive leisure is encouraged. It seems certain, however, that a laissez-faire attitude toward these problems will result in wasted human resources that are vitally needed to cope with accelerating social change. At worst, such an attitude may result in rapid deterioration of health and early death for many individuals thrown on the scrap heap when their services appear to be no longer needed.

Economic and educational organizations in advanced industrial societies are, perhaps, as important and influential as agents of socialization as the nuclear family unit. Yet it is paradoxical in a society such as the United States, which values democracy, that its constituent organizations are frequently structured in such a manner as to discourage the practice of democracy. John Stuart Mill (1963) pointed out that it is no use having universal suffrage and participation in national government if the individual has not been prepared for this participation at the local level; it is at the latter level that the individual learns how to govern himself. Quoting Mill, "A political act, to be done only once every few years, and for which nothing in the daily habits of the citizen has prepared him, leaves his intellect and his moral dispositions very much as he found them" (p. 229). One may speculate that the low voter turnout in U.S. elections (approximately 55 percent in the 1972 presidential election and an even lower percentage in state and local elections) is, in part, the result of the lack of training in democracy (or, conversely, a training in authoritarianism) provided by American educational and economic organizations. Kornhauser (1965) presents data on auto workers who are employed in an industry containing the prototype of nondiscretionary, repetitive work. These data suggest that such workers hold attitudes that are more authoritarian than the U.S. population as a whole.

Evidence suggests that changes in educational practices are presently taking place in the United States in the direction of greater participation of students in the learning process (Kohl 1969). It is less clear whether similar trends are occurring as rapidly in the structure of jobs or in the attitudes and assumptions that management holds about workers. It is unlikely, however, that such arrangements can remain undisturbed for long while so much change in a democratic and participative direction occurs in other types of organizations and at other societal levels.

SHARING THE COSTS AND BENEFITS OF JOB DESIGN

The reader may have gained the impression in the last section that job redesign, in the various forms discussed, leads only to positive consequences for all constituent parts of society as well as for the society as a whole. While such a possibility is conceivable in a small, homogeneous society, it is not likely to occur in a complex, pluralistic society such as the United States or in the countries in Western Europe. In the latter societies, economic and political power is shared among several semiindependent constituent parts of the society whose interests and philosophical values are likely to clash. For example, the interests of stockholders, managers, workers, and consumers may clash (we must recognize, however, that members of any society may simultaneously occupy more than one of these roles). Clashes in philosophical values may occur because such values support and promote the economic and political interests of their purveyors. They may also derive from the varying religious, ideological, and cultural experiences of a plualistic society's members. While such clashes may be inevitable or even necessary in complex societies for adaptation and growth to occur, the increasing interdependence between a society's constituent parts may no longer allow any of them to achieve their objectives without guidance from a shared image of and strategy for the society as a whole.

It is easy to envision job designs with consequences that are incompatible with one or more of the economic interests or philosophical values held by a society's constituent parts. At the beginning of this chapter, we discussed conflicts between management and workers resulting from job specialization. The outcome of this conflict was disproportionately favorable to management when viewed from a simple bilateral economic framework. Increased specialization reduced the worker's wage rates, job security, and control over the work process. There was little evidence to suggest to management that this framework was inadequate because any secondary consequences of specialization such as absenteeism, turnover, and boredom were economically unimportant to it. Labor was in abundant supply and easy to train, production standards were crude, and productivity could be sustained by external threat. Other consequences of specialization such as reduced mental and physical health and passive use of free time were unknown to management and had little impact, as yet, on other organizations and institutions of society.

By the 1940s management was discovering that there were limits to job specialization, and experiments have been undertaken since that demonstrate the benefits to be derived from jobs with increased variety, discretion, and opportunities for participation. However, the framework that prompted these experiments was primarily economic, and the impetus for change came almost exclusively from management. It is unlikely that management would undertake a job-redesign experiment that showed benefits to some other constituent part of society without showing benefit to itself. However, the distribution of power in society has changed since the early conflicts between management and workers, and new values have arisen and less prevalent ones have been strengthened. As a result of the redistribution of power in society by the reduction of economic scarcity and by recognition of the complexity and interdependence of the decisions and actions of a society's constituent parts, it is unlikely that management will continue to be the main impetus for job redesign or that the impetus will be primarily economic. For example, workers with rising expectations about the quality of their work may, through their union's countervailing power, demand changes that decrease productivity but make their work more interesting and challenging. Or legislators, aware of the social costs of repetitive unchallenging work under authoritarian supervision, may pass laws prohibiting certain practices or encourage change by providing tax credits to organizations that undertake job-redesign programs. The problem has now become very complex. It is more than likely that there is some point at which the costs of job redesign will exceed its benefits in productivity increases but yet, at the same time, accelerate personal growth and the learning of social and cognitive skills for coping with change, early retirement, more leisure, and so on. Who is willing to bear how much of the costs for the latter benefits? Are workers, who are also consumers, willing to see the costs passed on in higher prices for goods and services? Are workers willing to accept smaller wage increases if productivity grows at a slower rate than before? Are taxpayers willing to see tax dollars spent or forgone through tax credits on programs that have immediate returns to only a few segments of society?

Answers to the above questions cannot be provided without knowing the value premises of those who will make the required choices. Value premises are not easy to discern during periods such as the present when social structure and values are in transition. For example, once a society has conquered the scarcity of basic economic necessities, new values may emerge among its members to supplant those prevalent during less abundant times. Also, the range of problems a society acknowledges may increase as greater complexity and interdependence is apprehended by the society's members.

SCHEMATA OF REALITY AND VALUATION

The sociopolitical choices made by a society's leaders during a particular historical period are based on the world-view then prevailing. Among the characteristics of the mechanical world-view outlined earlier were assumptions held among a society's members concerning the nature of man and his role in the production process. Assumptions such as these consist of what Vickers (1965) calls schemata. Although Vickers never quite defines what he means by the term, his use suggests that schemata are clusters of concepts organized into meaningful wholes. This definition means somewhat the same as Bartlett's (1932, p. 201) definition of schemata as "an active organization of past reactions, or of past experiences." Boulding (1956) uses the term "image" in somewhat analogous fashion.

Schemata that directly or indirectly contribute to or undermine the prevailing world-view are under constant pressure for revision and elaboration. Chapter 1 suggests that pressures undermining the mechanical world-view have increased during the past 20 years. A new organic world-view is emerging in its place. Pressures such as rising affluence, the changing nature of work, and social legislation lead to incoherence between and within schemata. Such incoherence is observed when societal members perform "acts of appreciation," which are matches between new experiences and schemata built up from the past. The latter serve as norms against which new experiences may be comprehended and assimilated. Some incoherence arising from mismatches between new experiences and schemata is inevitable, but if sufficiently pervasive societal members may eliminate it by changing the way reality is perceived or by changing the norm. This is done either by changing the schemata used for classifying reality or the schemata used for classifying values, respectively, or by changing both (see pp. 160-65, Vickers 1970).

Changes in schemata of reality involve extending or shrinking the number and kinds of objects, events, or persons to which given schemata apply. Changes in schemata of reality that are consistent with and may facilitate the emergence of an organic world-view include the following:

(1) Extension of the schema "democracy" to include the industrial as well as the political sphere.
(2) Extension of the schema "efficiency" from application to a society's constituent parts to application to the society as a whole.
(3) Extension of what is acknowledged as the "consequences of job design" to include the mental and physical health of the worker, effects on socialization, development of social and cognitive skills for becoming a more effective citizen, and so on.
(4) Extension of the schema "corporate asset" to include what an organization's employees know, their capacity to learn new skills, and the organization's current investment in training.
(5) Extension of the schema "job" to include not only the tasks at which the worker is currently employed, but what other tasks he can perform and plans to learn to perform over a given period of time.

Changes in schemata of valuation involve revision or alteration of the "rules" by which a situation is judged right or wrong, fair or unfair, good or bad, and so on. While such changes can be understood in their own right, they influence and are influenced by schemata of reality. Changes in schemata of valuation that are consistent with and may facilitate the emergence of an organic world-view include the following:

(1) Workers allowed to control their own job and share in decision making based on the principle of affected interest. This supplants management's right to direct workers based on the principle of property ownership.
(2) Change from work designed to maximize production to work designed to maximize human growth potential.
(3) Change from economic organizations as maximizers of profit to producers of social utility.

At the end of the preceding section of this chapter, it was suggested that answers to questions concerning who was willing to bear what costs depended on knowing the appreciative judgments of those who would make these choices on behalf of their society. As discussed in this section, the schemata underlying these appreciative judgments are under constant pressure for change. If the schemata of reality and valuation outlined above were to become the basis for the appreciative judgments of those who will make society's choices, the quality of work would be given basic consideration in judging the quality of the society as a whole.

CHAPTER

3

DIRECTED ACTION, MOTIVES, AND WORK PERFORMANCE

The objective of this chapter is to develop a framework for understanding behavior at the work place. The kind of behavior with which this chapter is concerned might be called motivated behavior. However, save for knee jerks, sweating, and so on, nearly everyone upon introspection would acknowledge that most of their behavior seems "motivated" to attain something, thus making the expression "motivated behavior" usually redundant. Discussions of motivation and "how to motivate" arise, perhaps, most frequently in the literature of industrial psychology. However, the frequency with which discussions of motivation arise within the context of work performance suggests that these discussions may be significantly influenced by how contemporary organizations design work and manage those who perform it. One is less likely to question whether behavior is motivated when observed in spheres beyond the work place. For example, the spontaneous involvement of children in play activity and of adults at sports, dating, hobbies, and so on suggests that, perhaps, such spontaneity is more the norm than the exception. The appropriate question to ask may be, What is it about our current methods of work design that take away what is intrinsic in most spheres of human activity beyond the work place? Has it perhaps been the conditions under which contemporary organizations design jobs that require these organizations to search for how to put back into behavior what the job design has taken away?

Although knowledge of behavior in nonwork spheres may offer clues as to why some kinds of behavior are more spontaneous, involving, and persevering than others, this does not imply that a framework for understanding behavior at the work place need offer equal understanding of all behaviors in all other spheres of activity. The behavior of primary concern in this discussion is work performance—that is, behavior that is coordinated and directed with varying degrees of tenaciousness toward the production of socially valued products or services. Less attention is devoted to understanding behavior motivated by hunger, oxygen, or sex* or behavior taking place within contexts where love and affection are paramount, such as in the marital dyad and the family. To understand behavior at the work place, it is not necessary to have an all-encompassing theory that explains all behavior in all settings. Following R. S. Peters (1958) in this regard, the search for such an all-encompassing theory may be neither desirable nor, indeed, even possible.

Acceptance of a more limited framework for understanding behavior at the work place does not imply that love, affection, or any strong affect-laden behavior does not occur at or is unrelated to work. However, what leads an individual to involvement in the performance of the work itself is more easily explained by the framework presented in this chapter than by theories explaining primary group behavior; psychosocial development; unconscious, unresolved conflicts; and so on. While not denying that such theories may be useful for explaining behavior in specific work settings, they are not considered to be of sufficient generality to be a primary explanatory framework for work-related behavior.

THE WORK PLACE AS A CONCRETE SETTING

This chapter discusses a method for predicting and explaining behavior at the work place that differs from methods predominantly used in industrial psychology. The latter generally consist of collecting cross-sectional data and then abstracting variables considered relevant for predicting and explaining behavior. Such methods are appropriate when we are interested in populations rather than single cases or groups. If we wish to describe the characteristics of a population, we may be interested in what the relationship between two or more variables is, on the average, recognizing that a number of individual cases deviate from the average. Invariate relationships may be found, on average, between several variables if multivariate techniques are used. However, the majority of cross-sectional studies restrict their interest

---

*The distress or pleasure associated with psychological states is a drive as distinct from a motive. It will be explained shortly that motives are subordinate parts of a directed action leading to the elimination of a particular drive. Drives and the distress to which they give rise are not activities but conditions of being (see Chein 1972, p. 25).

to two of three variables—for example, the relationship between job variety and mental health, job satisfaction and mental health. Cross-sectional methods are also useful in operations research when we may be seeking to optimize populations characteristics—that is, when, on average, we wish to achieve an optimal outcome. The designer of work faces a problem in acquiring knowledge by cross-sectional methods. He designs work for the individual or the group, each within a concrete setting with a different configuration of variables that influences behavior.

If the designer of work is also a practicing manager, as well he might be, cross-sectional methods applied to a sample of work sites informing him that his design produces positive rather than negative results at a better than chance level may not be adequate to his needs. For example, he may be responsible for managing only one work site, and the mean and standard deviations of a sampling distribution tell him nothing about the configuration of variables at his site that may produce results at the mean of the distribution or three standard deviations from it.

A related question is whether knowledge gained by studying a sample of work sites can ever capture the manner in which variables are related to each other in a particular concrete setting. Inferences drawn from data collected across settings are based on choices by the researcher as to what variables to abstract from these settings. Hypotheses about how variables interrelate are either deduced from theories (in which case the hypothesized interrelationships need only agree with other parts of the theory) or induced from analysis of the data once collected. In the latter case, the inferences are based on choices already made as to what to abstract from a concrete setting. While inferences based on such data may be plausible psychologically, they may not bear any particular relationship to any concrete setting in which behavior is observed.

The study of the concrete case does not imply an atheoretic approach to understanding behavior at the work place. However, the theory or framework used should allow us to go, in Lewin's words (1935, p. 35), "from the particular to the general without thereby losing the particular in the general and thereby making impossible the return from the general to the particular." The essential feature of this framework is that forces directing behavior do not originate solely within the individual but are a function of a total situation at a particular time, consisting of forces within the individual and his enviornment. Unless the full concreteness of the particular situation is captured in one's conceptualization of it, features critical for generalizing will be distorted or lost. It is, perhaps, due to ignoring the total situation and focusing exclusively on the individual that theories of work motivation have developed that attribute high performance to various qualities in the individual, such as "Motive X." This is frequently the case in studies that test the relationship between productivity and Maslow's need deficiencies (Porter 1962; Lawler and Suttle 1972). Conversely, scientific management said little about forces in the individual beyond postulating a naive model of economic man and attributing high performances to qualities of the environment such as incentives, work measurement, and technology. An adequate framework for work design must integrate both the individual and his psychological relevant environment.

BEHAVIOR AS A FUNCTION OF CONTEMPORANEOUS FORCES

The proposition that behavior is a function of contemporaneous forces acting on a given situation at a given time has confused many readers of Lewin's field theory and has resulted in much misinterpretation of what this proposition implies. At least part of the confusion results from the fact that the concept of contemporaneity is open to several interpretations. This section summarizes these different interpretations, in order, it is hoped, to eliminate the confusion.

The proposition of contemporaneity can be interpreted within the context of strict causality. Virtually all social scientists would agree that past events are not "causing" present behavior; there are no mechanisms by which past events travel through time to affect present behavior. However, past events that make virtually irreversible alterations in the structure or functioning of the individual—for example, an industrial accident leading to amputation of a limb—may influence present behavior. Psychic traumas, in the Freudian sense, may do the same. Furthermore, any images or memories of the past can potentially influence present behavior; such images and memories are not static but are subject to alteration by the vagaries of time, selective forgetting, integration with other memories, and so on. Also, future events do not "pull" present behavior toward predetermined ends "existing" in the future. However, images of the future existing in the present are crucial in influencing the individual's present and future behavior. Evered (1976) has called behavior that is guided by contemporaneous images of the future "prospective causality."

The proposition of contemporaneity is demonstrated by Lewin's (1935) conception of behavior as resulting from a field of forces whose configuration may change with changes in the concrete situation. For example, the "path" an individual may take to reach a particular goal is not necessarily known from the field of forces existing the moment the action begins. In Lewin's scheme, each action the individual takes toward the goal changes the strength and direction of field forces existing in a particular situation.

FIGURE 3.1

Situational Determinants of Force Fields

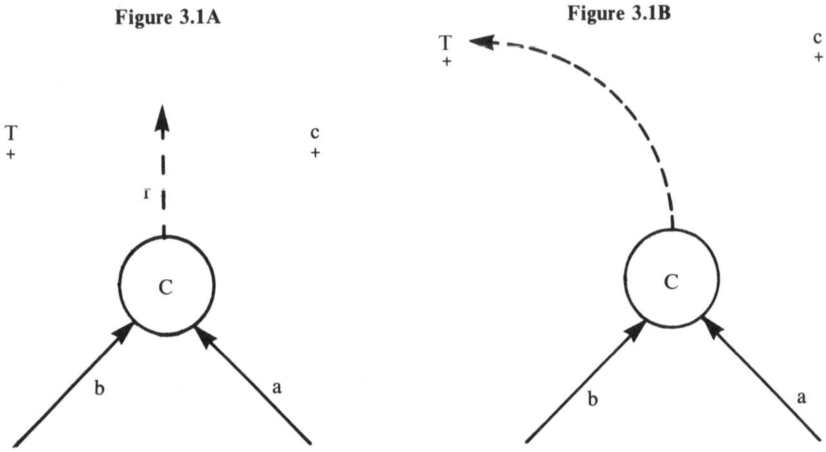

Source: "The Conflict Between Aristotelian and Galileian Modes of Thought in Contempororary Psychology" in Lewin (1935).

A great deal of attention is devoted to goal-directed behavior in Chapter 7. However, it might be useful to introduce some elementary properties of force fields with the following example that Lewin used to demonstrate the point of the preceding paragraph. In Figure 3.1A, a child C stands before two attractive objects (say a toy T and a piece of chocolate c), which are in different places. According to Lewin, there exist force fields in the direction a and b. Based on the resultant of the two forces existing at the moment described in Figure 3.1A one would predict (by resolution of vectors assuming a parallogram of forces) that the child would take direction r which leads to neither T nor c. However, once the child begins to move toward one or the other of the two attractive objects, the strength of the two forces changes—for example, T may take on stronger valence and c a weaker one as the child moves toward T. The resulting path to the toy would resemble that shown in Figure 3.1B. These two figures illustrate that to predict and understand the direction of behavior, one must be able to refer to the whole situation in its concrete individuality, to the state of the situation at every moment of time.

The third issue raised by the proposition of contemporaneity is whether this notion differs from what is referred to as the ahistorical. Many writers (for example, Vroom 1964) do not make a clear distinction between the two terms, interpreting "ahistorical" within the context of the first issue discussed in this section. In his article "The Conflict Between Aristotelian and Galileian Modes of Thought in Contemporary Psychology," Lewin criticized Aristotelian thinking for confusing the historical-geographic accidents associated with a particular case as an expression of its essential character. Lewin felt this was due to the Aristotelian inclination to seek laws by discovering statistical regularities in nature. The Aristotelian use of classifications for defining the essence of the cases contained within them offers no criterion for separating accident from essence. An example of Aristotelian thinking in contemporary industrial psychology would be to conclude from data showing a high correlation between authoritarian structures and moderately high production that authoritarian structures are essential for achieving moderately high production. An Aristotelian would not see this relationship as resulting from the particular history of the Industrial Revolution discussed in Chapter 2.

In Galileian thinking, laws are established from the concrete case and are invariant even if these cases occur only rarely. As the work designer deals almost exclusively with persons and tasks in a concrete setting, intensive study of single cases would appear to be the most appropriate method for discovering the laws governing their behavior. Allport (1937) called laws derived from the single case ideographic, to distinguish them from nomothetic laws that are generated from the study of populations. The rationale for single case studies is that each person or group constitutes a behavioral universe that operates according to its own laws. Each person or group generates its own laws (or rules for possible functional relationships). These laws are derived from the nature of the person's or group's own psychophysical structure and his or its transactional relationship with the environment (see Herbst 1970, pp. 3-13). Such generating rules may be discovered either by studying a subject doing the same task over a prolonged time period or studying a subject doing a different set of tasks during the same short time periods.

The generating rules of ideographic laws are constant, but the functional relationships they generate may take a specific form in different concrete settings (so may parameters). Either of the latter may change with changes in attitudes, skill level, and so on. In Aristotelian thinking, functional relationships must be constant for a law to exist at all—for example, the relationship between productivity and job satisfaction. In contrast, the Galileian might view the same data and try to predict what kinds of behavior workers might exhibit if new organizational forms were created.

DIRECTED ACTION

Our primary unit of analysis is human action taken in a concrete setting. In particular, we are concerned with "directed action," defined by Chein (1972, p. 70) as "action, the course of which is, in fact, particularized with respect to an object, regardless of the syntactical form used to describe it." This definition specifies the molar quality of a directed action; it stands by itself as a total unit of action regardless of the verb form or object specified. The existence of a directed action may be verified by observing whether the course of action is maintained by compensation or adjustment when the object's location changes or barriers are placed along the action's course. Thus, if, at the work place, we observe a worker assembling an amplifier from several electronic components, we would describe his action as directed toward the completion of the amplifier; this description does not change if the worker varies the sequence, timing, or types of skeletal-muscular movements he chooses to complete it.

The things, events, processes, symbols of a concrete situation are not objects until an action is directed toward them. The object of a directed action might more properly be called an object relationship, because a directed action is completed only when a future relationship between the subject, the originator of the action, and the object of interest has been realized. Thus, completion of the directed action "to eat an apple" is not to walk over and stand next to an apple, but to establish a consummatory relationship to the apple by biting into it, chewing it, and swallowing the apple pieces. While the taste of the apple itself may be pleasurable and may be a reason for eating it in the first place, the future relationship the subject seeks to establish with the apple is that it entered within his gastrointestinal tract. He learns to bring this about by establishing subsidiary relationships between himself and the apple. Thus, at first, the relationship between himself and the apple is spatiotemporal. Upon reaching the site of the apple, a relationship exists between his muscular-skeletal, proprioceptive system and the apple as a physical, relatively hard object. After the apple reaches the location of the subject's mouth, the relationship consists of his oral-masticatory system and the apple as a semisoft object. In each of these subsidiary relationships, he has learned from prior encounters with apples under varying, but relatively similar situations, what relationships to establish between himself and the apple's changing attributes.

The object relationships illustrated in the apple-eating example are no different in principle from those one learns in transforming objects (from "raw material" to completed product) at the work place. Object relationships in the work place are more constrained by criteria of efficiency and effectiveness than those contained in the apple-eating example, but the difference is primarily one of degree. One learns, in either case, the "rules" by which he may relate himself (the parts of himself) to changing object attributes and develops, with practice,"skill" in carrying out the rule-complying actions.

Although the subject is likely to be conscious of his directed actions at the point of their initiation, he need not be. The "wish" is the antecedent of action, and within the Freudian scheme, wishes may be unconcious. However, if the subject's wish is conscious, it takes the form of an imagined future relationship between himself and his object of interest. In the apple-eating example, where the subject is separated from an apple by a few feet, the future is immediate, and, unless a barrier exists between the subject and the apple (for example, it is on a very high shelf beyond his reach), he may not be aware of the image. In fact, unless an obstacle or barrier to the object exists, what Chein calls "a snag in the smooth progress of a behavior," the action, according to field theorists (such as Lewin 1951 and Ryan 1970), would not be called intentional. If one leaves aside the existence of barriers, obstacles, or snags to establishing object relationships and if the object is not physical but is a process, event, symbol, and so on, the further into the future the realization of the imagined object relationship, and the more vulnerable the imagined object relationship is to shifting definitions and the meanings imparted by the individual and by his related social groupings. Another important influence on the nature of imagined future object relationships not yet mentioned is the importance of the object to the feeling, needing subject. This influence will be taken up in a latter section.

MOTIVES

The reader has learned from the above section that directed actions may vary greatly in duration. Minimally, the duration may be so short that an observer would charaterize the subject's actions as "impulsive": Each action appears unconnected to the others. However, even actions of such short duration are directed, requiring the subject to focus his eyes and turn his head and shoulders toward the object of interest. In contrast, the duration of a directed action may be very long, lasting for years—for example, the decision of a student to pursue a Ph.D. degree while he is still a freshman in college.

The directed action of the freshman pursuing his coveted doctorate differs from the directed action of minimal duration in that the former contains within it a hierarchically arranged sequence of directed actions each possessing an "in order to" quality in relation to those that follow in the sequence. For example, the student will diligently study for his examinations "in order to" earn a passing grade in each course of a particular semester. He will maintain a high grade-point average "in order to" get a bachelor's degree with honors. He will apply to graduate school "in order to" pursue a doctoral program, and so on. It is the "in order to" quality of a directed action that defines it as a motive; any directed action that requires a subordinate expediting act to be included in it is a motive.

Defining a motive as an act or as a behavior differs from how the concept of motive has come to be conceived in most theories of motivation in contemporary psychology. A motive as conventionally conceived is an energizer of behavior; it is something "behind" or "prior to" behavior. While energizers may raise the tension level of an organism, by themselves energizers could lead only to random activity. Even if one adds directionality to the conception of motive as energizer, if it continues to be conceived as something "prior to" or "behind" behavior, it cannot be a necessary and sufficient explanation of behavior in a given situation. There are just too many different behaviors that a human organism can elicit to accomplish the same end. Some of these behaviors result from emergent conditions or barriers not foreseen at the time that behavior was predicted.

The dilemmas that arise from conceiving of a motive as "behind" or "prior to" behavior disappear if a motive is conceptualized as a subordinate part of the molar unit, directed action. The following considerations lend support to this belief.

1. Directed action is a transactional concept. This means that such action does not originate or reside exclusively within the subject but is a jointly determined outcome of the characteristics or properties of the object and the definition or meaning the subject imparts to the situation in which the object is embedded. This was implied in the discussion of establishing object relationships—for example, apple eating. Within the molar unit of a directed action, neither subject nor object is considered the sole originator of action; each is a "prompting force" (Angyal 1941) for the other.

2. The definition of a directed action includes a future object relationship the realization of which "completes" the directed action. The future object relationship represents the end or goal toward which behavior is directed; it informs us of its purpose. If the observer knows the end or goal of an action, he possesses a molar unit of understanding within which the subject's specific and varied behaviors "make sense."

Frequently, the reason an observer cannot predict a subject's behavior is that the observer has arbitrarily selected a time frame for a completed action that does not coincide with that of the subject. For example, suppose we observe a man leave his house, walk down the street to a newsstand, and purchase a newspaper. If we end our observation at the point at which the man picked up the newspaper and paid for it, our inference might be that the motive for his action was to find out about the world beyond his immediate experience, the world of sports, art, politics, finance, and so on. If our inference were correct, we would predict that before long he will return to his house or search for a public bench on which to sit and read his newspaper. Suppose, however, we observe that instead of proceeding to do either of these activities, he continues down the street, stops at an empty store front, lights the newspaper with a match, and tosses it in the store's doorway. Obviously, our initial inference that he bought the newspaper to read it would be incorrect.

Another reason an observer may not be able to predict a subject's behavior is that the observer does not share with the subject the same definition or meaning of the situation or the same "universe" of moral concerns. Management, as the observer, may be surprised that its workers are not "motivated" to produce more units of output when a new incentive system is installed that pays the worker an additional amount of money for each additional unit of output produced. The incentive system that management believes is "in the worker's best interest" to comply with, may be defined by the workers as a management device to "make us fight among ourselves" or to "hold a whip over us." What management might see as "the way a man can prove his self-worth," workers might see as "a way to make another guy look bad or get him laid off."

In order to understand the transactional character of a directed action, it is necessary that the observer share with the subject the latter's time frame for action and definition of the situation. When we do not share these with the subject, we do not "understand" the "in order to" quality of his behavior and may, as a result, fall back upon a more primitive type of thinking by explaining his behavior as the result of something that resides solely within him, such as an energy called motive X.

3. The hierarchical character of motives is implicit in the definition of a motive as a directed action requiring subordinate behaviors for its completion—that is, the motive of the subordinate behavior is its superordinate directed action. In the example above of the freshman who aspires to attain a Ph.D. degree, we could trace the "in order to" quality of his behavior down to the bottom of the hierarchy, where we would reach the motive for his taking his pen in hand. Carrying out such a procedure may lead the reader to ask several questions: (a) If we trace the freshman's motives "upwards" in his hierarchy of motives, will we not reach a point at which the "in order to" quality of his behavior will end and he will tell you the reason for an action is "just because"? (b) Is human behavior as rational as is implied in the hierarchy of motives? The freshman may not be able to tell us the reason for actions that are several "steps" removed from what he is currently doing or may not be able to tell us any reasons for action at all. (c) During the next eight years, the freshman is not directing all of his actions toward the Ph.D. degree. Is he not pursuing other ends or goals simultaneously?

Question (a) will be discussed at length in the next section, but a preview of the answer can be provided here. There is a lack of agreement in contemporary psychology as to whether a motive should be conceptualized as energizing behavior or as giving behavior its directionality. The theory of directed action outlined in this chapter explains the direction of behavior by the concept of directed action with its implied hierarchy of motives. Motives do not energize behavior, *condition of being* do that. The first condition of human experience is the discomfort associated with hunger and thirst. This condition in the newborn infant leads only to crying and randomized thrashing of the body and limbs, not to directed action. The infant will learn directed actions after discovering that the nipple removes his initial discomfort and replaces it with the experience of relative well-being. The means by which the child obtains milk, warmth, and love are prototypes by which directed actions are learned. As the infant matures, his behavior will be increasingly oriented towards objects bearing no relationship to physiological drives at all. The objects in his world will increasingly take the form of symbols as well as will the network of relationships that define the situations in which we will take actions. Because of its symbolic nature, his world will extend beyond the momentary present into the future. He will develop what Lewin (1935) calls "action-wholes," by which the goals that influence behavior are thrown continually into the future.

Conditions of well-being may initially arise from physiological drives and their satiation, but they are also the existential qualities of living and are equally experienced throughout adult life in the form of distress, anxiety, pleasure, or mild pleasantness. One's most comprehensive directed actions, those that justify one's life and give it meaning as well as the short-term directed actions one takes daily are oriented to moving away from or toward these conditions of being (or their anticipation). We shall return to discussing these within the context of work shortly.

Question (b) can be answered in several ways: The freshman need not be aware at all times that the reason he is in the library at 11 p.m. is because his ultimate goal is to attain a Ph.D. degree. The latter goal may be the reason he enrolled in the university, but he is not thinking about this while he is studying to pass his chemistry examination tomorrow morning. We might say he has forgotten why he is doing what he is presently doing, knowing that if we prompted him to trace the "in order to" quality of his actions, he would inevitably "remember" his reason. We will leave aside the basic question of why he considers it important that he should have a Ph.D. —for example, to have a meaningful life, to satisfy his parents, and so on— until we discuss conditions of being in the section below.

The objection that the freshman does not plan the steps toward his future as rationally as implied by a heirarchy of motives may be based on the computer program as the paradigm for how humans plan. Although humans know how to make some plans the way a computer can does not mean that humans plan this way in general. Humans may guide their actions relative to principles or abstractions that lack the completeness and precision that computers require of their programs (see Hatt 1968; Hayek 1969). Humans need not be as literal minded as computers in carrying out their actions. There is an incompleteness to their action-wholes that guides subsidiary actions, allowing improvisation through a series of concrete situations to achieve the same ends in different ways. Hayek offers a theory that concrete human acts are the product of the brain's capacity to organize and reshuffle deeply structured, perhaps inarticulable abstractions. These abstractions function as organizing principles for lower-level abstractions, eventually leading to principles by which the individual can organize intentional action. More recently, see Powers (1973) for an empirically based theory similar to Hayek's.

As question (c) implies, a human life is filled with the simultaneous pursuit of and escape from present and anticipated outcomes. It is the human condition that many coveted outcomes cannot be pursued without the potential loss of other equally coveted outcomes or without enduring, at the same time, outcomes that are unpleasant. Life is a process of orchestrating one's actions by combining, where possible, the pursuit of several outcomes by the same action, of compromising and choosing between outcomes when it is necessary to do so. Justification and rationalization for the choices one makes may help to soothe the pain of desired outcomes foregone.

An individual's span of foresight permits him to anticipate the things, events, and processes that his present course of action will lead him to encounter and permits him to choose, as best he can, the courses of action that produce more satisfaction and less despair. A greater span of foresight does not imply than one can prevent some encounters from happening. When an individual believes himself powerless to change the future, his prevailing sentiment many be resignation or hope. As Sennett and Cobb (1972) attest, powerlessness may be too painful a condition for many to accept. One may deny this condition by believing that he has *chosen* to sacrifice for others. This act of denial may be the final rationalization when one feels powerless. As we shall see, the self as the agent or originator for directed action is a key to the design of meaningful work.

DIRECTED ACTION AND CONDITIONS OF BEING

As previously discussed, there is lack of agreement in contemporary psychology as to whether a motive energizes behavior or gives direction to behavior. The concept of directed action was introduced to explain the latter. The energizer of behavior, if that is an apt metaphor, is a condition of being or existential state that, upon introspection, an individual would characterize by varying degrees of pleasantness or unpleasantness, pleasure or unpleasure, anxiety or exhilaration, and so on. The individual is most likely to take action to enhance, prolong, or recreate those experiences he would characterize as positive, and to take action to diminish or terminate those experiences he would characterize as negative. Depending on the nature of the affect he experiences, the individual will take directed actions that move him toward or away from objects in his environment. The object of a directed action is not the affect that the individual experiences but the events, processes, and things he has learned or hypothesized will enhance or diminish the affect.

In addition to whether the affect experienced is positive or negative, its relationship to a directed action depends on whether it is experienced before or during the performance of a directed action or in anticipation of its outcome.

Affect is experienced before a directed action commences if the individual has no warning or anticipation that such an affect will be experienced. If the affect is unpleasant, the individual will take action to diminish or eliminate the affect. The sudden appearance of a dangerous animal while walking in the woods, the commitment of a faux pas, or the unexpected or unintentional occurrence of an embarrassing, guilt- or shame-provoking situation produces the kind of affect the individual would try to diminish or eliminate, by running away from the dangerous animal, by avoiding those individuals who embarrassed him, by repressing the situation from memory, and so on. Chein (1972) considers repression of a thought to be a directed action; an unpleasant thought is the object to which another behavior, selective inattention, is directed. Chein assumes that subliminal awareness of the object exists, and the subject need not be conscious of his directed actions toward it.

Affect may be experienced *during* the performance of a directed action. Baldamus (1961) suggests the term "tedium" for the affect experienced while performing tasks of relatively short duration which must be repeated frequently, circumstances quite common to industrial production. Baldamus (1961) suggests the term "tedium" for this affect. It appears to be greatest when the required action consists of cycles of short duration. Although it may not be possible totally to eliminate industrial work of this kind, Baldamus suggests that tedium may be postponed or overlaid by "substitute satisfactions" subsumed under the label of "traction." "Traction," according to Baldamus (p. 59),

> is a feeling of being pulled along by the inertia inherent in a particular activity. The experience is pleasant and may therefore

> function as a relief from tedium. It usually appears to be associated, though not always, with a feeling of reduced effort, relative to actual or imagined situations where it is difficult to maintain continuity of performance.
>
> Example of traction include the following:

Object traction: derived from visualizing an object or its parts that one feels an urge to reproduce or complete.

Batch traction: connected with a desire to complete a batch of articles. It grows stronger as completion of the batch approaches.

Process traction: experienced in operations where the tempo and sequence of one's motions are determined by the chemical or physical nature of the production process. It is a pleasant sensation connected with being guided or pulled along by the process.

Affect may also be experienced in anticipation of the consequences of a directed action. If the individual anticipates that others will admire or be grateful for what he will do, then this may be one of the reasons he will undertake the action. If, however, he anticipates that he will be criticized or punished by others or that he will feel ashamed or punished for what he will do, then he will avoid actions that will make the undesirable outcome likely.

Expectancy theories (Vroom 1964; Atkinson and Feather 1966; Porter and Lawler 1967; Steers and Porter 1975), as they have come to be collectively called, are based on anticipation of future outcomes. Objects of directed action that are associated with particular conditions of being (because they augment or attenuate such conditions, as the case may be) may themselves take on "valences," which Vroom (p. 15) defines as "an affective orientation toward particular outcomes." The valence of a particular outcome is based on (1) the cognized instrumentality of an object for the attainment of the outcome and (2) the intensity and the nature of the affect associated with each outcome.

In addition to the valences they associate with a particular outcome, individuals also form "expectancies" concerning whether the outcome an individual is seeking (or avoiding) will be attained. Expectancies may vary from "0" for impossible to "1" for certain outcomes. Vroom's theory assumes individuals to be subjectively rational, and any act they choose to perform is "a monotonically increasing function of the algebraic sum of the products of the valences of all outcomes and the strength of (their) expectancies that the act will be followed by the attainment of these outcomes" (p. 18). This formulation is quite similar to the economist's theory of maximizing subjective utility.

Expectancy theories are consistent with the theory of directed action. The theories are similar in that (1) both view behavior as oriented toward future outcomes, (2) both view behavior as arranged into hierarchies where subordinate acts are instrumental to superordinate acts. Expectancy theories differ from the theory of directed action in that (1) the former do not consider motives as behavior but as affective orientations toward outcomes (for example, Vroom; Atkinson and Feather) and (2) the latter does not assume that choices between behaviors are made as rationally as do expectancy theories (Atkinson and Feather are exceptions). The theory of directed action is concerned not only with what objects an individual (or group) chooses to pursue, but why and how he ought to pursue them. The latter concerns values which have aesthetic and moral as well as rational aspects. Values influence "the selection of available modes, means, and ends of action" (Kluckholn 1951, p. 395). They influence action because the latter have consequences for maintaining coherence and consequence among values, the primary systemic dimension among values.

The theory of directed action is concerned with an action's "intrinsic appropriateness," a Gestaltic property, as it is with an action's rationality. Expectancy theories have been developed and tested in circumstances where subjects tend to behave more rationally than they might otherwise—for example, choosing an occupation (Vroom 1964) following incentive systems (Steers and Porter 1975) and might be viewed as special cases of a more general theory of directed action.

Many of the outcomes discussed in this section are desired because they enhance the self as originator of action. The directed actions and outcomes with which this book is concerned are those that produce socially useful products or services. A cardinal principle of work design is that self-enhancement be a natural byproduct of such production. Self-enhancement is the subject of the next section of this chapter.

THE SELF AS ORIGINATOR OF DIRECTED ACTION

The self evolves, according to Klein (1932, 1959), from the earliest mother-child relationship. Through this relationship, the child learns to reject those attributions to self that cause anxiety and accept those that lead to the experience of well-being. These feelings are inextricably bound to the mother's accepting or rejecting behavior toward the child as well as how the child reacts to his mother's behavior. The child's behavior, in turn, affects how accepting or rejecting the mother is, thus defining the reciprocal nature of the relationship.

The adult self emerging from this relationship relates itself to objects in its environment that are consistent with the "good self" and rejects those objects that imply a "bad self." The individual may do this by identifying with the object (projective identification) or by taking in attributes of the object as parts of oneself (introjection). More will be said in Chapter 7 about these mechanisms. Another way in which an individual may relate himself to objects is by directed actions whose outcomes (establishment of an object relationship) produce feelings of self-enhancement.

Implicit in the discussion of directed action is the actor or originator of action. Very early in life, the child discovers a distinction between himself and his surroundings. He discovers that he is the "cause" or originator of actions that alter in some way the events in his surroundings. White (1959) reports evidence that children are gratified when they discover the connection between a movement executed and the accompanying and subsequent sensations. This discovery "gives rise to the triumphant feeling of making an organ obedient to the will of the ego" (p. 64, White quoting Abraham Kardiner). White takes such observations as evidence of a "competence motivation," which leads individuals throughout their lives into actions by which they may experience competence and the positive affect associated with it.

Chein (1972) considers the self to be "the center of gravity of the being of the actor." It is the focal point by which the self locates events, processes, and things in time and space. Knowledge of relations between objects, processes, and things grows through encounters with them and through what others tell him about such relations. In addition to being a center of gravity or "hub" of activity, the self may also be an object of awareness—that is, the self focused upon itself as an object, the "self-concept." Quoting Chein (p. 219):

> It is probably true that most, perhaps all, motivation with regard to the self is either self-preservative, self-enhancing, or self-determining; self-preservative, not in the sense of protecting it from extinction but in the sense of preserving its status, reputation, competencies, base of operations, possessions, territorial and other rights and prerequisites, and so on, and securing the conditions that make such preservations possible; self-enhancing in the sense of obtaining more of whatever is involved in self-preservation, that is, improved status, reputation, competence, powers, and so forth; and self-determining in the sense that various writers have used inner-directedness, self-actualization, growth motivation and so on.

All action need not be initiated with the conscious intent of preserving and enhancing the self-concept, but it seems safe to say that preservation and enhancement of the self is a constraint to which directed actions must conform. When other objects are in *focal awareness,* self-enhancement, self-preservation, self-determination may be subconscious, or in what Gestalt psychologists call "distal" or "subsidiary" awareness. They are subject to awareness if attention shifts toward the self as object (see Heider 1958; Polanyi 1958).

We could devote many pages to the self-concept, and the effects of self-perception on an individual's behavior, but as this book is devoted to one type of behavior in particular, work performance, it would be appropriate to deal with the self-concept only where it is directly relevant to our subject matter.

The self-concept is relevant to work performance because of the role it plays in determining the significance and meaning the individual places on his work relative to his life as a whole. The pursuit of a Ph.D. degree is a directed action that is probably very central to the self-concept of the freshman because this course of action provides a means for demonstrating that he is a person worthy of his own and others' respect. There are, of course, other means by which he may demonstrate his competence, such as in sports and hobbies, but that to which he will devote so large a proportion of the next seven years provides him with ample opportunities for such demonstration. There are relatively few jobs in an industrial society that permit its occupants the same number of opportunities or any opportunities at all to demonstrate competence.

How can the worker enhance his self-concept and add meaning to his life, in general, if his job requires no skill, negligible use of intellect, and no meaningful way of relating to organizational goals? Obviously, this would be very difficult to do. However, humans live in a world of images that, under given sociohistorical circumstances, may be organized to allow the worker to relate even menial tasks to larger purposes. For example, during World War II, U.S. workers frequently displayed great commitment to menial tasks that could be construed as contributing to the war effort. Many public relations campaigns and much government propaganda were devoted to reinforcing such connections. A worker in a developing country may display the same commitment if he can relate what he does to building his country's future (see Riskin 1974). His government may appeal to nationalism or socialism as the larger purpose to which his work relates. In both examples, there is a larger purpose to which current activities relate, and one's self-concept may be enhanced by identification with a larger social entity and its successes. However, the conditions cited do not generally exist in advanced industrial countries. The United States, for example, is perhaps too large, heterogeneous, and affluent for nationalistic fervor to be a continuous source of work motivation (as Tausky 1973 suggests). One can only hope that nations will find other means than war to unite its people in common cause.

Nevertheless, these examples should provide clues to the importance of relating action to larger action-wholes, that is, to larger purposes. When work is designed so that it takes on the "in order to" quality discussed above, the activities that make up the work become motives for accomplishing desired outcomes.

INCORPORATING DIRECTED ACTION INTO WORK DESIGN

A directed action can transform its subordinate activities into motives of tenacious strength if the outcome of the directed action is valued by its originator and its realization can be attributable to him. In the world of the work place, outcomes that workers may value include the production of products and services that are of value to the organization, to its customers and clients, and to the larger society. Workers also value production requiring the exercise and demonstration of skill. Work will provide self-enhancing experiences to the one who performs it when he can observe, upon self-reflection, that "I am doing work that others respect," that "meaningful contributions to the products or services of this organization can be attributed to my actions," or that "I am the originator or 'cause' of actions and outcomes that are valued by others." When work is designed so that such observations of the phenomenal self are possible, directed actions draw subordinate activities together into larger action-wholes as a magnet would attract iron filings to itself.

An important work-design principle for reestablishing the connection between intention and action destroyed by traditional job design is that work must allow the worker to experience himself as the cause of outcomes that are valuable and that may be attributed to him. This principle is translated below into five operational statements concerning work design. Documentation of supporting studies are provided only where it might help to understand the points being made. Each statement is a synthesis of many theorists, notably Tolman (1932), Lewin (1935), and Chein (1972), and many hundreds of empirical studies. Collectively, the statements offer rules or guidelines for work design, rather than support or lack of support for any particular theory. The reader who is interested in more extensive documentation of supporting studies might refer to Argyris (1964), Vroom (1964), or *Work in America* (1972).

1. Workers are more likely to experience self-enhancement if their products and services are valued by their employing organization and/or by the larger society.

The employing organization demonstrates the value it places on its workers' products and services by the general manner in which it treats its employees (as in its personnel policies) and the extent to which it solicits and permits its employees to participate in decision making. Also, the value of the product or service itself is reflected in judgments made by the organization's customers and by the larger society in general—for example, values placed on the production of medical supplies versus deodorants or doing janitorial work versus drafting blueprints.

2. Workers can experience self-enhancing observations of the phenomenal self if the products or services they produce form "meaningful wholes."

Products or services form a meaningful whole when, as objects of directed action, they evoke strong visual images that "stand by themselves." Such images may result when the worker understands the uses to which his products or services will be put by customers or clients. If his work permits him to interact directly with customers or clients, as did frame men (Ford 1969) and service-order representatives (Ford 1973) employed in the Bell Telephone System, the worker will receive direct feedback of the use and satisfaction that clients receive from his products and services. Even if a worker's product or service does not consist of a completed product used by a customer or client, it will stand by itself as a meaningful whole if it is a vital part of a product or service without which the product or service would be incomplete.

3. Workers may have self-enhancing experiences if the production of outcomes allows them to experience competence and to demonstrate this to others.

In the view of Sennett and Cobb (1972), competence is experienced when action is "united with the real self," permitting one, in their words, "to carry out Nietzsche's injunction to unite love and power." One experiences competence, then, when action and intention are united around the self as originator of action.

Competence can be experienced by workers when their work has been designed so that tasks demand enough knowledge and skill to challenge their intellectual and sensorimotor skills but are not so demanding as to make failure a frequent occurrence. Competence is experienced when an individual's accomplishments are equal to or exceed his level of aspiration—that is, when they are equal to or exceed what he thinks he is capable of doing (see Lewin et al. 1944; and, more recently, Atkinson and Feather 1966; Zander 1971). If the worker finds that his task assignments permit him always to exceed what he believes himself capable of doing, he will lose interest in his work because it will provide him no opportunity to experience competence. However, if his task assignments are such that he nearly always falls short of what he is capable of doing, he will also lose interest in his work because it produces in him a sense of inadequacy. Under either of the two circumstances, the work place has lost any attractiveness as a site where self-enhancing experiences are likely to occur. The consequences may spread to the nonwork sphere in the form of generalization of inadequacy or of compensation by finding challenges at other activities such as sports or sex, and so on.

Work may be designed to permit a worker to test and revise his level of aspiration as he learns the knowledge and skills necessary to perform increasingly demanding tasks. This may be accomplished by providing the worker with a "career path" toward assignments of increasing difficulty. Over a sufficiently long time period, this may mean promotion into positions of increasing responsibility, but over the near term, a set of tasks, each requiring an equal but different kind of challenge, can be assigned to a group of workers. Group members possessing the skills and knowledge demanded of each set may become teachers of those assigned to other sets, allowing each the opportunity to acquire new knowledge and skills through guidance and systematic rotation. To ensure the success of such an arrangement, a reward system must be devised to reward those who teach and learn from each other. The tasks assigned to some groups permit group members to exchange these two roles continuously.

A large pet-food manufacturer designed and built a plant that incorporated many of the principles of work design being discussed here (see Walton 1972). Workers were assigned to work groups in which sets of tasks were designed to be equally challenging (although each set comprised unique skill demands). There was a single job classification for all work-group members, but pay increases were geared to members mastering an increasing proportion of the tasks, first in the work group and then in the total plant. Thus, group members were paid for learning more and more of the total system of which they were a part. Since there were no limits on the number of workers who could qualify for higher pay brackets, each was encouraged to teach the other.

4. Workers will have self-enhancing experiences if their work is designed so that they perceive themselves to be the cause of valued outcomes and if such outcomes can be attributed to them.

Self-enhancing experiences will result when workers are held responsible for the production of such outcomes and when they are permitted sufficient control over tools, machines, and information so that they can produce outcomes of acceptable quality and quantity

The attribution of outcomes to a particular worker or group of workers is reinforced when they occupy a common territory that is recognized within the organization as the location from which a particular valued outcome arises. This is reinforced by designing work places as self-contained units of production in which a sociopsychological boundary exists between the worker(s) and the rest of the organization. Miller and Rice (1967) refer to this sociopsychological boundary as a "sentient boundary." They theorize that when this boundary is weak, group members divide their loyalties among other groups within their organization and lack the commitment to accomplishing their own work group's goals. However, when the boundary is strong, the group members have difficulties coordinating their goals with those of other groups within their organization, creating, as a consequence, organizational conflict and loss of efficiency and effectiveness. Developing an optimal balance between these two forces is a problem for sociotechnical system design and will be discussed in Chapter 8.

Self-contained units form Gestalts in the minds of organizational members, particularly among those who work within the same unit. This is particularly so when group members are assigned the production of a particular product or service and responsibility for such production resides within the work group. The latter implies that management has designed a system of accountability so that "variances" or errors can be traced to those who produce them. Following Trist (1973), a variance is any deviation from a standard or specification (see also Chapter 5). A variance is key if it significantly affects (1) either the quantity of production or its quality or (2) either its operating or its social costs. A principle of sociotechnical system design is to assure that key variances can be controlled, as much as possible, by the unit responsible for the operations that produce them, thus minimizing their "export" to other units of the organization or its environment.

Workers will experience themselves as the cause of valued outcomes when they are autonomous and self-regulating. Workers are autonomous when they are permitted to decide on the activities necessary to produce the products or services for which they are held responsible and to regulate such activities so as to maintain an acceptable level of quantity and quality. If workers are not delegated discretion commensurate with their responsibilities, they will not experience themselves as the cause of the organization's valued outcomes. Self-regulation is intimately associated with autonomy and exists for workers when they are provided with sufficient tools, machines, and information to maintain the standards for which management has held them accountable. Self-regulation requires that workers be provided with feedback on the type and sources of variances they make so that they themselves can take corrective action. Immediate feedback also permits workers to increase their requisite knowledge and skills by providing them with opportunities for self-learning.

5. The association between directed actions and the self as their originator is strengthened to the extent that the worker perceives his directed actions as contributing to larger action-wholes with which he may identify.

As stated earlier, affluent, heterogeneous countries do not offer the circumstances under which a worker can easily make a connection between what he is currently doing and the larger national purpose. However, affluence also frees the individual from preoccupation with economic insecurity and increases the likelihood that he will shift attention to needs related to self-enhancement.

The longest self-related action-whole to which an individual may focus his attention concerns how he will make sense of or give meaning to his life. An individual lives his life from the same continuous frame of reference, his self, around which the events, processes, and things that impinge on him are organized into a temporal Gestalt. A temporal Gestalt makes sense out of isolated events, processes, things, and so on, by relating them to his self-concept through the dimension of time. These events and so on make sense because they fit in with an individual's conception of who he is and what he believes his future to be. They make sense as does a musical note when and only when it becomes part of a recognizable melody.

Work to which an individual may devote a half of his waking life for 40 years contributes significantly to the meaning an individual gives to his life. If an individual has been assigned to the same unchallenging dead-end job for his entire working life, he must find some way to come to terms with this experience and relate it to the rest of his life. Such a working experience may generate an anxiety fundamental to the self—that it is not in control of what happens, that it is helpless. As Sennett and Cobb have suggested, the ultimate defense under such circumstances is sacrifice; if an individual cannot change the course of events, he can believe he has chosen to sacrifice. In Sennett and Cobb's (1972) interviews with blue-collar workers in unskilled, low-paying jobs, many report to making meaning out of their working lives by sacrificing for someone else's future, that of their wives and children.

Work can be designed so that the individual can relate what he is currently doing to his conception of a desirable future. Just as an apprentice can make sense out of his current tasks because doing them will someday lead to his becoming a journeyman or just as the freshman can make sense out of studying for tomorrow's examination because it will bring him closer to obtaining his Ph.D., so might the present production of products or services provide opportunities for personal development if the work has been designed to encourage self-learning, if work assignments are related to each other so that each new assignment offers different challenges from the last, and if the organization offers a career path to workers by supporting outside and company-sponsored educational programs leading to promotions and higher pay.

Work can also be experienced as a temporal Gestalt by organizing it into a series of larger action-wholes. The completion of each action-whole represents a mission. Trist, Brown, and Susman (1975) collaborated with a labor-management committee to set up an autonomous section of a coal mine in this manner. Coal miners were given responsibility for mining a section of a mine called a "butt" and were supplied data on the productivity and cost of mining their section. Each butt took approximately six months to a year to mine. During this time, it was necessary, maybe 30 to 40 times, to break down, move, and rebuild one of the belts that conveyed coal from the underground to the surface. Miners were supplied productivity and cost data by belt moves, which they reviewed at day-long section conferences held every six weeks. When work is organized around time units that are intrinsic to the work to be done, rather than by units of the calendar, the time units will "stand by themselves" as bases by which tasks can be meaningfully organized.

THE WORK GROUP AS ORIGINATOR OF DIRECTED ACTION

Up until now, when referring to the self as originator of directed action, it was implied that the referent was singular rather than plural. However, more than one worker may be required to produce products or services that form meaningful wholes of value to the employing organization. When this is so, the work group rather than the individual can be the primary unit of work, and all that was said above concerning how to produce self-enhancing experiences for the individual are applicable to the work group as an originator of directed action.

It is no more difficult to design work with the work group as the center of action than it is to design work for the individual. Studies of primitive societies as well as studies of early childhood development indicate that the self as referent of action need not be coincident with the boundaries of the skin. Such coincidence predominates among the members of Western civilization, but it is a learned coincidence. The fact that the self as originator of action need not be bound by the skin explains the origin of the human capacity for identification with social units of varying size. When such identification takes place, the "I" becomes the "we." In grammar, both the I and the we are first person, the center from which action originates and to which action is done. When identification with a larger social unit exists, it becomes the referent of action. When the social unit is successful, the individual who identifies with it is successful. When the social unit fails or one of its members is attacked, the individual who identifies with the social unit fails or is attacked. Further, if the group is cohesive, a member starting one part of a task completed by another member may vicariously experience the satisfaction of completing the whole task (see Lewis 1944).

When the work group rather than the individual worker is the primary unit of design, the criteria developed above to promote self-enhancing experiences for the individual are as applicable to individuals as members of work groups. In the latter case, design centers on the work group as the producer of desired outcomes. As the production of products or services representing meaningful wholes frequently necessitates that the work group be the primary unit of production, the major focus of the remainder of the book will be on work groups. However, this should not suggest that the criteria for promoting self-enhancement need be applied only at one level of analysis or the other. The criteria are simultaneously applicable to both levels and will be jointly realized by shifting from the individual level to the work-group level as the nature of the work demands it.

THE ONTOGENIC CHARACTER OF MOTIVES

An objective of sociotechnical design is to establish conditions in work groups by which the means for achieving the group's goals and objectives become objects of directed action for the group's members. Such conditions exist when pursuing or attaining an object produces experiences of self-enhancement. It is not so easy, however, for the designer to know what objects will be invested with such emotion. One may discover what actions and outcomes are valued by understanding the group context and culture and by judging how difficult and visible actions and outcomes are to group members. One cannot always rely on asking group members what they value because they may not always be able to articulate what will produce such feelings. Individuals do not always know what is self-enhancing until they have been offered the opportunity to make difficult decisions or perform skillful acts. Thus, many individuals have to be led through such opportunities to the existential experience of competence and the self-enhancement this experience provides.

Motives are acts, not what is behind an act, but they are, nevertheless, inextricably bound with conditions of being such as experiences of self-enhancement. Human motivation then has an ontogenic character to it in that actions lead to conditions of being and conditions of being lead to new motives. The possibility of transcending one's abilities and limitations is always present, but frequently this possibility has to be discovered, for an individual accepts new goals and objectives when their achievement seems within reach. This view of motivation justifies Victor Frankl's (1959, p. 101) criticism of the term "self-actualization" to describe man's highest motive. In his view, a more accurate term is "self-transcendence."

PART II

THE ORGANIZATION AND THE WORK GROUP

INTRODUCTION TO PART II

The chapters of Part II of this book discuss the relationship between the work–group and higher-level organizational units. This relationship is discussed through the medium of a general systems framework. This framework is valuable because of the sophistication it offers for understanding the manner in which interacting social units deal with each other under conditions of uncertainty. Higher-level units greatly influence the degree of uncertainty that work-group members face and the degree to which higher-level units can program the activities that group members perform. Also, the discretion and information that group members possess have intended and unintended consequences for work-group performance.

Chapter 4 defines the nature of the relationship between systems at different hierarchical levels of the organization. The primary focus is on the relationship between the work group and the next highest hierarchical level. An aggregate of workers becomes an autonomous work group when the workers can make decisions affecting the relationship between themselves as a total production system and the enviornment they face. Chapter 5 discusses the effect of high-level organizational decisions on the variety and uncertainty that work-group members face. Chapter 6 discusses the types of decisions that members of autonomous work groups can make.

CHAPTER

4

PLANNING AND DESIGNING WITHIN COMPLEX SYSTEMS

This chapter introduces some general systems concepts that should facilitate our subsequent discussion of work groups and their design. Some of these concepts will be familiar to many readers, but the context is somewhat different from that in which they are usually presented. Here, they are used as a vehicle to discuss modes of planning and organizational design that are congruent with improving the quality of work that rank-and-file operatives perform. The position taken in this book is that improvement in the quality of work is marginal unless steps are taken to alter the work and conditions that operatives face as part of their daily experience. Unless opportunities are provided for challenging work and learning experiences and unless the possibility exists of being directly engaged in creating and modifying the conditions under which work is performed, the historical separation at work between intention and action discussed in Chapters 2 and 3 remains, as does its undesirable consequences.

This position doesn't mean that methods for improving the status of workers relative to management through indirect forms of participation such as workers councils, codetermination, and so on, are not useful or important. Such methods can serve important worker interests; for example, worker representatives on a board of directors could delay or modify a decision to shut down a plant, reduce the number of layoffs, influence the purchase of safer equipment. In each of these cases, labor is challenging management's prerogative to be the sole judge as to how capital and its proceeds are to be distributed. However valuable it may be for labor to share in making these decisions—and it is most valuable—they are made by too few workers, too removed from circumstances that might ameliorate alienation from the work itself.

This book is not a comprehensive survey of different approaches to improving the quality of work through redesigning the work itself, although a vast literature on this subject is developing. This book is admittedly partisan; it primarily presents concepts that are useful for developing the sociotechnical approach; and the reader should judge this approach in toto as presented and compare it with other approaches.

Before focusing our primary attention on the dynamics of work groups, it is important to understand the wider conditions that influence the social and technical conditions that work-group members face. Of particular relevance is the hierarchical structure of complex organizations and their modes of planning.

ORGANIZATIONAL LEVELS

At the most general level of analysis, it can be said that the end considered most desirable by a formal organization is its continued survival. There are many courses of action available to an organization to improve its survival chances, which action it chooses being dependent on what it perceives its environment to be (actual and potential) and the knowledge it possesses (by previous learning and present problem-solving capabilities) of cause-and-effect relationships between actions and desired outcomes. The alternative outcomes that are considered desirable and the outcome the organization chooses to pursue are constrained by the organization's environment consisting of customers, suppliers, competitors, and so on, who are themselves embedded in a larger social field made up of institutions, world views, systems of belief, and so on. The processes, events, and elements that make up the organization's environment are increasingly the products of man rather than nature and are considerably more complexly interrelated than in previous times, resulting in conditions that Emery and Trist (1965) call "turbulent."

Organizations survive within this turbulent environment of changing values and institutional relationships partly by helping to shape these new values through, in Selznick's (1957) words, acts of administrative leadership and partly through assessing or discovering changes taking place within it. This activity takes place at what Parsons (1960) calls the "institutional level" of the organization, and those who perform it engage, essentially, in acts of valuation or, as Vickers (1965) refers to them, acts of appreciation. An act of appreciation is essentially a "value judgment [that] cannot be proved correct or incorrect; it can only be approved as right or condemned as wrong by the exercise of another value judgment" (Vickers). An act of appreciation is not properly regarded as decision making, for it does not begin with goal states and sets of possible transformations to achieve them; it is an elemental act of assigning value by locating or noticing new dimensions of reality and assigning value to them. Acts of appreciation relevant to improving the quality of work were explored at the end of Chapter 2. Discussed were events and interrelationships of events calling for changes in schemata of reality and valuation consistent with a postindustrial society. It is generally at the institutional level of the organization that such appreciations are made and/or sanctioned. Examples of appreciative acts discussed in Chapter 2 were (1) reconceptualizing labor as a corporate asset rather than as a factor of production, (2) reconceptualizing labor as a producer of social utility rather than as a cost of production, and (3) supplanting the principle of property ownership with that of affected interest. Organizations may deal with the changes occurring in the progression toward a postindustrial society by adapting through understanding and accommodation or by seeking to ignore the presence of such changes or otherwise defend itself against what it cannot understand or cope with. Emery and Trist (1973) discuss a number of adaptive as well as maladaptive strategies used by individuals, organizations, and societies to cope with turbulent environments.

Appreciative acts when translated into specific policy absorb uncertainty regarding value questions within the institutional level and permit managers to operate within the prescribed domains of what Parsons (1960) calls the "managerial level." While the institutional level is concerned with what "ought" to be done, the managerial level is assigned the responsibility of translating these values into what can be done within a specifiable time period and within what is perceived to be the present political, economic, and social situation. Decision makers operating at this level and making decisions that most writers identify as strategic plans, face an environment that, although rendered less complex by the absorption of value questions at the institutional level, is still highly uncertain. It is uncertain not only because the immediate future can only be imperfectly estimated but because decisions take place in a reactive environment in which the decisions of various decision makers are mutually interdependent—that is to say, the decisions one makes are significantly modified by the decisions of others. Pricing decisions made by companies facing oligopolistic market conditions are good examples of decision making in reactive environments. Decisions at the managerial level also include, in addition to goal-setting, internal resource allocation (also political and reactive), and the selection of the basic means by which long-term objectives are to be met.

Parsons identified a third organizational level, which is subordinate to the managerial level and is qualitatively distinct. The "technical level," as Parsons calls it, is concerned with how decisions made at the managerial level are to be implemented. Implementation is not automatic, as decision makers at this level are always confronted with a fluid situation, day-to-day modifications in applying available means and resources must be made, and, as Parsons points out, this level frequently reacts to the managerial level in competing and coordinating ways. However, the prime function performed by decision-makers at the technical level is the supervision of risk (McWhinney 1960). Quoting McWhinney (p. 274):

> Risk-taking, making decisions based on data, samples and subjective expectations, is the province of the expert who studies the distributions and formulates appropriate decision paradigms. The ability to predict opens the possibility of delegation and control. If we have some idea of the future behavior of a system we can instruct another on how to handle a range of contingent events and on when he should return "control" to ourselves.... The techniques of identification in risk supervision may be more sophisticated than those Weber considered, but the basic activity is the same, and thus propositions concerning bureaucratic operations would usually apply to risk supervision.

The tasks that correspond to risk supervision are essentially "administrative" functions. These include technical staff such as production control, industrial engineering, personnel, much of applied research, and general supervision.

HIERARCHICAL STRUCTURE OF COMPLEX SYSTEMS

The nature of the decisions made at each of the three organizational levels creates a hierarchical structure in that the institutional level sanctions the ends and values of the managerial level, and, in turn, the managerial level specifies the goals and constraints within which the technical level functions. The relationship between these three organizational levels can be clarified by use of Ozbekhan's (1971) concepts of organizing and instrumental systems. According to Ozbekhan (p. 181):

> (1) In a hierarchical structure an *organizing system* is the system whose ends or values govern and determine the behavior of the whole structure.
>
> (2) In a hierarchical structure *instrumental systems* are those systems whose ends or values are determined in such a manner as

> to fulfill, besides their own ends, the ends or values of the organizing system.

An organizing system and one or more subordinate instrumental systems may jointly form the hierarchical structure of a complex system. A complex system as distinct from a simple system is one whose organizing and instrumental systems are controlled by different *deciders* (J. G. Miller 1965). A decider is the common locus from which decisions regarding a system's functioning originate. A decider is a system function; it is not a person. This function could potentially be filled by a computer or similar artifact, but at the highest organizational levels, it is performed by human beings. The decider of either the organizing or instrumental systems of a complex system may consist of several persons—for example, a board of directors as an organizing system—or the same person could be the decider for both an organizing and an instrumental system—for example, the same individual who functions as chairman of the board and president of a corporation. However, in the latter case, he must switch perspectives and behaviors to perform each of the different roles effectively. In contrast to complex systems, a simple system has only one decider; it has no subordinate instrumental systems, only an organizing system.

Ozbekhan states that, in relation to an organizing system, all others can be described as instrumental systems.

> 1. In hierarchical structures the objectives and goals of the organizing system represent the objectives and goals of the whole structure; whereas the objectives and goals of instrumental systems are set and attained with the aim of providing information to the knowledge/means elements of the next level, and ultimately, to that of the organizing system.
>
> 2. For a hierarchical structure to exist, it is not generally necessary that any of its component systems be symmetrical as to their elements or contexts, nor can the principles of operation applicable to any component system be necessarily derived from principles that are applicable to the other component systems.
>
> 3. For any component system of a hierarchical structure to attain its goal, it is necessary that the component system below it function correctly.
>
> 4. It is not possible to understand a hierarchically structured whole system with reference to any of its component systems if the latter are taken separately. It is, however, possible to say that "starting from any given [system] stratum, understanding of a system increases by crossing (boundaries): moving down the

hierarchy one obtains a more detailed explanation of its significance, [or meaning].*

Considering the organization as a whole as our unit of analysis, the institutional level is an organizing system for the managerial level, and the managerial level is an instrumental system of the institutional level. Furthermore, the managerial level is an organizing system for the technical level, and the technical level is an instrumental system of the managerial level. One can see that each decider below the highest in the organization has a dual function of being an instrumental system to a higher level as well as an organizing system for its own level.

HIERARCHICAL STRUCTURE OF PLANNING

Ozbekhan (1971) follows up these definitions and classifications of the hierarchical structure of complex systems by developing a hierarchical stucture of planning. "Normative plans" select the values, and "strategic plans" set the goals for the system as a whole. "Operational plans" are subordinate to strategic plans and correspond to administrative functions. In a simple system, all three types of planning are carried out by the system's only decider. When a simple system is differentiated into a complex system, operational planning is the first type of planning to be delegated to an instrumental system.

In a complex system such as an organization, differentiation has reached the point at which the hierarchical structure of planning coincides with the three organizational levels discussed above. Normative planning is the predominant activity of the institutional level of the organization, strategic planning is the predominant activity of the managerial level, and operational planning is the predominant activity of the technical level.

When this degree of differentiation exists, the managerial and technical levels perform their respective types of planning as instrumental systems of the organizing system that contains them.

The assertion that normative, strategic, and operational planning are the predominant activities of the institutional, managerial, and technical levels, respectively, needs further clarification. This does not and should not imply that members of these respective levels are the exclusive ones within the organization to do each type of planning. However, the implication that

*Ozbekhan is quoting Mesarovic and Macko (1969, p. 35).

they might do so follows from the bureaucratic model, which considers this to be the only proper way for such planning to take place. Within the traditional bureaucratic structure, normative planning—that is, acts of appreciation—carried out at lower organizational levels is "illegal." Such illegal activities may be suppressed by higher organizational levels, but these activities may also lead to innovations that are later incorporated into the planning activities of higher organizational levels. Examples abound of successful innovations in traditionally structured organizations that began at lower organizational levels. Trist (1974) refers to diffusion of this sort as "cumulative innovation," which is the accumulation of initiatives from below that ultimately produce an upper-level mandate.

Proctor and Gamble (Jenkins 1973) and General Foods (Ketchum 1975) are two corporations whose headquarters did not initiate the organizational design efforts that have had profound implications on how work is organized and employees are managed. Instead, both efforts began as "underground" efforts whose undeniable success led to ultimate formal acceptance by top management.

In the case of General Foods, an innovative manager designed a new plant on advanced sociotechnical principles and brought it into successful operation. High levels of work satisfaction and cost savings were achieved. Initial resistance to these results and their implications was great. However, the original plant manager who was transferred to corporate headquarters began working with a network of other interested plant managers and together they produced similar successful innovations that eventually made an impact on top corporate management. The corporate vice president for operations developed a document entitled "An Operations Philosophy for General Foods," which was sanctioned by the president. The philosophy not only commits the corporation to sociotechnical work design but to principles such as maintaining labor stability.

By contrast, at Shell UK Ltd. (Hill 1971), a top-level staff group in collaboration with the Tavistock Institute of Human Relations initiated normative planning by writing a document that outlined a new set of organizational values. This document was subsequently endorsed by the managing director of the company. Some key concepts of the document have far-reaching implications for the manner in which human and other resources are utilized by the company as well as how human needs are satisfied as technical performance is maintained—for example, that all resources used by the company are "social resources" belonging to the community and must be protected and developed as such. Endorsement from the top then led to a series of upper- and middle-management conferences where the document was discussed and a new philosophy of management and its implications were worked out. The overlapping membership at these conferences resulted in the cascading of new values throughout the hierarchy, each lower level reinterpreting these values for appropriateness to the conditions each faced.

The only implication of normative planning being placed in Parson's "institutional level" is that consensus on new appreciations is necessary at a level that coordinates for the organization as a whole, that is to say, if coherent and consistent relationships are to be maintained among the organization's parts. Normative, strategic, and operational planning can take place at any organizational level, and, indeed, Emery and Emery (1974) believes that all three types of planning should be encouraged at every organizational level to overcome the inertia created by excessive bureaucratic design.

As discussed above, new appreciations affecting the organization as a whole may originate at lower levels. In democratic organizations new appreciations may have to be legitimated by a majority vote among all organizational members. Friedmann (1973) has suggested that the most appropriate vehicles for promoting normative planning at any or all organizational levels are "learning cells" composed of those individuals closest to the issues to be dealt with. In the case of issues related to the quality of working life, operatives, supervisors, and technical staff who work with them are the most appropriate members of such cells. Emery and Emery (1974) have experimented with a similar concept, which they refer to as a "participative design workshop" consisting of relevant members from "deep slices" of the organization. Discussion of the redesign of the work place may frequently lead to manpower or personnel policy changes with organization-wide implications—for example, everyone paid a salary rather than wages, retirement or retraining policies, and so on. Implications such as these may be discussed and communicated upwards in sets of interlocking learning cells that Friedmann calls "assemblies." Whether the communication is upward or downward through learning cells, participative design workshops, or sets of conferences with overlapping membership as in Shell U.K., the intent is the same—that is, providing an opportunity for different organizational levels to "work through" implicit assumptions, learn new concepts, and internalize new values.

THE TECHNICAL LEVEL

Our attention now turns to the internal structure of the technical level of the organization. The technical level as a whole is responsible for planning, coordinating, and appraising the performance of activities that produce the basic products and services of the organization. It is that part of the organization having the chief responsibility for planning and administering of day-to-day activities, leaving the normative and strategic planning of the organization as a whole to the institutional and managerial levels, respectively. Unlike the managerial and institutional levels where responsibility is frequently shared and decisions are made by groups—as in the Executive Committee and Finance Committee of the Dupont Company (Chandler 1962)—responsibility for technical-level performance is generally assigned to a single chief executive officer who heads an administrative hierarchy.

A number of factors that the technical level of an organization faces makes it extremely unlikely that its chief executive officer with or without the aid of staff can make all the decisions with which this level must deal. Only the most extreme model of bureaucracy would imply that all of such decisions could or should be made exclusively by the top of the technical level. An organization that tried to make all decisions from the top would collapse from the sheer number of decisions and time limits under which they must be made. This would be so even with exclusive focus on the internal relationships between organizational parts and ignoring organization-environment relationships, as is done in classical thinking about bureaucracies. Readers familiar with Simon's (1962) article "The Architecture of Complexity" will note the similarity between his analysis and that presented below.

Internal Hierarchical Dimension

Operational plans limit the decision-making alternatives of lower hierarchical levels* by committing resources to the pursuit of specific courses of action. In general, the longer the time period required for the consequences of strategic decisions to be realized and evaluated, the less flexible are resources for commitment to alternative objectives. Furthermore, (1) the longer the time period in which strategic decisions operate as constraints on the decisions made by technical-level personnel and (2) the lower the complexity of the tasks required to carry out operational plans, the more likely that operational planning will take place at a higher level.

---

*Organizational levels refer to the institutional, managerial, and technical levels of the organization. Hierarchical levels refer to levels within the technical-level hierarchy. Unless otherwise specified, when the term "level" is used by itself, it refers to the latter.

FIGURE 4.1

Internal Dimensions of Technical-Level Hierarchy

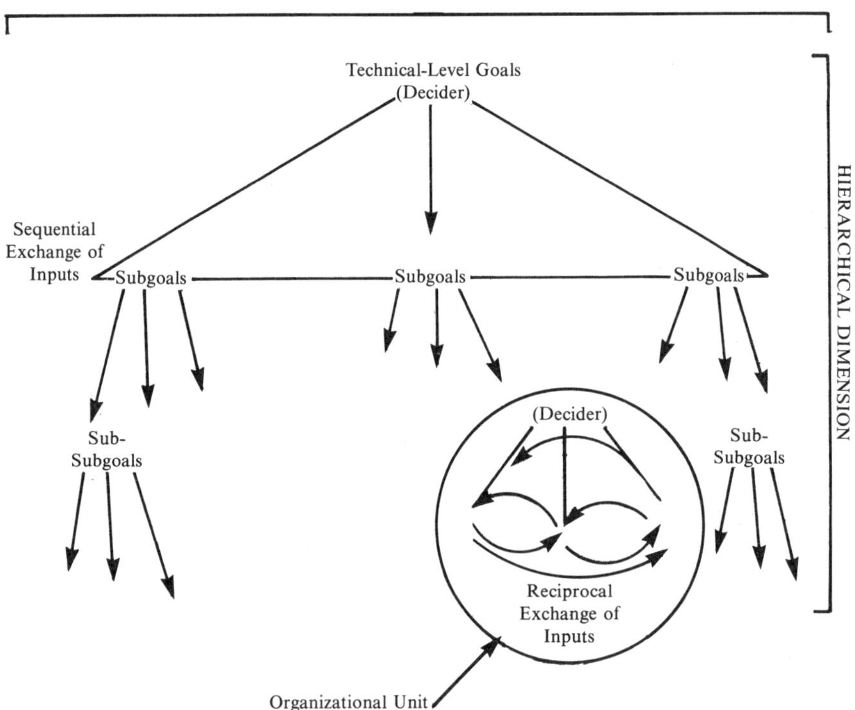

Source: Compiled by the author.

Figure 4.1 shows the manner in which operational planning takes place at the top of the technical-level hierarchy. A means-end chain is constructed in which organizational goals are partitioned into subgoals and then into sub-subgoals, and so on. The construction of a means-end chain is possible to the extent that organizational goals are operational—that is, if it can be determined whether and to what extent these goals will be realized if particular courses of action are chosen (March and Simon 1958). Each subgoal is then divided into a set of tasks that are programed to be performed by men or machines in particular sequences and at particular times. The extent to which tasks are programed depends heavily on the nature of inputs to which men or machines are directed to respond. The inputs of primary concern to those who perform subgoal tasks are the raw materials that the organization transforms into products as well as the resources necessary to do this.

If the technical level were a simple system, the top of the technical level would make decisions specifying the exact manner in which tasks assigned to each and every subgoal, sub-subgoal, and so on, were to be performed and would convey these specifications to all task sites. However, this would be conceivable only for a very small organization with simple tasks to perform. In most organizations, the stimuli to which responses are made (1) are too complex to anticipate all contingencies, (2) occur at unpredictable times, or (3) are not understood well enough to program an appropriate response.

Internal Lateral Dimension

There is a lateral dimension to the technical level as well as a hierarchical one. As Figure 4.1 shows, the tasks of two or more subgoals at any level of the organization may require the men and machines assigned to them to deal with inputs in sequences, each subgoal assigned responsibility for different responses to inputs. The most typical example of sequential exchange of stimuli is raw materials, which go through successive stages of transformation. In Figure 4.1, all branches of the subgoals on the left may be responsible for procuring raw materials and supplies and scheduling their arrival at production plants; all branches of the middle-subgoal may be responsible for producing finished products, and, finally, all branches of the third subgoal may be responsible for distributing products to customers.

If the technical level of the organization were a simple system, the top of the technical-level hierarchy would coordinate all lateral relationships between subgoals. This would be conceivable if all inputs could be transferred from one subgoal to the next in a predictable sequence and above a minimal time interval between successive responses. However, shown at the bottom of Figure 4.1, transfer between tasks may occur with high temporal and sequential uncertainty, and, instead of being unidirectional, transfer may consist of a continual and reciprocal exchange of raw materials, information, and so on. For example, if little is known about raw materials or the methods required to produce a customized product, an applied research department [R] may have to work closely with a product development department [D], which, in turn, works closely with a production department [P]. Under these conditions, there is no discrete separation between the responsibilities of one department and those of another. One department's responsibility doesn't end abruptly, and "title to the goods," so to speak, doesn't pass on to another department. Instead, the responsibility of one department ends gradually as another department takes over more and more responsibility for the product's completion.

Under the above conditions and as organizations increase in size and task complexity, it may be impossible for the top of the technical-level hierarchy to coordinate all transfers of inputs between subgoals because information between the top level and task sites must be exchanged too often and rapidly or is too complex to code or too costly for maintenance of a satisfactory level of effective and efficient performance.

THE TECHNICAL LEVEL AS A COMPLEX SYSTEM

Under the conditions of internal complexity and uncertainty described above, what can the top of the technical-level hierarchy do to ensure that tasks will be performed when and where required and that effective coordination takes place between the tasks assigned to two or more subgoals? If the top of the technical-level hierarchy cannot by itself make all the necessary decisions to maintain a satisfactory level of efficient and effective performance, it can delegate some of its decisions to a decider and direct the latter to make decisions as to how it will achieve the subgoal assigned to it. The decider and the subgoal and tasks assigned to it by the top of the technical-level hierarchy constitute an "organizational unit." (See bottom center of Figure 4.1.)

The decider function of an organizational unit is performed by one or more humans, who may be assisted by computers or other artifacts. The function of the decider is to choose between response alternatives so that the unit maintains critical performance standards in a "steady state."

The basis for creating organizational units may be the functions or services performed, products produced, customer or territories served. The criterion for choosing among these alternative bases is frequency of required performance, kinds and number of required personnel, and extent of interdependence among tasks.

The creation of deciders below the one at the top of the technical level of the organization transforms the technical level from a simple system into a complex system. Thus, the technical level depicted in Figure 4.1 is not a simple system, but a complex one. In a complex system, the organizing and its subordinate instrumental system(s) are maintained by different deciders. In a simple system, the functions of the organizing system and instrumental system(s) are carried out by the same decider. The implausibility of the technical level's remaining a simple system and continuing to plan and control all of its relevant activities as it grows in size and complexity was demonstrated above. Additionally, no system whether simple or complex contains more than one organizing system. If two or more organizing systems are observed in what was thought to be one organizational unit, then really two units exist, not one. A complex system may, of course, have many instrumental systems contained within it.

The top of the technical level deals with the organization as a whole. In addition to planning how to meet the goals set for the organization as a whole, the top of the technical level sets the goals (subgoals) of any organizational unit to which it has delegated a decider. The organizational units contained within the technical level are instrumental systems of the top. They do not deal with the goals of the organization as a whole but with the subgoals that have been assigned to them.

Let us switch perspectives and consider our unit of analysis to be one of the organizational units created by delegating it a decider. This organizational unit may itself be a simple or complex system. Depending on how uncertain its environment or tasks, it may be necessary for it (or the top level) to delegate a decider to a still lower level. If the latter is the case, our organizational unit is a complex system also. We could continue to switch perspectives to successively lower-level organizational units until one is reached that has not delegated a decider to a still lower level; that unit, when reached, is a simple system.

ORGANIZATIONAL UNITS

An organizational unit may delegate a decider to a support function or to subordinate organizational levels arranged in a hierarchy. The relationship between organizational units arranged in hierarchical fashion is reminiscent of the arrangement of Chinese boxes. The decider of any complex organizational unit makes decisions applicable to the unit as a whole, then transmits its decisions to any subordinate units to which it has delegated a decider. Any support or subordinate unit performs the dual function of being instrumental to the unit that has delegated it a decider as well as organizing itself to meet the subgoal it has been assigned. It is this characteristic to which Koestler (1967) and Lazlo (1972) refer when they write of the "holon" or Janus-faced quality of complex system functioning. This managerial function of mediating the internal and external relationships of an organizational unit is called "boundary maintenance."

An organizational unit at any level either transmits its decisions to lateral or subordinate units or delegates a decider to them. At some point, an organizational level is reached when a unit does not delegate a decider to its components, it is a simple system. Formally, when organizational units are also simple systems, they are called work groups. The only exception is when an individual constitutes a unit unto himself. As we shall see in Chapter 6, this is a rare organizational arrangement. This restrictive definition precludes calling just any collection of organizational members a work group. Any collection of organizational members that only receives or passes on information without making decisions, is not functioning as a system at all, the members are components of the next highest system that contains them. According to the above definition, any collection of individuals that functions as a simple system, that is, is delegated a decider, is also conditionally autonomous.

What unites a set of diverse individuals is that they are under the direction of the same organizing system. This commonality allows us to use the term "organizational unit" for units whose members share nothing else other than that they perform activities in the same geographical territory—such as a sales division some of whose members may never see each other and whose manager limits his decisions to assigning territories and rewarding salesmen's contributions to total division sales. The term "organizational unit" applies also to units whose components are highly interdependent in producing the unit's products—such as an oil-refining unit whose technical staff and operatives continuously modify each others' information about the unit and adjust to each others' activities.

In addition to being simple systems, three other characteristics generally distinguish work groups from other kinds of organizational units: (1) each member knows that, together with all other members, they constitute a single entity that is, they perceive themselves to be a group; (2) each member can potentially engage in two-way communication with every other member, although channels of communication may not be open at all times; and (3) the members usually, although not at all times, occupy a common territory, which permits them to see and hear each other.

ORGANIZATIONAL UNITS AS SYSTEMS

We have already stated that organizational units are systems but have not defined what a system is. Ackoff (1960, p. 3) defines a system as "any entity, conceptual or physical, which consists of interrelated parts." System parts may consist of concepts, objects, or operations; they can also represent the conceptualization of objects or operations. An organizational unit,being a system of human action in a concrete setting, consists of objects as well as conceptualizations. The most significant parts of an organizational unit as a system consists of human beings who interact among themselves and/or with other system parts to produce outcomes. As discussed in Chapter 3, the outcomes of a system of human action are achieved by pursuing objects of directed action, and, therefore, the behavior of members of such systems is purposeful. Organizational units are also open systems, which means that interaction occurs not only among system parts but also between system parts and elements of the system's environment. The system is separated from its environment by a boundary across which some "breakpoint" occurs in the nature of the interdependencies that exist between system parts and those that exist between system parts and the environment. Although the placement of a system's boundary sometimes seems arbitrary (its placement usually depends on the nature of the problem studied or a criterion that permits efficient coordination between systems), its effect is to divide a set of interacting parts into two entities: a system and its environment. In Chapter 8, the role of the decider in maintaining a dynamic boundary between the system and its environment is explained.

TRANSACTIONS OF AN ORGANIZATIONAL UNIT WITH ITS ENVIRONMENT

Some general comments should suffice concerning the internal system properties of an organizational unit, as this subject is discussed in detail in Chapter 5. An organizational unit is a system of human action whose components are coordinated toward a common outcome. The objective is to produce an output that its environment will accept and to produce it in such a manner that the unit over the "long run" receives more from its environment than it expends. Production consists of "importing" raw materials (matter and/or information) from the group's environment, taking actions to alter the form, shape, location, or meaning of raw materials, and "exporting" them back into the unit's environment. For group tasks such as problem solving, "importing" raw materials may consist of no more than an act of observation by group members or noticing that a problem exists; "exporting" a solution may consist of no more than verbalizing the solution to another organizational unit.

In addition to raw materials to transform into products and services, organizational units must import resources from their environment to create and maintain a "structure of means" that will produce the unit's output.

These resources, called maintenance inputs, consist of matter and/or information. Maintenance inputs consisting primarily of matter include tools such as hammers, pencils, and machines such as lathes, typewriters, and photocopiers. Human beings are maintenance inputs consisting of matter and energy when muscle power is required, but they also possess information-processing capacities for learning new skills, solving problems, and storing knowledge. Maintenance inputs consisting of information include feedback about consequences of actions taken to produce products or services, and information necessary for making decisions and coordinating and controlling members' activities. Maintenance inputs consisting of either matter or information may possess symbolic as well as instrumental value for unit members. For example, activities required to produce outputs, such as learning new skills, may also produce intrinsically rewarding experiences, prestige, comradeship and so on. Although procurement of maintenance inputs is a recurrent concern for most units, some maintenance inputs, such as knowledge and skills, decay so slowly or are latent properties of human beings, being produced as byproducts of the unit's pursuit of its goals, that, for practical time periods, the unit need not be concerned about replenishing them. This applies only to knowledge and skills in units facing relatively stable environments. When a unit's environment is dynamic, there is continuous need for importing new skills and knowledge.

HIERARCHY AND ENVIRONMENT

Up to this point we have discussed the implausibility of the technical level's remaining a simple system because of the complexity of relationships between an organization's internal parts. However, just as critical is the fact that organizations must deal with multiple environments of varying degrees of complexity and uncertainty that emerge as a result of the partitioning and assigning of subgoals to organizational members. The existence of different environments of varying degrees of complexity and uncertainty within the technical level increases the likelihood that deciders must be delegated to lower-level members of the technical-level hierarchy.

As discussed earlier, the organizations of any nation—or, as is increasingly the case for multinational corporations, the world—are embedded in a social field of sociopolitical beliefs, contracts, laws, customs, and so on. The social field, being a system in and of itself, has dynamics of its own whose elements and the relationships between them change as customs, beliefs, and so on change. Many of the changes discussed in Chapter 1 leading to an advanced industrial society have been taking place for decades and centuries and will continue to take place independently of what any single organization does. For example, although U.S. economic organizations in the aggregate have produced national affluence, the effects of such affluence on attitudes toward work, increased life-span, relationships within the nuclear family, and so on as well as the mutual interpenetration of these effects on each other are produced by sociopsychological dynamics of their own that have little to do with the specific objectives and goals pursued by any particular organization. Changes may also occur in social fields as the unforeseen consequences of several organizations competing against each other in pursuit of limited objectives—for example, industrial pollution has given rise to the environmentalist movement, the creation of new governmental agencies, and so on. Whether or not any particular organization has influenced such changes, they must be taken into account as premises upon which future planning is based. Emery and Trist (1973) have called such interrelationships between elements within social fields the "contextual environment" of the organization. The contextual environment of an organization is dealt with through new appreciations of changing conditions—that is, through normative planning.

Against the background of the contextual environment is the "figure," to borrow the terms from Gestalt psychology, of an organization's "task environment." An organization's task environment (Dill 1958) consists of those parts (elements) of the environment that are relevant to the setting and attainment of specific goals and objectives. What becomes an element in the organization's task environment is determined by the specific values and objectives that the organization adopts.

Following Dill's definition of task environment, Thompson (1967) specifies that, as goals shift, so do the elements making up the environment. The task environment that an organization faces is created and subsequently influenced by the strategies and objectives that an organization pursues.

The relationship between an organization and its contextual or task environment is more than simple adaptation to minimal survival conditions; it is a kind of mutual interpenetration between an organization and aspects of its environment: As Emery and Trist (1973) have pointed out, planning and instrumental action by an organization are externalizing some aspects of the organization into its environment, while learning is the means by which aspects of the environment are internalized by the organization.

Normative and strategic planning at the institutional and managerial levels of the organization reduce uncertainty over the basic values and objectives that are pursued by the organization as a whole. Planning at these respective levels provides members of the technical level of the organization with a framework of "givens" within which members of the technical level of the organization can pursue the subgoals they are assigned. The top of the technical-level hierarchy (whether the position title be president, executive vice-president, or general manager) and staff assistants translate strategic objectives into operational goals; for example, they might translate the strategic decision to pursue a new product line into specific methods for production and introduction by a given target date.

As discussed previously, one of the most significant aspects of operational planning is the creation of organizational units through partitioning the goals pursued by the organization as a whole into subgoals, and assigning these, along with raw materials, supplies, and personnel for their pursuit. Simultaneous with the organizational unit's creation, the assignment of a subgoal and resources also determines the task environment the unit faces. The task environments facing organizational units are unlikely to be the same as those facing the organization as a whole, since organizational units, not being concerned with overall strategy for the organization, look at different elements or different attributes of elements than do the institutional and managerial levels of the organization. For example, the managerial level may focus on the strategic plans pursued by one of the organization's suppliers, while an organizational unit within the technical level might only be concerned with when raw materials and other supplies will be delivered at the organization's receiving dock.

In addition to the policies, rules, and commands issued by higher-level units, boundary-spanning organizational units (Katz and Kahn 1966) may face environments consisting of customers, suppliers, government, unions, and so on. Units that deal only with elements internal to the organization such as work groups might face an environment consisting of other work groups preceding and succeeding it in the product flow.

Figure 4.2 summarizes the relationship between organizational units of the technical-level hierarchy and between organizational units and their environments. The top of the technical-level hierarchy has been differentiated into two first-level instrumental systems. The first-level instrumental system in the upper left of the diagram has not delegated a decider to any of its components, it is therefore a simple system. The other first-level system is a complex system, having created second- and third-level instrumental systems within itself. Each second- and third-level unit has the Janus-faced quality of being instrumental to the unit that contains it, but organizes itself.

The top of the technical-level hierarchy makes decisions dealing with the technical level as a whole and faces an environment labeled the "micro-environment." The first level below the top doesn't deal with the technical level as a whole, and organizational units contained within this level face environments labeled E_{1a}, E_{1b}, and so on. The first-level unit on the left might be a dispatching center, which is not further differentiated into lower-level units. The first-level unit on the right might be a manufacturing division. This latter unit might have further delegated a decider to one or more second-level units each containing one or more third-level units dealing with various stages of production. There is only one second-level unit

FIGURE 4.2

Relationship Between Organizational Units of the Technical-Level Hierarchy and the Environments they Face

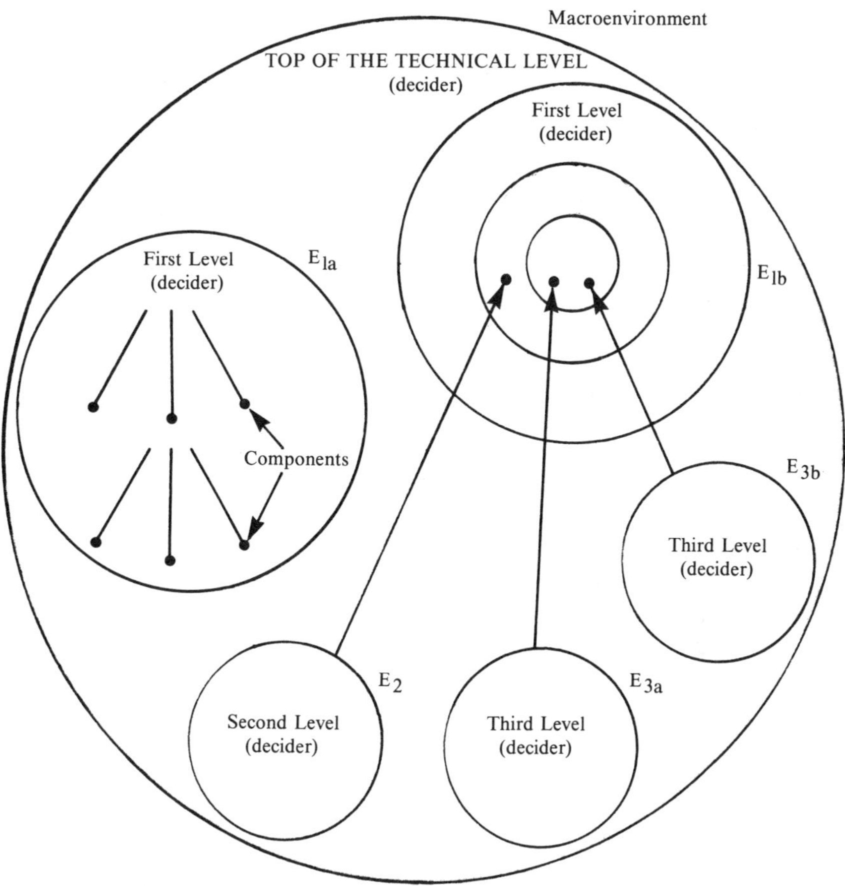

Source: Compiled by the author.

depicted in the figure so as to minimize visual confusion, but if there were more than one unit at this level, their environments would be labeled E_{2a}, E_{2b}, and so on. Any one of these second-level units may be further differentiated into a third level. The two third-level units depicted in the figure are work groups each of which faces an environment labeled E_{3a} and E_{3b}, respectively.

THE NATURE OF WORK-GROUP ENVIRONMENTS

The organizational unit to which our attention will shift in the following chapters is the work group. The purpose of the preceding discussion was to lay the groundwork for the major thesis of the following chapter—that organizational units at any level of the organization, including units at the level at which goods and services are produced, may face environments containing more, less, or the same qualitative range of uncertainty as faced by any other level of the organization. Even though the elements dealt with at each organizational level differ, as has already been pointed out, it is the abstract nature of the relationships between environmental elements and between such elements and organizational units that determines the type of uncertainty that such units face.

The Emery and Trist (1965) typology of environmental types is based on the abstract nature of relationships between environmental elements —what they refer to as an environment's "causal texture." Their analysis of environmental types is at the macroenvironmental level—that is, their examples concern the relationship of the organization as a whole to its macroenvironment. However, the abstract nature of their environmental types makes them applicable to any system level. Indeed, Emery and Trist acknowledge that the expression "causal texture of the environment" is derived from an analysis at the level of the individual by Tolman and Brunswick (1935). The reader is referred to the two references to Emery and Trist already cited (1965 and 1973) for examples of macroenvironmental relationships. Environmental types and their relationship to work-group dynamics are discussed in Chapter 5.

The discussion in this and the following chapter aims at correcting an impression given by several writers on organization theory (Parsons 1960; Thompson 1967; McWhinney 1960), perhaps unintentionally, that reduction of uncertainty increases unidirectionally from the periphery of the organization to its core interior. This would only appear to be the case if one looks at successively lower-level units from the perspective of the macroenvironmental issues facing the organization as a whole. However, this is not true if one looks at the environments faced and decisions that must be made at the various levels of any complex organization.

As the next chapter will show, the environments with which any unit at any level of the organization must deal are determined by the nature of the subgoals and tasks assigned to a unit—in particular to our concerns, work groups—as well as by the properties of the raw materials, supplies, or other resources allocated to them. Furthermore, the assumptions that technical staff hold about human behavior influence how they believe work should be designed, what kinds of information should be provided to workers, and whether opportunities for participation and learning should be encouraged. As will be discussed in the following chapter, traditional design assumptions developed when the mechanical world-view dominated lead to specifying the detailed operations required of all tasks as well as the relationships between tasks. Traditional designers believe that such procedures will render certain the environments faced by work-group members—an ideal state of affairs for traditional designers—but, in fact, residual uncertainties as well as unintentionally created uncertainties remain with which work-group members have no resources nor motivation to deal.

PARTICIPATIVE UNIT DESIGN

The position of the sociotechnical designer is that any organizational unit whether at the work-group level or higher in the organization must be free to develop responses that are appropriate to the type of environment the unit faces. Such responses are best discovered by the unit members themselves through a learning process that encourages direct and committed engagement with the environment that must be dealt with. The sociotechnical designer seeks to foster organizational values that encourage those most directly involved in carrying out the goals of a unit to discover for themselves a structure of means to achieve these goals.

Adopting Herbst's (1974) discussion on sociotechnical design to our purposes, operational planning by the top of the technical-level hierarchy should be limited to the creation of organizational units. This is achieved by assigning raw materials, supplies, personnel, and technology to the pursuit of specific organizational subgoals and specifying the critical performance standards that unit members are expected to meet. Beyond this type of planning, technical-level managers and staff should then provide the conditions for participative unit design. The vehicles for lower-level normative planning discussed previously may be extended to deal with issues related to the design of actual work places. The values that have been shaped by normative planning at each respective level may then become the premises upon which the design process is carried out. The sociotechnical designer, whether he be an outsider or a technical staff member, may play an effective role in the process as a resource person to the members of current or future organizational units. He can, among other things, translate the concepts discussed in this book into concrete proposals for unit design. As Herbst points out, as unit members become more deeply involved in learning about the tasks and environments they face, they become more fully able to utilize experts as consultants.

CHAPTER 5

RELATIONSHIPS WITHIN AND BETWEEN ORGANIZATIONAL UNITS

This chapter deals with the influence of higher-level unit decisions on the internal and external conditions that work groups face. Our analysis will proceed from the organizational unit one level removed from the work group, although, of course, many decisions that affect the conditions that work groups face are made at much higher levels than this. Most of the examples are of work groups that produce physical products, but these will be interspersed with examples from service organizations or departments that deal with less tangible raw materials and resources. The principal effect that higher-level decisions have on work groups is the degree of uncertainty and variety that may be reduced before raw materials and resources are dealt with by work-group members.

FRAMEWORK FOR ANALYSIS

Figure 5.1 can be considered an elaboration of Figure 4.2 of the previous chapter. It had been suggested that one of the first-level units in the organization's technical-level hierarchy be a manufacturing division. Decisions made at this or higher levels significantly influence the variety and uncertainty faced at lower levels. These decisions will be discussed in the next section. Contained within the designated first-level unit and subordinate to it could be several parallel second-level units each responsible for a type of production process; one of these units is shown in the figure. Finally, contained in the depicted second-level unit are three third-level units or work groups, each of which could be responsible for a production stage or each for producing a similar product.

FIGURE 5.1

Relations Between Higher-Level Units and Work Groups

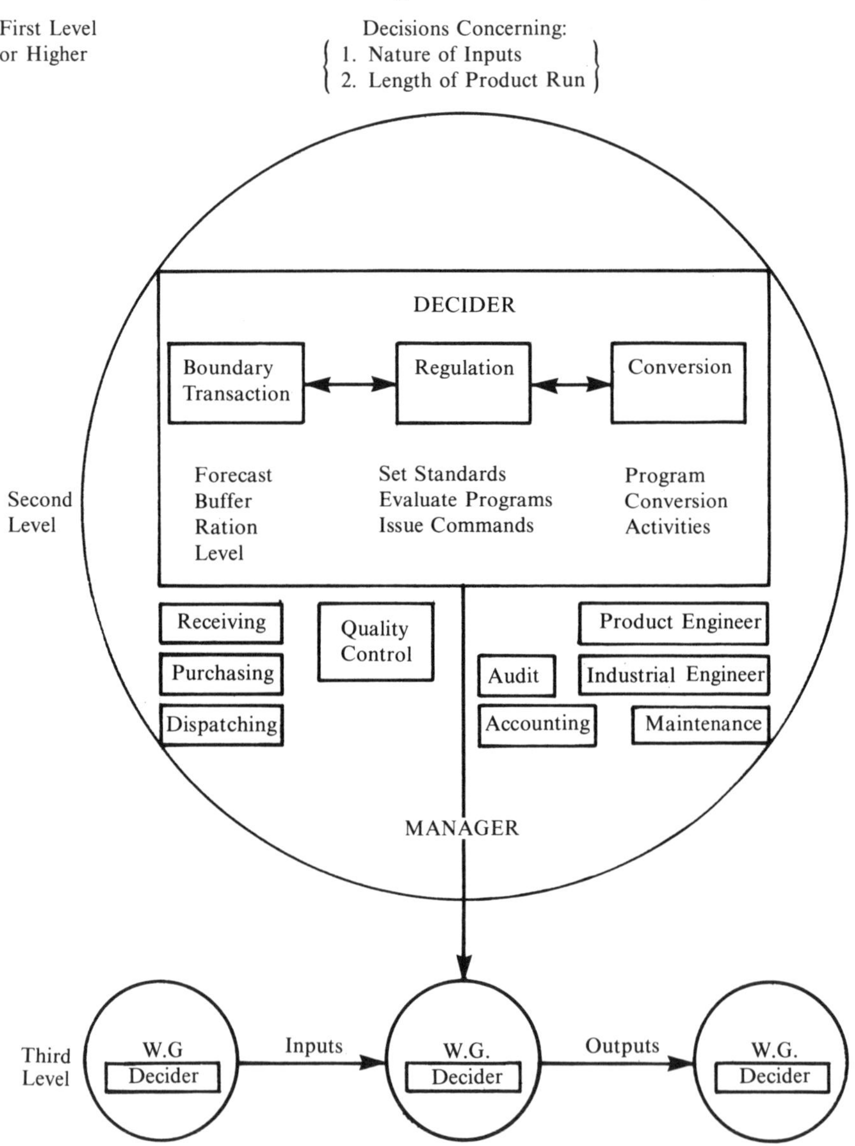

Source: Compiled by the author.

STRATEGIC DECISIONS

At the top center of Figure 5.1 are shown the strategic decisions made at the first level or at the higher levels of the organization. These decisions concern, among other things, what products to produce, what markets to enter, and what customers to serve. These decisions influence the nature of decisions and activities carried out within the second- and third-level units depicted in Figure 5.1. The major influence of strategic decisions on lower-level units results from their impact on (1) the nature of inputs to be processed and (2) the length of product run.

The Nature of Inputs Processed

The decision of what products to produce or services to perform influences what inputs the organization acquires for transformation. Inputs are raw materials or resources consisting of matter or information carried on or by human or nonhuman objects. Human inputs may be job applicants processed by an employment agency or the clients of other people-processing organizations such as universities, hospitals, or welfare agencies.

Independent of definitions and prior to any organizational actions, inputs have initial properties that may be unknown to decision makers or have varying degrees of instability. For example, some of the newer metals used in manufacturing aerospace vehicles have more unstable or unknown properties or require more transformation stages to produce a final product than is the case for older, more well-known metals. In general, human inputs are initially more unknown, unpredictable, and complex than inanimate ones, regardless of the definition organization members may give to the former.

Strategic decisions influence three major attributes of inputs with which members of our organizational unit must deal. These attributes are (1) the variety of input properties requiring conversion activities, (2) uncertainty over how to convert input properties, (3) uncertainty over what, where, or when input properties require conversion activities. Conversion activities alter the shape, size, location, or pattern of inputs.

Perrow (1970) limits the concept of variety of input properties requiring conversion activities to "novel" stimuli or exceptional cases, which evoke search behavior. However, this concept may be broadened to encompass any attribute of an input property to which organizational members have learned to elicit a response—that is, a conversion activity. Variety may arise from the diversity of products produced or from the number of conversion activities required to produce or to maintain the unit. Variety increases rapidly if the organization decides to produce many products, each product requiring many conversion activities for its completion.

The second attribute of inputs concerns whether there are known ways of dealing with their properties. If there are not known ways to deal with them, the search process requires experience, judgment, intuition, or problem-solving to find conversion activities that will alter stimuli in an acceptable manner. Uncertainty of this type is called conversion uncertainty. It is presumed that the longer the time available to organizational members to search for activities to convert input properties, the greater the likelihood that appropriate activities will become known to them.

The third attribute of inputs—refers to uncertainty over what, where, or when input properties enter an organizational unit or leave it as outputs. An

TABLE 5.1

Sources of Uncertainty and Variety Dealt with by Organizational Units

Uncertainty	Variety
Boundary-transaction uncertainty	
1. Uncertainty over what, where, or when inputs and outputs cross the unit's boundary.	1. Number of products. 2. Number of conversion activities required per product.
Conversion uncertainty	
2. Uncertainty over how to convert input properties.	

Source: Compiled by the author.

example of such uncertainty is the inability to predict product demand, which, in turn, reduces the ability to predict arrival of inputs at the organization's boundary. Uncertainty of this type is called boundary-transaction uncertainty. Organizational members may reduce such uncertainties by searching for boundary-transaction activities that alter the flow of inputs and outputs to and from the unit's boundary.

Table 5.1 lists the sources of variety and uncertainty dealt with by organizational units. Column 1 lists the two sources of uncertainty described above, while column 2 lists the two sources of variety described above.

Length of Product Run

Strategic decisions concerning what markets to serve affect whether the organization is to produce customized or standardized products. Customized products are made in "short runs" tailored to product specifications and delivery dates set by customers (usually after some negotiation). Interaction between the organization (especially the sales department) and customers is high, and orders for what to produce and when are uncertain, leading to scheduling problems for those responsible for production. Variety is high due to the number of different products the organization produces and boundary transaction uncertainty is high due to the difficulty of predicting the time and sequence of customer orders. If the organization is in a seller's market, it may be able to reduce boundary-transaction uncertainty by, for example, queuing its customers and rationing its output on a first-come-first-serve basis.

Standardized products are produced in "long runs" to be distributed later to customers from inventory and through impersonal channels. There is little or no direct interaction between the organization and customers—for example, store clerks, self-service, and so on—and production subsystems are buffered from the uncertainty of customer demands by warehouse storage capacity. Variety is lower for standardized products than for customized products because a smaller variety of different products is usually produced; boundary-transaction uncertainty is lower for standardized products because storage permits production engineering to schedule production sequences.

In addition to reducing the degree of boundary-transaction uncertainty that members of work groups face, the decision to produce standardized products reduces conversion uncertainty by increasing the time available to technical staff to learn how to convert inputs into products effectively and efficiently. The longer the time available to technical staff, the more likely they will find appropriate activities to convert inputs. Alternatively, the longer the time available to technical staff, the more likely that techniques will be developed to eliminate or alter unstable input properties so that previously known activities can be used to convert them. In either case, the probability increases that technical staff will be able to program work-group activities.

The extent to which technical staff can program activities or modify input properties depends on the initial instability of or the lack of knowledge about the input properties selected for conversion. For any given amount of time available to technical staff, the more unstable or uncertain the initial input properties, the less complete the process of centralizing the planning and controlling of work-group activities.

Variety is not considered as important as uncertainty for determining the programability of conversion activities and will not be explicitly discussed in the remainder of this chapter. Many highly programed jobs require conversion of inputs with high variety—for example, assembling printed electronic circuits. However, variety may be the deciding factor as to whether programed activities will be performed by humans or machines. The greater the variety of inputs, the less likely that a machine can be built economically to substitute for the human capacity to discriminate and vary its programs to variations in input stimuli (see Browne 1965).

FUNCTIONS PERFORMED BY UNIT DECIDERS

An organizational unit's decider performs two basic functions for its own unit, and it may perform one or both of these functions for subordinate units: (1) it searches for appropriate conversion and boundary-transaction activities to deal with inputs and outputs, (2) it sets and maintains standards. If the search process leads to appropriate conversion and boundary-transaction activities, the decider sets and maintains activity and/or outputs standards. If the search process does not lead to appropriate activities, the decider sets and maintains output standards. Regulatory activities, as they may be called, that return "deviant" activity and outputs to standards may themselves be more or less programable. Chapter 6 deals with the kinds of regulatory decisions a unit's decider makes and, in the case of a work group, how such decisions may be distributed among its members. This chapter primarily deals with the search for conversion and boundary-transaction activities.

Units at any level may be linked to upper, lateral, or lower level units in varying degrees of dependency or symbiosis depending on the manner in which regulatory and search functions are dispersed between them. For example, a unit's decider may perform the regulatory and search functions for its own level as well as for subordinate units, or it may delegate either or both functions to subordinate units. Furthermore, any unit's decider may laterally disperse one of the functions performed at its own level to a support unit. In a unit as small as a work group, it may be possible for one individual to make all the decisions affecting conversion, boundary transaction, and regulatory activities. A larger unit, such as the second level unit depicted in Figure 5.1 or any unit that grows in number of members, number of products, etc., may create support units, for example, departments, by laterally dispersing one of its decider functions to them as the figure shows.

Boundary Transaction

The second-level departments on the left of the figure whose functions are collectively identified as boundary transaction staff are concerned with directing the flow of resources and raw materials to work groups and removing them as products or wastes. Their search procedures may lead them to reduce boundary transaction uncertainty through forecasting, leveling, buffering, or rationing (Thompson 1967, pp. 20-23).

Buffering of inputs is illustrated by the stockpiling of inputs acquired in an irregular market and their steady insertion into the production process. Buffering of outputs is illustrated by maintaining warehouse inventories that permit production at a constant rate but distribution to fluctuating market conditions. Leveling involves taking actions to reduce fluctuations in the environment—for instance, airlines charging lower rates in winter than summer to level out peaks and troughs in demand. When leveling is not possible, forecasting anticipates demand. Rationing, usually the last resort, involves assigning priorities to alternative uses of inputs or eliminating some products or services.

Conversion

The second-level departments on the right of the figure whose functions are collectively identified as conversion staff are concerned with searching for ways to alter the properties of inputs before or during their introduction to work groups. Conversion staff may alter input properties in a number of ways before they reach the boundary of any particular work group. One way to alter input properties is through research or by changing inputs judged to be of inferior quality. An example of the former is reported in Hill (1971), who cites improvements in quality in a bitumen-molding unit by adding a white coloring agent to molten bitumen to make it easier to fill molds to the correct level. An example of the latter is provided from the Chemical Pulp Department of the Hunsfos Pulp and Paper Mill studied in the Norwegian Industrial Democracy Project (Emery and Thorsrud 1975). Although problem solving by department members helped improve pulp quality, improvements were significant only when the mill began to use spruce and fir inputs of higher quality. A second way conversion staff may alter input properties is to modify the conversion procedures used by work groups that precede other groups in the work flow. This seems to have been done in the metal-fabricating department included in the Norwegian Project. Improvements were made in the way metal was surface-treated in one group so as to make it easier to assemble in a succeeding group. A third way is to plan for all the conversion activities that will be required in a particular work group. Planning consists of programing the activities required to produce a product and passing these programs on to workers or machines in the form of instructions. In the case of machines, instructions are embedded in the choices of technology, layout, and so on. What inputs cannot be altered by conversion staff must then be dealt with by the second-level unit manager and his regulatory staff or discretion for dealing with them delegated to work-group members.

Regulation

The departments shown in the center of the second-level unit of Figure 5.1 are collectively known as regulatory staff. Together with the manager of this unit, the regulatory staff members compare the actual activities and/or outputs of the work group against a set of performance criteria. These criteria may be set by any departments within the second-level unit or at a higher level or by elements in the organization's macroenvironment such as governmental agencies—for instance, the Food and Drug Administration, the Federal Trade Commission.

Regulation is a residual function that remains to the unit manager and his regulatory staff because of the inability of boundary-transaction and conversion staff to perform completely their functions to reduce uncertainty over the flow and conversion of inputs to the point where all required work-group activities can be planned and programed. It is because of the inability of staff to perform these functions completely that variances occur between what has been planned and what actually occurs. Plans establish standards by which work-group activities and/or outputs may be monitored by the second-level unit manager and his regulatory staff. Regulation of variances consists of monitoring standards for variances or deviations and when variations or deviations are observed issuing directives to technical staff and/or work-group members to increase or decrease deviations. Directives issued to technical staff generally initiate problem solving to deal with chronic variances, while those issued to work-group members are intended for short-term corrections. Problem solving may temporarily increase deviations from standards and is called "positive feedback." Positive feedback can lead to improved system performance if the problem is ultimately solved, but it can also lead to system extinction if it is not. Participative design workshops, discussed in Chapter 4, which allow group members to participate in solving these kinds of problems will increase the likelihood of the former outcome. Short-term corrections generally decrease deviations from standards and are called "negative feedback." Procedures that permit work-group members to deal effectively with short-term corrections are discussed in Chapter 6.

The second-level unit manager and his regulatory staff will monitor work-group performance for variances in whatever activities can be programed. Either boundary-transaction or conversion activities will be so monitored if conversion and boundary-transaction staff can successfully reduce their respective uncertainties to the point where programing of work-group activities is possible. If either type of uncertainty remains, discretion for dealing with it may be delegated to work-group members, and, if so, the unit manager and his regulatory staff will monitor work-group performance for variances in outputs produced. March and Simon (1958) list specific criteria that higher-level units may use to determine whether subordinate units should be evaluated by activity or output specifications.

The potential reductions in boundary-transaction and/or conversion uncertainty lead to four combinations of boundary and task conditions that work groups might face. These conditions and the likely distribution of conversion and boundary-transaction functions that are likely to follow are discussed in the next section. One of the chronic problems in traditionally designed organizations is that technical staff members assume or wish to assume that less uncertainty exists at the work place than is actually present. The result is overprograming and overmonitoring of work-group performance for variances in activities rather than in outputs. The larger number of variances in activities that occurs when uncertainties remain cannot be dealt with by work-group members, as they lack appropriate resources. Second level unit members try to deal with these variances by continually intervening into work-group affairs, thereby further reducing the group member's capacity for self-regulation.

TASK AND BOUNDARY CONDITIONS FACING WORK GROUPS

The concepts introduced so far in this chapter allow us to understand the sources of uncertainty with which the various levels of the organization must deal. We saw that strategic decisions influence the initial uncertainty faced by second-level technical staff and the time they have to reduce it. This initial uncertainty is concerned with transactions across an organizational unit's boundary and the methods for converting inputs into desired outputs. Influenced by strategic decisions and combined with the resources at their disposal, conversion and boundary-transaction staff may be able to reduce one or both types of uncertainty. The potential for so doing creates four sets of task and boundary conditions that ultimately influence the distribution of decision-making between work-group members and higher-unit members. These four sets of conditions are depicted in Figure 5.2 and are described below.

Cell 1 represents conditions that result when technical staff can reduce uncertainty over both conversion and boundary transaction uncertainty. If such conditions exist, there is little or no uncertainty remaining for group members to deal with, and the second-level unit will find it easy to program

FIGURE 5.2

Task and Boundary Conditions Facing Work Groups

CONVERSION UNCERTAINTY	BOUNDARY-TRANSACTION UNCERTAINTY: LOW	BOUNDARY-TRANSACTION UNCERTAINTY: HIGH
LOW	assembly lines typing pools (1)	job shops bank tellers telephone operators refinery monitoring rooms (2)
HIGH	surgical teams construction crews (3)	dispatching centers customer complaints depts. temporary emergency groups (4)

Source: Compiled by the author.

FIGURE 5.3

Distribution of Decider Functions Between a Work Group and a Higher-Level Unit Under Cell 1 and Cell 2 Conditions

CELL 1 CONDITIONS

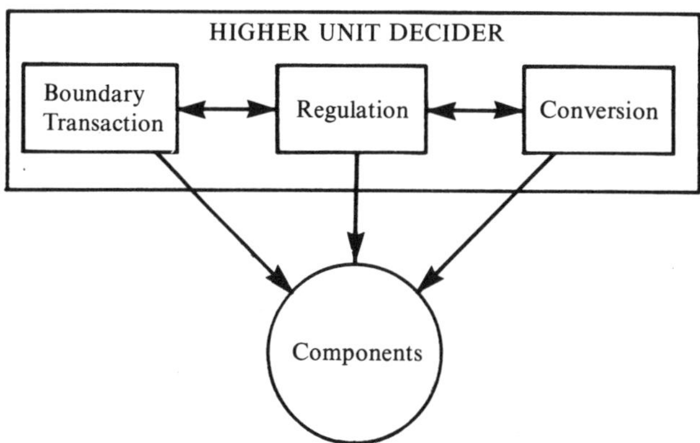

CELL 2 CONDITIONS

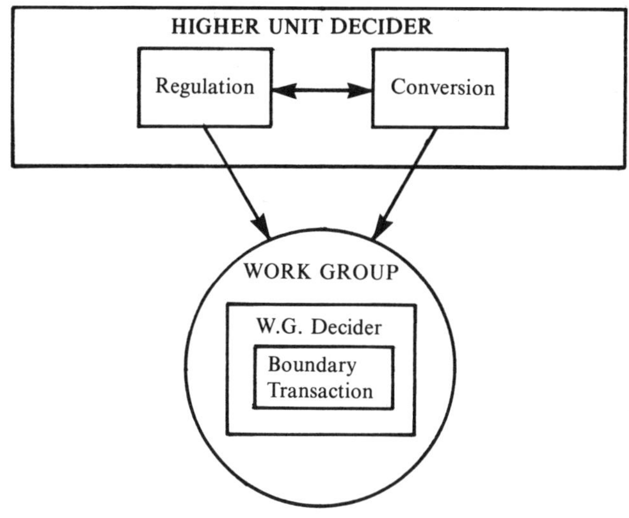

Source: Compiled by the author.

boundary transaction and conversion activities; little or no discretion will remain to delegate to work-group members. Regulatory activities are also easy to program, and what little discretion remains will likely be dealt with by second-level managers and regulatory staff. The distribution of decision-making types between the second-level unit and the work group is depicted in Figure 5.3A. Under such circumstances, members of the third organizational level do not belong to a work group as we have defined it but are components in service of the second-level unit. Cell 1 conditions are found on the automobile assembly line.

Cell 2 represents work-group conditions resulting when technical staff are able to reduce conversion uncertainty but not boundary transaction uncertainty. Under such conditions, conversion activities can be easily programed, but the timing and sequence for performing them cannot. As a consequence, questions of what, where, and when inputs and outputs will cross the work-group boundary are not settled substantially prior to the time that conversion is required. Under these conditions, the second-level unit might delegate the boundary transaction function to the work group, as shown in Figure 5.3B.

Cell 2 conditions are typical of job shops in which conversion activities are programed to the degree of standardizing and timing them as a basis to set wages. However, the scheduling of activities is a continuous preoccupation of the production manager who assigns jobs to work-group members. Typically, his scheduling arrangements are the result of negotiations with the sales manager as well as with the members of other units. Up to a point, the shorter the lead time between recognition of inputs and when a response from the work group is required, the more likely it is that work-group members rather than the production manager will perform the scheduling function. However, as the lead time between inputs and required responses becomes shorter, the scheduling of conversion activities is more likely to be on a first-come-first-serve basis, as with bank tellers, telephone operators.

Cell 3 represents conditions that result when technical staff can reduce boundary transaction uncertainty, but not conversion uncertainty. Under such conditions, the flow of inputs to the work group can be programed by boundary transaction staff, but conversion uncertainty cannot be programed by conversion staff. It is much easier, in this case, to move inputs to the work group than to program responses to convert them. Sophisticated techniques for routing inputs to the boundary may be developed by boundary-transaction staff, but once they have crossed the work-group boundary, discretion, judgment, and intuition are required to convert them. Under this set of conditions, the boundary-transaction staff is likely to be well developed, but there will be very few if any conversion staff departments within the second-level unit. Figure 5.4A shows the likely distribution of

FIGURE 5.4

Distribution of Decider Functions Between a Work Group and a Higher-Level Unit Under Cell 3 and Cell 4 Conditions

CELL 3 CONDITIONS

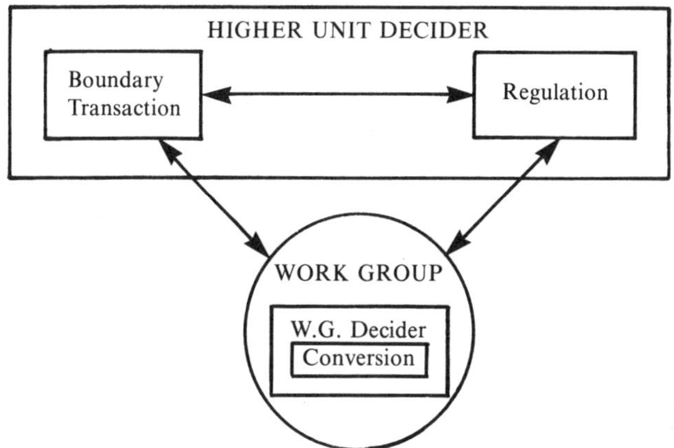

CELL 4 CONDITIONS

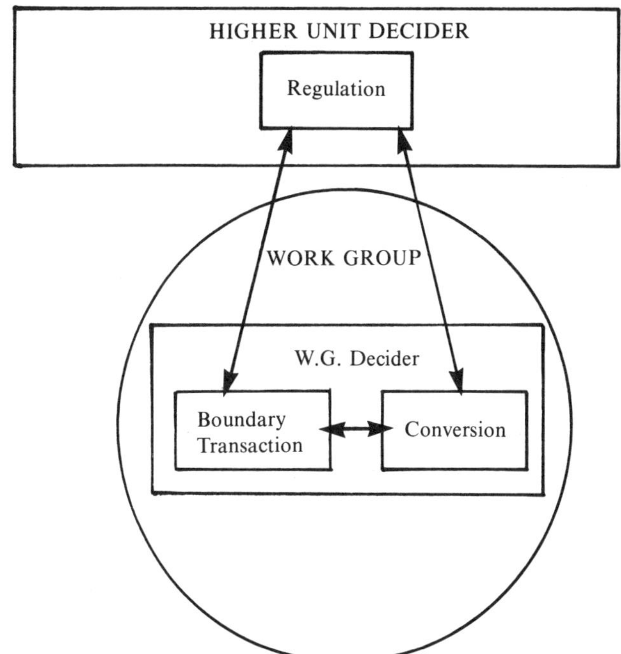

Source: Compiled by the author.

functions between the second-level unit and the work group. Surgical teams in large medical hospitals face conditions such as these. Surgery may be scheduled according to routine bureaucratic procedures, but the surgery is done by highly trained professionals.

Cell 4 represents conditions in which boundary-transaction staff cannot reduce boundary-transaction uncertainty and conversion staff cannot reduce conversion uncertainty. Under such conditions, neither the flow of inputs nor conversion activities are programable. Not too many groups that produce physical products are likely to face such conditions, except, perhaps, groups that deal directly with customers who make highly individualized requests. Dispatching centers and groups set up to handle emergency situations, such as natural disasters, might also face similar conditions. When these conditions are found, there is little reduction of conversion or boundary-transaction uncertainty prior to the time that work groups must deal with inputs. As a result, there is little development of conversion and boundary-transaction staff, and both the boundary-transaction and conversion functions will be delegated to work-group members, as is shown in Figure 5.4B. What regulation remains to the second-level unit will be done on the basis of monitoring the group's output.

TRADITIONAL DESIGN ALTERNATIVES

The desire of technical staff members to program conversion and boundary-transaction activities and, thus, to leave work-group members with virtually no discretion is based on their assumption that the decisions they make at the time of programing are superior to those that group members would make at the time action is required. Aside from the question of its superiority, programing is possible only if the staff members can predict what inputs work groups will face as well as the consequences of actions programed to deal with these inputs. Such conditions are necessary for staff to program and assign these activities to work-group members. However, except under the task and boundary conditions depicted in Cell 1 of Figure 5.3, one or both of these predictions is not possible. Under conditions 2, 3, or 4 in which it is not possible for a staff group to program all activities to be performed by a work group, there is a dilemma for the staff members who believe that extrinsic control of work-group activities is the most effective way to improve work-group performance. Such control assumes that the staff members have superior knowledge and perspective on what work-group members are supposed to do, and, therefore, the former rather than the latter, should make decisions concerning group activities.

The dilemma for the staff members is that unless they can program activities, control must take place in real time. In that case, so much time is spent coordinating work-group activities that little time remains for planning future activities or diagnosing chronic problems that require long-term solutions. One obvious answer to this dilemma is to delegate decision-making for what cannot be programed to work-group members and monitor their performance on the basis of output only. However, traditional design assumptions generally lead staff to reject this solution. Instead, staff will seek a solution that attempts to approximate conditions similar to those in Cell 1 by redefining or changing the inputs that work groups convert. This solution, however, overlooks the question whether creating these conditions will result in producing the product at its highest level of quality or quantity or in the most effective and efficient way.

When conversion and boundary-transaction uncertainty cannot be reduced because of the initial uncertainty associated with inputs or because insufficient time is available to learn to reduce such uncertainty, technical staff may choose to approximate conditions of reduced uncertainty by choosing new inputs or selectively ignoring properties of present inputs by redefining them. For example, work groups producing customer services may have customer requests redefined by technical staff into more limited

FIGURE 5.5

Trend of Changes in Task and Boundary Conditions due to Efforts by Technical Staff to Approximate Conditions of Reduced Uncertainty

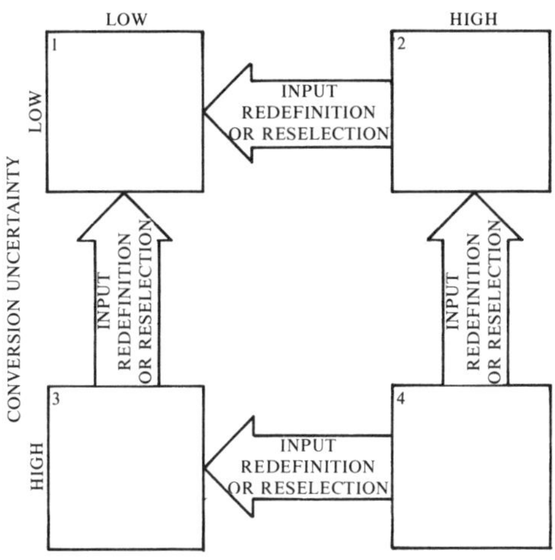

Source: Compiled by the author.

and predictable categories so that conversion uncertainty is reduced and responses easier to program. Another example is a psychiatric hospital, which redefines it inputs (patients) as certain and simple rather than uncertain and complex by changing its goals from therapy to custodial care (Perrow 1965).

If technical staff members are successful in programing boundary-transaction or conversion activities because of their efforts at input redefinition or reselection, the trend or direction of changes in the task and boundary conditions that work groups face will be as depicted in Figure 5.5. Cell 4 conditions will approximate those of either Cell 2 or 3, and Cell 2 and 3 conditions will approximate those of Cell 1. If technical staff are successful in redefining inputs, the distribution of decision-making functions between the second-level unit and work-group members will approximate that for each of the respective sets of conditions shown in Figures 5.3A, 5.3B, and 5.4A.

TRADITIONAL REWARD STRUCTURES

As was discussed in Chapter 4, technical staff members start with the goal of their organizational unit as given and partition it into subgoals, assign each subgoal to a work group, and then attempt to program activities to accomplish the subgoal. A reward structure is then developed to reward work-group members for carrying out the activities assigned to them in the manner in which they were so instructed. Like the programing of activities, these reward structures are a form of extrinsic control based on traditional design assumptions. Consistent with these assumptions, technical staff assume that work-group members will perform their activities reliably when each is rewarded for achieving his or her group's subgoals. The performance of these various activities will then be checked and balanced by the staff, for example, through quality control.

The trouble with this method of control is that instead of each work group pursuing its activities in the manner the staff members assume will "add up" to the goal of the organizational unit, each work group may pursue its subgoal and attempt to increase its rewards in a manner not initially anticipated and in a manner that may be incompatible with the pursuit by other work groups of their goals. Control is maintained by providing group members with extrinsic rewards rather than by designing the work so that it encourages group members to pursue intrinsically meaningful or purposeful activities. As we shall see, reliance on extrinsic rewards may produce unintended consequences with which neither higher units nor work-group members are prepared to cope.

UNINTENDED CONSEQUENCES OF TRADITIONAL DESIGN

Any programing of work-group activities has the potential for producing unintended consequences. This is because any conditions that technical staff members assume work groups face are, in a sense, artificial since all inputs with which work groups may deal require definitions that may only more or less accurately reflect their properties. The inputs that cross work-group boundaries are bundles of properties, some of which staff and work-group members "see" and for which they will select appropriate responses and others they choose to ignore. This selective process is promoted by the definitions that are attached to inputs and by the rewards given to work-group members for seeing inputs as technical staff have defined them. The important point to remember about the potential for producing unintended consequences is that "relevant" and "irrelevant" properties cross the work-group boundary simultaneously, usually on the same object, and all may potentially affect work-group activities and outputs.

Emery and Trist's (1965) typology based on the causal texture of the environment is useful for describing the task environments that work groups face. "Causal texture" refers to the nature of the interdependence between elements with which a work group must deal. In the following analysis, elements are (1) inputs and the properties of inputs converted by the work group or (2) the organizational units from which inputs are procured. Inputs may be within the work-group boundary or outside of it depending on whether the group's task, at a particular moment, is one of boundary transaction or conversion. Generally, third-level work groups that produce physical goods spend more time dealing with inputs after they are physically within the work-group boundary, so their task environment is more internal to the group than external. The reverse is true of boundary-spanning units at any organizational level.

Emery and Trist's four environmental types can be conviently grouped into two pairs; one pair is useful for describing internal task environments and the other pair for describing external task environments. Placid-randomized and placid-clustered environments are useful for describing the relationship between inputs and conversion activities taking place within the work-group boundary. Disturbed-reactive and turbulent environments are useful for describing the relationship between organizational units and boundary-transaction activities taking place across the work-group boundary. The environmental type and relevant elements change as the task of the group alternates between boundary transaction and conversion. Actions taking place within the work-group boundary are embedded in a different field of elements than those taking place across the work-group boundary. When the task of the work group is to convert inputs into products, the causal texture of the task environment consists of the consequences of group actions on the patterning of inputs and their properties. When the task of the work group is boundary transaction, the causal texture of the task environment consists of the consequences of group actions on the existing relationships between the various parallel or higher-level units from which inputs are procured. The external task environment of such third-level work groups seldom extends beyond units internal to the organization. In dealing with either boundary-transaction or conversion tasks, the degree to which work-group members can predict the consequences of their actions depends on the knowledge and skills possessed and the opportunities and resources available for learning.

Placid-Randomized and Placid-Clustered Environments

Placid-randomized environments are created by designers who wish maximum predictability in the task environments that work-group members face. Maximum predictability allows the designer to make "operating units" out of group members by instructing them to perform only those actions that meet what Boguslaw (1965) has called the "customer's requirements." To many designers, the customer is the designer's immediate superior whose primary requirement is the lowest labor cost per unit of product produced.

If conversion uncertainty is low, as it is under Cell 1 and Cell 2 conditions or as it is defined to be under Cell 3 and 4 conditions, the traditional designer will partition all the tasks required to produce the group's products into limited and isolated sets of tasks, each of which is assigned to an individual and labeled as his job. Required coordination between jobs is assumed to be minimal as jobs and relationships between jobs (for example, conveyors, fixed work flows, and so on) are assumed programable. Whatever coordination happens to be required is assigned to a supervisor. Under the conditions the designer has created, each job-holder perceives no relationship between his own job and the job of others. He knows only how to do the job assigned to him but not the way in which the various jobs fit together to produce a complete product. Furthermore, little or no information has been provided to him that would permit him to learn how the jobs are related to each other.

Environments of this type are labeled "placid-randomized" for two reasons. They are called placid because the relations between input properties remain stable throughout the production process, and thus the pattern of required actions does not shift; in these environments, any particular action is known to be the "right" one or the "wrong" one. The difficulty with such environments is that the entire set of tasks required to produce a complete product is known only to the original designer of the environment. Each job-holder only knows how to do his own job, and, from his perspective, the relationship between his job and the jobs of others is random—hence, the second name of the environmental type. To paraphrase Emery and Trist, his job is a localized tactic, which is not embedded in an overall strategy to produce a complete product. Jenkins (1973, p. 252) quotes a Norwegian welder who faced conditions such as these: "I stood here for eight years welding together metal plates, always on the same spot and with never any change. I hardly knew what the plates were being used for. I never thought about the job and never asked anybody—I just did what I was told. The work was a vacuum...."

The job-holder facing this environment has not been provided with the information that would permit him to learn the relationship between his job and jobs assigned to others. If a breakdown or problem occurs, he cannot suggest how to modify his actions so that the overall group task will be completed. He can only continue or stop doing what he has been instructed to do. In the words of Emery and Trist, he cannot subordinate tactics in pursuit of an overall strategy; he just doesn't know enough about how the group's product is produced to do more than his own job.

McWhinney (1968, p. 270) describes the placid-randomized environment as having the "double aspect of placing the member...in a position totally dependent on his environment for the inhabitant of an organized area has no ability to predict what his environment will do—and totally independent of it for there is nothing to know about it so concern with it is useless."

The reaction that McWhinney describes is quite similar to reactions generally referred to as alienation—namely, apathy and withdrawal. Additionally, the possibility exists that an individual will react to such an environment by rebellion or by searching for ways to "beat the system."

Placid-clustered environments are different from placid-randomized environments in one important respect and similar in another. They are similar in both being placid—that is, the relations between input properties remain stable throughout the production process with similar consequences for actions taken. However, in a placid-clustered environment, the whole pattern or a significant part of it is known or can become known to each individual job-holder. This takes place because individual job-holders may informally learn about each other's job, or such information becomes available from higher-level units. When such learning has occurred, group members may together pursue a common strategy by modifying the actions of their own jobs to assure that the overall group task is achieved—that is, subordinating tactics to strategy. An example of this would be doing a job in an unauthorized or, in the short run, a less efficient way that may ultimately lead to improving overall group performance—for example, a group taking actions for the sake of preventive maintenance, which slows production now but avoids a longer and more costly breakdown in the future.

The response of "just following your nose," which is demanded of placid-randomized environments is certainly less than what intelligent human beings are capable of, and they will generally make an effort to respond to such environments in a manner more in keeping with their capabilities. Roy (1955) demonstrated this by his efforts to play a competitive game against himself when faced with a highly monotonous task. He would speed up his production for short periods to achieve self-imposed goals, then take it easier later on.

When every member of a work group knows and can perform all of the tasks required of the group, his task environment is transformed from placid-randomized to placid-clustered. Two procedures, in particular, will encourage group members to do on behalf of the group what Roy's experience suggests they are capable of doing spontaneously: (1) encouragement of participation in problem-solving sessions aimed at correcting or modifying chronic sources of variance and (2) systematic rotation between jobs within the group. Both procedures will encourage group members to identify with the goals of their group rather than those associated with a particular job. As will be discusssed in Part III, a change in values as well as in organizational rewards is required for individuals to shift their identification from the job they hold to the task of the group as a whole.

Disturbed-Reactive and Turbulent Environments

Our perspective now shifts to consideration of the group relative to its external task environment, which consists of, among other things, other work groups or higher-level units. In a disturbed-reactive environment, the work group and other organizational units are assumed to be in conflict with each other over scarce resources, and the actions that one unit takes to move itself closer to its goals may impede or prevent other units from achieving their goals. This conflict adds a new dimension to a disturbed-reactive environment that is not found in the two environments previously discussed. The new dimension is uncertainty created by each unit's efforts intentionally to deceive other units as to the course it is pursuing. Such competition can be self-defeating because in addition to planning strategies and tactics, the group must devote its energies to what Emery and Trist call "operations" —that is, trying to outmaneuver or deceive other units as to its intended actions. Traditional design fosters the development of such environments by devising fixed rules for allocation of resources between units and then limiting the interactions between units to those considered "legal." A likely outcome of such procedures is for each unit to devise plans to increase its rewards at the other's expense, leading to an overall reduction in organizational performance. An example of such an outcome existed in the coal mine studied by Trist, Brown, and Susman (1975). Mine management rewarded individual mining shifts for their production. This resulted in competition between shifts to maximize the tons of coal each produced. Coal was mined out of cycle when the face* area scheduled to be mined had bad conditions. Each shift tried to outmaneuver the other to get the good areas and leave the bad areas for the next shift. Each shift was also tempted to leave cleanup activities for the next shift, which invariably resulted in retaliatory actions by the others. Another example of such interunit conflict leading to an overall reduction in performance is provided by Walton et al. (1966). The managers of the production and sales departments of a manufacturing firm each pursued their own unit subgoals to the detriment of deadlines for delivery of goods to customers.

In most cases of competition between organizational units, uncertainty caused by competition between organizational units may be reduced by any of the units entering into coalitions with other units (Dalton 1959), by bargaining directly with other units, or by searching for a superordinate goal that all units can accept as a guide to coordinated effort. The second and third alternatives might be considered more stable than the first, as coalitions break up quickly when their members believe they have more to gain by a competitive action than by a cooperative one. The search for a superordinate goal will be facilitated if a vehicle exists through which the parties to a conflict can discuss their differences. The vehicle provided to the three coal-mining shifts discussed above was called the "section conference," which met every six weeks during the first experimental year. All 27 men, 9 from each of three shifts, attended the day-long conference to discuss events of the previous six weeks. Among the topics discussed were the negative consequences of competition. As a result of these discussions, commitments were made to cooperate between shifts. To reinforce these commitments, upper management revised its method of reporting production and cost data from a shift basis to a section basis.

There is still an additional dimension in turbulent environments that is not found in the other three. Up until now, unit actions directed toward inputs or the possessors of inputs have been taken against a background that

---

*The end of a drift or excavation where the work either is going on or has stopped.

was stable and could be taken for granted. For example, the background of a competitive "game" among units is consensus concerning what is a "winning" or "losing" state of affairs. In a turbulent environment, not only do the actions of competitive or uncoordinated units create uncertainty as to what each unit is going to do, but the background itself begins to change in unpredictable ways. Walton et al. (1966), in the case already cited, provide an example of how the background of a competitive game can shift—for example, when the customers began canceling orders for products not delivered on their promised dates. A similar shift in background might occur if a common superior cracks down on two or more competing units in conflict.

Backgrounds are equally unstable when unit members are professionals with extensive differences in training. In such cases, no consensus exists on values or what is, from the perspective of the organization as a whole, a win or loss; industrial engineering and organizational development are two departments interacting in such an environment. Each unit may take actions that are incomprehensible or unacceptable to the other. If these groups try to collaborate, their independent actions may end up increasing the degree of uncertainty faced by both.

Efforts of a higher-level unit to reduce the uncertainty of a turbulent environment may leave the situation no better off than before. The higher-level unit may try to force a common definition of goals among the work-group members or try to restrict the actions of some or all interacting groups. However, efforts of this kind are unlikely to be successful because the definitions that professionals may be asked to accept are superficial, considering the depth of differences that exist among individuals trained in disciplines as disparate as, say, engineering and psychology. Group members themselves may try to deal with the turbulence they and members of other groups have created by denying the existence or value of the other group's contribution.

The most effective means of reducing uncertainty in a turbulent environment is for all the units within it to agree on common values to guide their respective actions. In this way, the shifting background upon which units take actions is stabilized. The effect of shared values among units in a turbulent environment is different than the effect of acceptance of a superordinate goal, which was the solution suggested for disturbed-reactive environments. Generally, a superordinate goal of two or more third-level groups is a goal of the second-level unit that contains them. At the latter level, goals are usually operationalizable into targets for product quantity and quality within the constraints of cost and delivery time. Goals such as these may be partitioned into subgoals, each of which is assigned to a separate work group. Within the constraints of existing technology, members of each group, if allowed, can plan how their assigned subgoal will

TABLE 5.2

Environmental Types, Basic Characteristics, and Typical and Adaptive Responses

Environmental Types and Basic Characteristics	Typical Responses	Adaptive Responses
Internal Task Environment Placid-randomized:		
Actions appear randomly distributed; the structure of rewards and punishments is stable.	Only local tactics are possible; there is no way to organize local tactics in pursuit of an overall strategy; disengagement or rebellion is likely.	
Placid-clustered:		
Actions appear correlated; the structure of rewards and punishment is stable.	Tactics may be embedded into strategies—that is, action-wholes; learning through pattern recognition, generalization, and so on.	Members within each work group participate in problem-solving sessions; there is systematic rotation between jobs.
External Task Environment Disturbed-reactive:		
Action toward goals is uncertain because the environment is shared with other actors pursuing the same goal; the structure of rewards and punishments is stable.	In addition to strategy, "gaming" activity takes place—for instance, coalitions, bargaining.	Representatives from each relevant work group meet, along with members of superior unit to develop a superordinate goal as well as strategy and tactics to pursue it.
Turbulent:		
Action toward goals is uncertain because the environment is shared with other actors who have different frames of references; the structure of rewards and punishments is unstable because the "background" upon which actions are taken begins to shift.	Uncertainty is reduced by ignoring elements and relationships between elements, forcing a common definition upon the actors.	Representatives from each relevant work group meet to achieve value consensus through normative planning.

Source: Compiled by the author.

be achieved. To summarize the relationship between units, the subgoals of work groups are subordinate to the second-level unit goal as tactics are to strategy or as goals are to objectives. These pairs represent ends each of which is achievable within the respective time frames in which superior and subordinate units operate.

Values are different from goals in not being achievable ends; rather, values are guides to behavior—for example, fairness, respect for individual opinions, nurturance of one's own and other's learning opportunities, and so on. Values have the conceptual character of "power fields" (Lewin 1951)—that is, one does not try to reach a value but rather permits values to guide behavior. Values are in Kluckholn's (1951, p. 422) words, "conceptions of the desirable." This gives them their "ought" character, distinguishing them from what is simply "desired" without regard to its morality or immorality, its "goodness" or "badness." As Kluckholn puts it, a value "organizes a system of action" (p. 395). When values are shared between units in a turbulent environment, the background of their overlapping external task environments becomes stabilized, permitting superior, subordinate, and lateral units to set shared goals and achieve them by devising complementary strategy and tactics.

Values cannot be dictated by a higher-level unit; they must be "appreciated" by all the units whose actions affect each other. Such shared appreciations can be developed if a setting is provided in which the members of the various units can examine in an unthreatening manner the value premises underlying the actions that they have taken and that they propose for the future. Similar procedures have already been suggested for members of the same unit by which they might devise strategy and tactics for the internal task environments they jointly face. What is further suggested is that representatives of each group, or all group members if their number is not too large, meet to attain a value consensus to guide their respective actions. Essentially, what such a setting provides is an opportunity to carry out the recommendation of Emery et al. (1974) and Friedmann (1973), mentioned in Chapter 4, that all levels of the organization engage in normative planning. This arrangement not only permits members of each organizational level to establish the "ground" upon which their respective strategy and tactics can be devised but also provides a means to nurture and sanction innovations that might later be adopted by the organization as a whole. The redundancy of planning functions that this arrangement promotes increases the adaptive capacity of the organization by increasing the adaptive capacity of each of its units (see Emery and Trist 1973).

Table 5.2 contains a summary of the discussion in this section of the chapter. Summarized are the environmental types, their basic characteristics, and typical and adaptive responses.

CHAPTER

6

DECISION MAKING IN WORK GROUPS

WORK GROUPS AS DECISION-MAKING UNITS

Chapter 4 defined the smallest decision-making unit in the organization as the work group. However, a qualification is necessary because there are cases in which the individual may be the smallest decision-making unit. For example, take the salesman belonging to the organizational unit mentioned on page 84. He is assigned a territory by his unit manager, given an expense account, an automobile, product samples, and any other resources he may require to achieve the goal assigned to him. It is not likely that his unit manager or unit staff can program the techniques he uses for selling his product, although "selling tips" may be suggested to him at headquarters meetings. His performance is regulated by output measures—that is, he receives commissions based on how much his individual sales contribute to the total unit revenue.

This salesman is an organizational unit, but a rare one because few individuals are able to be what he is. He faces an environment in which he, as the decider of a system as a whole (himself), plans and decides on behalf of his organizational unit (himself). He is a "system unto himself" as well as a part-system of the organizational unit that contains him. He is rare because few individuals within organizations can be systems unto themselves.*

---

*This statement refers only to what higher organizational units formally permit individuals to do. It refers to neither the reality of informal organizational life to which an individual continually adjusts as a system

However, his position should not be confused with that of individuals who singularly make decisions on behalf of larger organizational units. In the latter case, the individual does not make decisions on behalf of himself as a system, but on behalf of a system or unit that may contain tens, hundreds, or thousands of individuals.

The reader should be clear that what follows in this chapter and in the following chapters of the book is a framework for work-group design, not for job design. Job design is, of course, an important problem area in and of itself, but it can seldom be discussed without considering the implication for group dynamics of placing and rotating jobs. Additionally, criteria developed for the design of individual jobs are frequently as applicable to the group when it is the focus of design, for example, meaningful pattern of tasks that gives a semblance of a single overall task; some scope for setting standards of quantity and quality of production and suitable feedback of results; inclusion of tasks requiring some degree of care, skill, knowledge, or effort that is worthy of respect in the community; a job that makes some perceivable contribution to the utility of the product for the consumer Emery and Thorsrud (1965) discuss, in addition to these job-design criteria, how various jobs might be related to each other. The framework developed in this book is intended to supplement and build upon previous work in job design, but it does so at another level of analysis, the group. The work group is chosen because, within it, a dimension is added to the qualiny of working life that differs from what the individual job can contribute. Design of work groups can only be adequately dealt with at its own level of analysis because decisions required within a work group are more than the sum of decisions required of individual jobs; they are qualitatively different.

A number of reasons can be offered as to why the work group is a more appropriate unit from which to approach the improvement of the quality of working life. It is an organizational unit that is small enough to allow the individuals employed in the occupational categories in Chapter 1 an opportunity to make decisions on behalf of a group, to manage an organizational unit. It is a unit large enough to contain sufficient tasks for producing complete products that are valued by unit members and the organization. It is also a unit large enough that meeting its goals and objectives requires sufficient variety, complexity, and uncertainty for challenging decision making. It is a unit large enough to allow individuals to exercise interpersonal skills for problem solving, consensus building,

---

unto himself nor how he reacts to any extraorganizational environments—for example, to his family or to unique biological or existential conditions he faces.

planning, and conflict resolution. On the other hand, the work group is an organizational unit small enough that group members can see the relationship between decisions made and goals achieved. Finally, the possibilities for innovative restructuring of work-group tasks and relationships are much greater at the group level than at the job level. Since the work group is a more complex entity, there are more alternative structures and social relationships possible that can meet the equivalent performance standards (see Von Bertalanffy's [1950] concept of finality). Some of these structures and relationships may be explored and created by the group members themselves, giving them an opportunity for growth and learning that individual jobs cannot always provide.

The objective of this book is to discover methods for the design of autonomous work groups. Autonomous work groups permit their members to exercise skills and make decisions that are similar in form to—although obviously different in content than—those made at higher organizational levels. Like the deciders of higher-level units, the deciders of autonomous work groups make decisions relative to the environment the group faces as a whole. A defining quality of an autonomous group is that it has a decider that makes decisions on behalf of itself as a whole. Although the decider of an autonomous work group can engage in normative, strategic, and operational planning, the choice of alternative values and goals is greatly limited at the level of the organization, where products and services are actually produced; the main type of planning is operational. Work groups at this level are invariably part-systems of higher-level units, and, therefore, autonomy is conditional. But this says very little, of course, because any autonomy is conditonal; no system can operate without constraints. What determines whether a unit at any level is autonomous is not the kinds of decisions that are made; there is no checklist one can consult. Autonomy is determined by whether the unit can make decisions for the unit as a whole and thus allow the unit to maintain certain critical performance standards at steady-state levels. "Steady-state" refers to maintenance of a range of critical performance standards that larger organizational units, work-group members, and the environment that the group faces consider acceptable. Unacceptable variation may lead one of these three to cease contributing resources that are vital to the continued existence of the autonomous work group. If this happens, the group may no longer exist or may no longer remain autonomous. For example, if higher management is not satisfied with the quality or quantity of output from an autonomous work group, it may no longer allow the group to make its own decisions—that is, it may withdraw its decider by reassigning group decisions to a higher organizational level.

CRITICAL PERFORMANCE STANDARDS

Let's assume the manager of a production department is willing to allow his operatives to form autonomous work groups. We will assume that the manager will do so because he believes this will increase departmental productivity and efficiency—not, for example, because he has a value commitment to democratic practice or because of his views on the nature of man. Leaving aside for the moment what kinds of decisions work-group members are making or how they are made, what would the manager consider as minimal conditions for allowing the continuation of autonomous work groups in his department?

The most obvious minimal condition is a level of quantity and quality of output that is at least as high as it was before the group became autonomous. The manager may also believe that output levels should be higher or costs lower than they were previously if he has incurred investment costs in training group members to make decisions that he or others once made or if he has tolerated a period of low performance during the group's initial learning phase. Costs can be broadly defined to include savings due to reduced turnover, absenteeism, accidents, and so on. Also, costs may be reduced because the group is wasting less, losing fewer tools, and so on. The range of variation in level of quantity and quality of production as well as costs that are acceptable to the manager may be narrow or broad depending on tolerances in production quality and the competition his products face from other organizations.

It should not be taken for granted that work-group members will automatically wish to be or continue to be members of autonomous work groups. They may consider the gains made in satisfaction or income not worth the psychic and physical effort expended. Thus, both parties to an autonomous work-group relationship may evaluate the desirability of continuing such a relationship in reward-minus-cost terms (see Herbst 1962). An economic exchange model should not be too strictly interpreted; however, it is a useful paradigm for viewing the relationship between the parties. It is extremely difficult, for example, to measure the satisfaction work-group members gain from making decisions they consider challenging or from doing meaningful work. The likelihood that satisfactions will be greater than effort expended will increase if sociotechnical design is permitted before commitments are made for new equipment, plant layout, information systems, and so on. Probably the greatest source of frustration that members of autonomous work groups experience is not having sufficient feedback of information concerning the performance standards they are responsible for maintaining. Group members either may not know how well they are doing or may lack sufficient information to take corrective action. Sociotechnical design principles are discussed in Chapters 7 and 8.

DECISIONS IN AUTONOMOUS WORK GROUPS

Assuming that management and group members are satisfied with their exchange of mutual rewards and costs, the next question concerns the nature of decisions made by the group. The decisions that work groups can make can be loosely grouped into three categories.

There are decisions that are intrinsic to the production process itself. Allowing group members to make these decisions directly affects the group's capacity to maintain performance standards within acceptable ranges. Making decisions of this type allows the group to be *self-regulating*. The justification for allowing group members to make these decisions is that group members are closer to relevant information and better able to take quicker and more appropriate action; they will make better decisions than decisions made by someone external to the group. Hopefully, acceptable output levels will become objects of directed action if achieving them is challenging and meaningful. Directed action is assumed to have a synergizing influence on group members, leading them to coordinate themselves better than they can be coordinated externally.

There are decisions that group members can make that are not intrinsic to the production process, but the ability of group members to make them influences how much freedom from technological or organizational constraints group members experience. Group members may be permitted to make decisions in this category because making them involves little or no cost to the production process or because the production process itself creates the conditions that allow them to be made. An example of the latter situation is the freedom that an oil refinery worker experiences because he can make his rounds of the tank farm or eat his lunch at his own discretion (Blauner 1964). The favorable sentiments that group members experience is, in a sense, negative; it is freedom from constraints. This freedom allows group members a "free space." Decisions in this category allow group members to be independent (Susman 1970a).

Group members can make decisions in a third category that is not mutually exclusive of the other two. These decisions may be related to the production process, but the reason for making them is not because group members can make them better than higher organizational units can. Group members make decisions in this category because they increase the group's capacity for self-governance. These are decisions concerned with who shall make what decisions and by what process these decisions shall be made. The justification for permitting group members to make these decisions is not efficiency or effectiveness. They are permitted to make them because group members have the political power or expertise to claim the right to do so, because it is congruent with the political values of the wider society, or because it provides a training ground from which group members can learn the interpersonal skills required for good citizenship or organizational advancement. Examples of such decisions are the following: Will the group elect a single leader? Will leadership be shared with others? What will tenure in leadership positions be? To whom will tasks be allocated? Who will make allocation decisions? Who will be a member of the group? How will deviant group members be disciplined? Examples of how such decisions are made include (1) election of a group member to make decisions within the group for a limited period of time and (2) election of a representative who will consult with higher management concerning decisions that affect the group.

The ability of the group to make any or all of the three categories of decisions discussed has been cited by different researchers as evidence that a work group is autonomous. But, as we shall see, each of the three categories of decisions may exist and be justified for different reasons. The lack of distinction between these decisions has created confusion in the literature as to what group autonomy is as well as the conditions for and consequences of its existence. At the end of Chapter 4, it was stated that an autonomous group must be able to make decisions according to ends and values that govern and determine the behavior of the whole structure. Many decisions of independence as well as of self-governance are not based on their contribution to such ends and values but are made on behalf of the interests, grievances, and so on of particular group members. Decisions of self-regulation would be most likely to qualify as the criterion of autonomy because they are made on the basis of their effect on the relationship of the group as a whole to its environment—that is, the maintenance of critical performance standards within acceptable ranges of variation.

Decisions of self-regulation, self-governance, and independence all contribute to making work groups more autonomous. The analytic distinction between categories of decisions is useful for helping management and work-group members to know the values or reasons for delegating a particular decision to work-group members and the consequences that are likely to follow. It is a matter of convenience that the generic term "autonomy" be retained; the more the decisions from each category are delegated, the more autonomous the work group. It is the writer's belief that decisions of self-regulation should be given the heaviest weighting.

DECISIONS OF INDEPENDENCE

One category of decisions was concerned with group-member independence. Work groups can make decisions in this category unless specific constraints prevent them from doing so. In this section, examples of decisions that affect independence are listed, and each is followed by analysis of organizational and technological conditions that may facilitate or impede them. The constraints that are listed are not "givens" that must inevitably compromise the group's independence. Each is viewed as one constraint in a network of constraints in a particular concrete environment. Higher-level organizational units may alter any of these constraints based on a change in technology, the nature of products produced, or an explicit organizational effort to alter priorities in terms of allowing greater work-group autonomy. Whatever the reasons for such alterations, it is important that there be an awareness of the impact these alterations have on work-group autonomy.

Where Will the Product Be Produced?

Work groups cannot make this decision when conversion activities require heavy or automated machinery, nor can groups whose conversion activities are tied to a particular geographical area. Logging work groups are a possible exception in that they can decide what trees to cut within a wide area of the forest (Gulowsen 1972). Assuming that neither of the two restrictions applies, work groups may be able to make this decision if raw materials are light in weight and easy to transport, maintenance supplies are few and infrequently used, and conversion activities are manual or require the assistance of few tools. If the raw materials and products consist of information rather than matter, it is more likely that the group can decide where it will work; for example, if the group's output is a report or policy decision, deliberation and problem solving can take place where the group chooses. Work groups whose members are employed in the occupational categories listed in Chapter 1 would seldom be able to make this decision.

When Will the Product Be Produced?

If a group can decide where to work, it is very likely it can decide when to work. Assuming the group cannot make the former decision, the group can decide when to work if particular conditions hold. It may do so if there is sufficient lead time between production requisition and delivery time to allow group members to decide whether to speed up work now and take it easy later or vice versa. The technology or the properties of inputs may prevent the group from doing the latter—for example, in wool-dyeing, the quality of dyed wool deteriorates rapidly unless each step of the dyeing process is completed according to a tight time schedule (E.J. Miller 1959). Even if lead time is short, work groups can still make this decision if an inventory of products can be built up allowing for steady distribution of outputs to the group's environment. An inventory of products allows group members a time buffer if products are standardized so that the "next" unit of production is always acceptable to the work group's environment.

In What Order Will Products Be Produced?

This decision is relevant only if the work group is assigned responsibility for producing more than one product. Two conditions must hold if the work group is to make this decision. The first is one of the conditions mentioned for *when* products will be produced; there is a sufficient lead time between production requisition and delivery time or there is sufficient inventory of raw materials within the group. Second is that, if raw materials are transferred between two or more work groups, the sequence of transference must be known and the same for each of the products produced. The sequence can be quite complex. For example, suppose the outputs of several preceding groups converge as inputs to one group or the outputs of one group diverge and become inputs into several succeeding groups. The production manager of a plant containing such groups need only concern himself with flows between groups, leaving product-scheduling decisions to be made within the groups themselves (Reeves and Turner 1972).

In What Order Will Conversion Activities Take Place?

This decision is relevant to the production of any single product. Whether group members can make this decision depends on how fixed the sequence of conversion activities leading to product completion is. In many cases, the nature of the technology or raw materials fixes the sequence of production. For example, an automobile worker on an assembly line cannot tighten a set of bolts attaching a fender to a car body until the fender has been placed in proper position on the car. Also, dyed wool cannot be spun until the wool has adequately dried, nor does drying take place until all the phases of the dyeing process have been completed.

In determining whether the work group can make this decision, the sociotechnical designer must ask whether the technology or raw materials actually determine the sequence of conversion activities or whether development or production engineers assumed this early in the design process. If the sociotechnical designer is allowed to contribute early to the design process, he may influence the choice of product design, raw materials, equipment, and so on, that allow group members to make conversion-sequencing decisions with minimal costs in development and, perhaps, substantial benefits to production. The separate assembly areas within Saab-Scania and Volvo automobile plants have been designed with such considerations in mind. A small group of workers receives formed engine cases and parts for assembly. An engine is scheduled for completion in one half hour, but the group members can vary the pace and divide the work among themselves as they wish (Jenkins 1973).

Even when the overall sequence of production appears fixed, there may be discontinuities at particular stages of production that allow choice in the order in which stages of production are produced. In such a case, "modules" of work each containing fixed sequences can be assigned to the work group permitting group members to choose the order in which modules are produced. An Italian manufacturer of office equipment has undertaken such a work design (Butera 1975). Workers build self-contained parts (modules) of adding machines but may vary module sequences if they so choose.

SELF-GOVERNANCE

Self-governance means that the group makes decisions that serve its members interests, and the right to make these decisions is limited to those who are deemed members of the group. The decisions that the group makes need not be relevant to work-group performance, and that makes the concept of self-governance applicable to a wider range of decisions than decisions of independence or self-regulation alone. The justification for self-governance is political, while the justification for self-regulation is economic; the latter is assumed to result in more effective and efficient work-group performance. Decisions of independence need not usually be justified since they are generally permitted by default. However, if the right to make them does come under dispute, work-group members may justify their right on political or humanitarian grounds—for example, mental and physical health or other claims of affected interest (see Chapter 2).

The difficulty of isolating justifications from each other contributes to conflict between management and the work force. Each claims the right to make decisions based on different justifications. For example, in decisions concerning who shall be assigned to the group or who shall be assigned to perform what activities, management may claim it has superior knowledge that permits it to make these decisions better than work-group members can. This claim may or may not be accurate, but the truth of the claim may not be the reason why work-group members seek to make it. Decisions as to who will represent group interests to higher levels of the organization—as with grievances, determination of whether overtime is required, and who assigns it—are more clearly based on political considerations.

The process by which decisions are made by the work group is as critical an issue of self-governance as who makes the decisions. Assuming that the group has been delegated the right to make a decision, will it make that decision by democratic vote, by seeking consensus, or will one member be elected by the group to make decisions on behalf of the group for a limited period of time? Decisions such as who will present grievances to management on behalf of the group, how group members will be disciplined, and what and how sanctions will be administered may be made by any method that is congruent with the preferences and values of work-group members. Such preferences and values emerge from the social dynamics of work groups and will be discussed in Chapter 7.

DECISIONS OF SELF-REGULATION

The term "decider" is unfortunate in one respect. It connotes an entity rather than a process as well as something concentrated rather than diffuse. The decider at various times may be characterized by any of these qualities. The decider was defined in Chapter 4 in fairly abstract terms as the locus from which decisions in a system originate. It has already been suggested that the decider may be diffused among all group members if a decision is to be made by democratic vote. The decider may also shift from member to member if the nature of the group's responsibilities demands it. Some group members may also make only certain decisions on behalf of the group, while other decisions are made by the group as a whole.

When the group makes decisions that directly affect work-group performance, the degree of diffuseness group members give to the decider depends on whether group members are making decisions immediately before or after or during the performance of activities or whether they are making decisions at leisure, perhaps removed from the work place. The latter type of decisions generally concern policy matters having long-term effects on work-group performance; the former type of decisions have immediate and generally short-term effects on performance. Decisions concerning policy matters are more likely to be diffused among group members than are regulatory decisions. Group members may make policy decisions by consensus or democratic vote after periodically reviewing performance data. This procedure has been followed in the coal-mining study already referred to in Chapter 3. Every six weeks, as part of a year-long training program, the 27 members of the autonomous work section spend an eight-hour day in an above-ground classroom reviewing performance data of the last six weeks and making plans and decisions concerning the next six weeks. In contrast, short-term regulatory decisions are generally made at the work site by one group member or a few group members. The nature and distribution of such decisions depend on the environmental and technological conditions that work groups face. This is discussed below.

TYPES OF SELF-REGULATION

If work-group members were sufficiently trained and motivated to carry out conversion and boundary transaction activities that were so perfectly programmed that no variances from standards ever occurred, there would be no need for a discussion of regulatory decisions. There would be no regulatory decisions to make. Of course, work groups never face such conditions, and choices must be made concerning the distribution of regulatory decisions between higher-level units and work groups and between the members of work groups. The focus of this section is more on the latter kind of distribution than the former. The topic of distribution of regulatory decisions between work-group members is distinctly separate, although related to the topic of division of labor. The latter topic concerning the assignment of activities to be regulated is discussed in Chapter 8.

In addition to regulatory decisions affecting long-term performance, there are three basic types of short-term regulatory decisions. (1) Coordination refers to decisions altering the nature, sequence, or timing of conversion activities. There are three basic types of coordination decisions to be discussed in the next section. (2) Allocation refers to decisions conveying raw materials, supplies, group members, and so on, to sites where activities are required. (3) Boundary maintenance refers to decisions altering the flow of inputs and outputs across the boundary.

Shown within the circles of Figure 6.1A are the three types of regulatory decisions (C, A, BM), each of which represents a function that must be adequately performed if the group is to achieve and maintain steady-state conditions. These functions are group properties, not individual properties. Each is necessary for effective work-group performance whether or not there are humans there to perform them. In fact, some of these functions might or could be performed by a computer. When humans perform these functions, they are carrying out a *role* on behalf of the group. The discussion below concerns these latter circumstances.

FIGURE 6.1

Varying Degrees of Separability Between Types of Regulatory Decisions and Bewteen Such Decisions and Activity/Resource Sites

FIGURE 6.1A

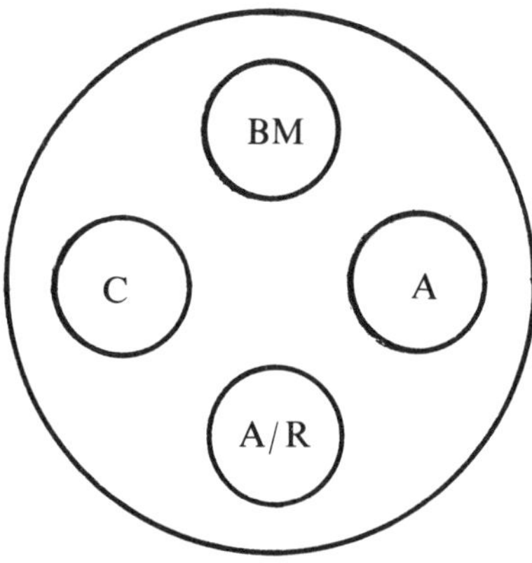

FIGURE 6.1B

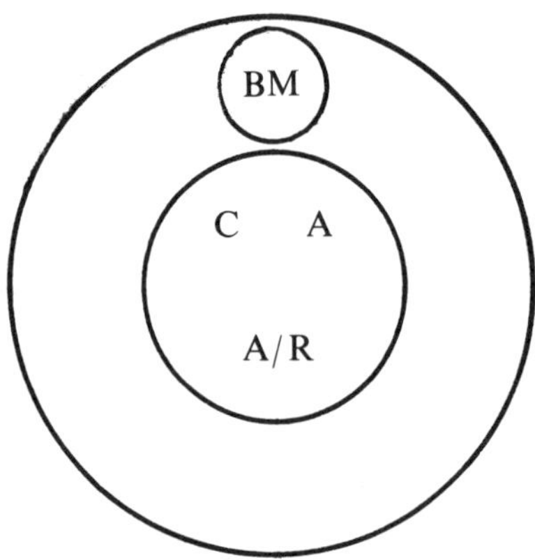

Source: Compiled by the author.

Whether one group member or several members jointly make coordination, allocation, or boundary-maintenance decisions depends on how separable each decision is from the other decisions or how separable each decision is from the activities they regulate. Two regulatory decisions are separable if each decision-type can be assigned to a different group member at no loss in group performance. Such a possibility is illustrated in Figure 6.1A by drawing separate circles around the decision letters C and A. Each circle then represents a role that one or more group members may perform on behalf of the group. Similarly, a regulatory decision is separable from the activities regulated if the decision type can be assigned to a group member who does not also carry out the regulated activities. This is illustrated in Figure 6.1A by drawing separate circles around the activity/resource sites (A/R)—that is, sites where activities are performed and resources utilized. In such circumstances, the members who make coordination and/or allocation decisions are not the same group members who actually perform the activities regulated.

The three types of regulatory decisions are difficult to separate from each other when each type of decision must be frequently revised on the basis of the other type decisions. The decisions are difficult to separate from the activities regulated when the activities themselves and the relationships between them are unclear or unpredictable—that is, conversion or boundary-transaction uncertainty is high. Figure 6.1B illustrates both of these difficulties by not drawing separate circles around decision letters C and B or between these decision letters and activity/resource sites but instead containing them all within one large circle. Various combinations of separability and inseparability could be illustrated by drawing circles of varying degrees of inclusiveness. Frequently, the conditions that make it difficult to separate these decision types from each other also make it difficult to separate the decisions from the activities they regulate. When decisions are not separable from other decisions or from regulated activities, decisions and activities must be made and carried out by the same group member or by group members in close interaction with each other.

When a type of regulatory decision is separable from the activities regulated, a group member may perform the specialized role of making these regulatory decisions on behalf of the group. For example, boundary-maintenance decisions are shown contained within their own circle in Figures 6.1A and 6.1B. If boundary-maintenance decisions are separable from the other types of decisions, they may be most appropriately assigned to a supervisor since he is more likely than any other group member to have ongoing relationships with relevant members of the work group's environment. A supervisor, nominally a member of the next highest unit, may make decisions in the capacity of being one of those to whom the group's decider is diffused. He has a specialized role to perform just like any other work-group member. This distribution of decision making is suggested in Chapter 8.

CONDITIONS AFFECTING THE DISTRIBUTION OF SELF-REGULATORY DECISIONS

The most appropriate distribution of regulatory decisions for a particular work group depends on the nature of the environmental conditions and the technological conditions that the work group faces. Two environmental conditions facing work groups discussed in Chapter 5 were boundary-transaction uncertainty and conversion uncertainty.

Boundary-Transaction Uncertainty

When higher-level units cannot reduce boundary-transaction uncertainty, work-group members may have to deal with the following kinds of questions to meet their production responsibilities: (1) When will raw materials, supplies, requests for production, or completed products cross the work-group boundary (for example, a dispatching center receiving incoming calls for orders)? (2) If the group's technology or product requires that the group be responsible for a large geographical territory (for example, coal mining), where will raw materials, supplies, requests for production, or completed products cross the work-group boundary (enter the group's territory)? (3) If the group is responsible for producing more than one product each requiring different conversion activities, uncertainty over the time and sequence in which production orders are received raises the question, When will the activities required to produce each product be organized? (4) If those who are to receive the group's output cannot articulate specifications without consultation with work-group members, then the question of what to produce cannot be determined prior to receipt of an order (for example, as with customers wishing customized products).

Conversion Uncertainty

When higher-level organizational units cannot reduce conversion uncertainty, the essential question facing work-group members is how to produce the product. If raw materials contain properties that are unknown to work-group members, the members will have to search for appropriate conversion activities (see p. 95).

Technically Required Cooperation

In addition to boundary-transaction and conversion uncertainty, a third variable related to work-group conditions must be introduced before proceeding with discussion of the distribution of regulatory decisions among work-group members. This variable is *technically required cooperation* (see Meissner 1969). Technical cooperation is required when, for a given technology or production time, any or all of the group's products cannot be produced by a single individual because of limits in individual capacities to perform the necessary conversion or boundary transaction activities. Therefore, responsibility to produce a given product is assigned to two or more individuals. These limitations may be due to the size of the area for simultaneous surveillance or action or the required physical strength of multiplicity of skills. These are limiting factors in the short run although sufficient learning time may lead to innovations in technology or improved skills that alter these limiting factors. Under these conditions cooperation among individuals is necessary and, according to Barnard (1938, p. 23), "justifies itself... as a means of overcoming the limitations restricting what individuals can do."

Meissner (1969, pp. 26-27) describes cooperation as a "relationship between two or more parties where the parties share certain properties of their environment and their behavior displays certain arrangements which regulate the distribution of whatever is shared." More specifically, he uses the term "technically required cooperation" "when... operators perform acts necessary for the attainment of technical ends" and when operators must share, in addition to time, the same equipment or "work piece." Meissner considers "work piece" to refer to any material that is worked on and may not have the discreteness implied by the term. For example, refinery operators or coal miners may be jointly responsible for petroleum flowing through a cracking plant or coal moving on a belt, respectively.

DISTRIBUTION OF SELF-REGULATORY DECISIONS

In combination with boundary-transaction and conversion uncertainty, the third variable, technically required cooperation, permits the creation of the three-dimensional matrix depicted in Figure 6.2. This figure is an

FIGURE 6.2

Three-Dimensional Matrix of Conditions Derived From Boundary-Transaction Uncertainty, Conversion Uncertainty, and Technically Required Cooperation

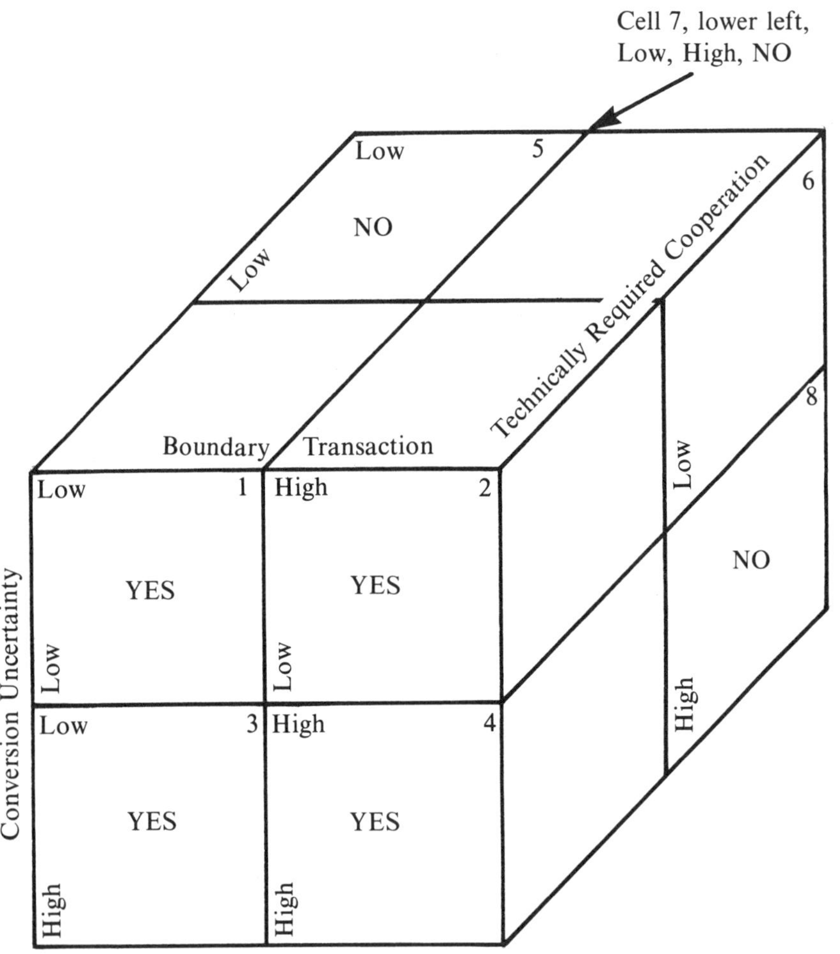

Source: Compiled by the author.

TABLE 6.1

Type of Interdependence and Coordination Following From Conditions Facing Work Groups

Cell Number	Boundary-Transaction Uncertainty	Conversion Uncertainty	Technically Required Cooperation	Type of Interdependence	Type of Coordination	Are Regulatory Decisions Easily Separable from Activities Regulated?	Are Regulatory Decisions Easily Separable from Each Other?
Cell 1	Low	Low	Yes	Sequential-dependent or simultaneous-independent	Scheduling	Yes	Yes
Cell 2	High	Low	Yes	Sequential-dependent or simultaneous-independent	Scheduling	Yes	No
Cell 3	Low	High	Yes	Reciprocal	Mutual Adjustment	No	Yes (BM)
Cell 4	High	High	Yes	Reciprocal	Mutual Adjustment	No	No
Cell 5	Low	Low	No	Pooled	Standardization	Yes	Yes
Cell 6	High	Low	No	Pooled	Standardization	Yes	Difficult
Cell 7	Low	High	No	Pooled	Standardization	Yes	Yes
Cell 8	High	High	No	Pooled	Standardization	Yes	Difficult

Source: Compiled by the author.

elaboration of Figure 5.2. The introduction of the third variable doubles the number of cells representing environmental or technological conditions from four to eight.* It would be visually confusing to try to put any descriptions within each cell. So the eight conditions have been listed in Table 6.1.

The remainder of the chapter discusses the distribution of regulatory decisions that seems appropriate under each of the eight cell conditions. Appropriateness is a judgment based on what evidence or logic suggests would be the most effective and efficient way to meet acceptable performance standards. As was previously discussed, coordination, allocation, and boundary-maintenance decisions may or may not be easily separable from the activities they regulate or separable from each other. When they are separable, they may be assigned to supervisors, or work-group members may elect or appoint one or more of their members to make decisions on behalf of the others. If a work group has a supervisor, he may be the best person to whom boundary-maintenance decisions are assigned; however, the fact that conditions are discussed under which coordination and allocation decisions could be easily dispersed upward to higher-level units is not a recommendation that they be dispersed. Work-group members may be able to make these decisions at no loss in work-group performance, while the satisfaction group members experience from making these decisions is one of the objectives for implementing work-group autonomy. It is not necessary that work-group members make all three types of decisions for the

---

*It is possible to consider boundary-transaction uncertainty, conversion uncertainty, and technically required cooperation as continuous rather than dichotomous, and therefore, to locate group conditions on a point in three-dimensional space. However, nothing is gained by doing this since recommendations for distributing regulatory decisions are dichotomous—for example, assigning a decision type to the same or different individuals, and so on. The three variables for determining conditions are best conceived as dichotomies; there is some point at which it is more advisable to assign decisions one way rather than another.

Additionally, recommendations for distribution are based on the assumption that conditions remain the way they are most of the time. This may not always be true, of course; however, if conditions change, the reader should look up recommendations for distribution under the new conditons. Some work groups may regularly face changes when, for example, new and different products are introduced. Work groups may vary their distribution of regulatory decisions as frequently as there are variations in the conditions the work group faces.

group to be considered self-regulating. However, group members must be able to make at least one of these three types to be so considered.

Cell 1 Conditions

Under cell 1 conditions, boundary-transaction and conversion uncertainty are low, but technical cooperation is required. Because conversion uncertainty is low and because raw materials are stable, sequences of conversion activities are known and predictable. Under such circumstances, two limiting factors influence the type of interdependence between conversion activities. Interdependence between group members may be simultaneous-independent or sequential-dependent. Simultaneous-independent relationships occur when the limiting factor is *time*—that is, for example, two workers may be needed to perform simultaneously two or more separate actions on semimolten billets in a hot-strip rolling mill in a time period too short for one worker to perform these actions (Walker 1957). The simultaneous-independent activities assigned to two or more group members need have no relationship between them, other than that they occur during the same time period.

Sequential-dependent activities can be assigned to two or more group members, but the activities assigned to one cannot begin until completion of those assigned to the others. Different group members will be assigned sequential-dependent activities when the limiting factor is skill. This may be due to differences in type of training or to union restrictions over who may be assigned to what activities; for example, a craftsman such as a glass-etcher may lack the skills of a glass-blower and must wait until the latter has completed his activities before beginning his own. Organizations may, of course, set up sequential-dependent situations such as the assembly line manned with narrowly trained workers. When this occurs, it frequently results from scientific management assumptions held by technical staff rather than from technological limitations.

Under cell 1 conditions, the low boundary-transaction uncertainty permits the three types of regulatory decisions to be separable from each other (contained in separate circles in Figure 6.1A). This is because knowledge about what, where, and when to convert inputs is relevant for a time period of sufficient length for different group members to share such knowledge and use it independently to make coordination and allocation decisions that are consistent with each other. Additionally, coordination and allocation decisions are separable from the activities to be programed (C, A, and A/R are contained in separate circles in Figure 6.1A). Therefore, these decisions may be assigned to group members who will make them on behalf of the group. Group members may have little or no need for boundary-maintenance decisions as higher-level units have already reduced boundary-transaction uncertainty before inputs and outputs cross the work-group boundary. The ease with which regulatory decisions are separable from the activities regulated makes the continuation of autonomy precarious as it is very likely that higher-level units will upwardly disperse such decisions, no longer permitting the group to be self-regulating, as for example, on assembly lines.

If a work group under cell 1 conditions produces more than one product, it may be feasible and economical to retain coordination and allocation decisions within the group. Different group members or the same group member may make each of these types of regulatory decisions.

1. Coordination decisions: Coordination of simultaneous-independent and sequential-dependent activities is through *scheduling* the time of their occurrence. If the group produces only one product, scheduling will be done, no doubt, once and for all by higher-level units and is no longer a concern of the work group. Even when the group produces more than one product, higher-level units may program scheduling decisions, providing only a signal to group members to change schedules to match the appropriate product—for example, if a sedan comes down the assembly line, fenders are bolted on before trunk lids, but if the car is a convertible, the trunk lids go on first. With these exceptions aside, when the group produces more than one product and each product requires a different schedule of activities, the likelihood increases that such decisions should be made within the work group.

2. Allocation decisions: Like scheduling decisions, allocation of raw materials and resources will be made routinely if the group produces only one product. However, if the group produces more than one product and each requires a different combination of resources to produce it, such allocation decisions could be made by a work-group member. One allocation decision that the work group might always retain is the right to assign themselves to activities. The right to make job-rotation decisions is frequently more an issue of self-governance than self-regulation, since making them is not always critical to meeting performance standards. It will be assumed that the right to make job-rotation decisions is retained within all work groups discussed below.

Cell 2 Conditions

The only difference between cell 1 and cell 2 conditions is that now boundary-transaction uncertainty is high. The latter means that questions of what, where, or when inputs and outputs will cross the group's boundary are not settled by higher-level units before the work group must deal with them. A number of factors must be considered before determining whether work-group members or higher-level units will deal with uncertainty questions on a real time basis.

Since conversion uncertainty is low and activities are programable, the coordination decisions need not be made by the same group members who perform the conversion activities regulated. Generally speaking, when boundary transaction uncertainty is high, the three types of regulatory decisions are not separable from each other. This is because knowledge about what, where, or when to convert inputs is not relevant for a time period of sufficient length for different group members to share such knowledge and use it independently to make coordination and allocation decisions that are consistent with each other. When boundary–transaction uncertainty is high and technical cooperation is required, then group members perform boundary–transaction activities that are "reciprocally interdependent" (Thompson 1967). Under reciprocal interdependence, the actions taken by one group member may modify the conditions under which any or all group members take action.

Coordination under reciprocal interdependence is by "mutual adjustment" (March and Simon 1958); constant updating about the state, nature, and consequences of boundary transactions must be communicated to all group members to maintain effective performance. Coordination by mutual adjustment involves decisions that cannot be separated from the activities regulated without incurring serious losses in efficient and effective performance—for example, the cost of transmitting information from activity/resource sites to a separate coordinator is high relative to the cost of time lags. Moreover, the information-processing capacity possessed by a separate coordinator is unlikley to be adequate to the varied and complex information that must be transmitted to and from such sites. Under such conditions, no one group member is likely to occupy a specialized role for making boundary–maintenance decisions or coordination and allocation decisions affecting boundary transaction activities. Such decisions may be widely spread among work group members.

Under particular variations of cell 2 conditions, the three types of regulatory decisions may be separable from each other (Fig. 6.3). The variations leading to separability between types of regulatory decisons are as follows:

(1) Production of one product: If the group produces only one product, scheduling may be done once and for all by higher-level units and no longer be a concern for work-group members. Furthermore, when one product is produced, work-group members may make few or no allocation decisions. Finally, boundary maintenance decisions may have been simplified because it is no longer relevant to ask the question of what to produce. These three decisions are likely to be upwardly dispersed to higher level units when the group produces only one product.

(2) Buffer within the work group: A buffer refers to an amount of time, raw materials, supplies, or finished goods that permits work-group members to delay their responses to environmental demands. Unless such a buffer is possible within the work-group boundary, boundary-maintenance and allocation decisions are difficult to separate from each other and should be made by the same group member.

(3) Site of boundary transactions: If all boundary transaction activities enter or leave the work–group at the same location—for example, a dispatching center having only one telephone, the question of where inputs and outputs cross the work group boundary is no longer relevant. One group member may be assigned the specialized role of making all three types of regulatory decisions affecting boundary-transaction activities.

FIGURE 6.3

Distribution of Regulatory Decisions Under Varying Conditions Faced by Work Groups Within Cell 2

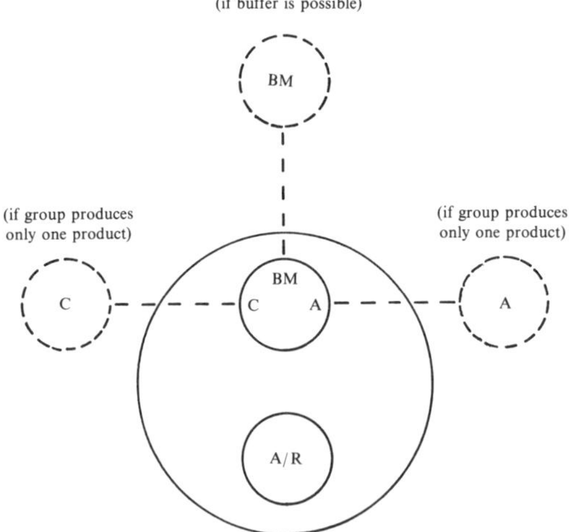

CELL 2: Conversion uncertainty low, boundary-transaction uncertainty high, technical cooperation required.

Source: Compiled by the author.

Cell 3 and Cell 4 Conditions

When conversion uncertainty is high and technical cooperation is required, as both are under cell 3 and cell 4 conditions, then the conversion activities that work group members perform are reciprocally interdependent. As uncertainty arises from the task and not from the boundary, reciprocal interdependence is required regardless of whether boundary-transaction uncertainty is low, as in cell 3, or whether it is high, as in cell 4. Reciprocal interdependence occurs when work-group members share a "work piece" whose properties are unstable or unknown. The members of surgical teams face cell 3 conditions. For example, patients may be routinely scheduled for surgery; however, their physical condition may be sufficiently unpredictable to require search for appropriate conversion activities. The members of a psychiatric team assigned to a single patient may experience similar conditions. Patients may be routinely scheduled for interviews, but the information received from each interview must be interpreted and shared among all team members to achieve a common diagnosis and treatment regimen. Rescue crews that are temporarily created to handle natural disasters, basic research groups, task forces, and so on may face cell 4 conditions.

As under cell 2 conditions, coordination of reciprocally interdependent activities (in this case, conversion activities) is by mutual adjustment and involves decisions that cannot be separated without incurring serious losses in efficient and effective performance. Thus, no group member is likely to occupy a specialized coordination role. Allocation decisions are as likely as coordinator decisions to be widely dispersed among work-group members.

Under cell 3 and cell 4 conditions, coordination and allocation decisions are difficult to separate from each other as well as difficult to separate from the activities regulated (Figure 6.4). Under cell 3 conditions, there may not be enough boundary-maintenance decisions to assign to a particular work-group member because higher-level units have reduced boundary-transaction uncertainty before inputs and outputs cross the work-group boundary. Under cell 4 conditions, boundary-maintenance decisions may be separable from coordination and allocation decisions and assigned to a work-group member *if* a buffer of time, raw materials, resources, and so on exists within the group's boundary.

Even if boundary-maintenance decisions are upwardly dispersed to a supervisor, this would not reduce the need for group members to make coordination and allocation decisions by mutual adjustment as uncertainty arises from the nature of the task itself. The effectiveness with which group members jointly make these decisions is facilitated by maximizing the number of group members who can effectively communicate with each

FIGURE 6.4

Distribution of Regulatory Decisions Under Varying Conditions Faced by Work Groups Within Cells 3 and 4

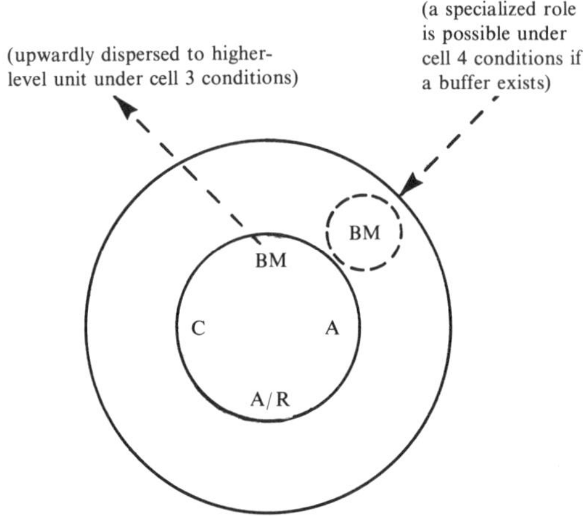

CELL 3: Conversion uncertainty high, boundary-transaction uncertainty low, technical cooperation required.

CELL 4: Conversion uncertainty high, boundary-transaction high, technical cooperation required.

Source: Compiled by the author.

other, minimizing status and wage differentials between group members, and maximizing the distribution of skills among group members (see Miller and Rice 1967, pp. 255-57).

Work Groups Dealing with Advanced Technologies: A Digression

This section discusses the task and boundary conditions facing work groups that deal with highly mechanized or automated technologies, for example, oil refining, chemical processing, continuous mining. With increased mechanization, raw materials are transformed by physico-chemical processes rather than by human action, that is, machines rather than humans perform the appropriate conversion activities. The human contribution to the production process is to monitor it and intervene at specified points. Monitoring requires being alert to relevant cues about the state of the production process by watching dials, gauges, or developing the five senses to attend to certain stimuli. Automation continues the trend of substituting machines for human action; in this case, self-correcting devices or servo-mechanisms take over more and more of the monitoring function.

The changing nature of the human contribution to the production process raises questions as how to best conceptualize the task and boundary conditions facing work groups that deal with these advanced technologies. The answers are provided in the following outline form:

1. Operators of these advanced technologies perform no conversion activities as such. Conversion activities and their coordination have been designed into the machine. However, operators do perform boundary-transaction activities that do not occur at any consistent time or in any consistent sequence. Lack of knowledge about the time and sequence for the occurrence of variances is a problem of boundary-transaction uncertainty (see p. 95). Thus, the work group can be conceived as a system whose environment consists of inputs (variances which cross its boundary and whose occurrence in time is subject to high uncertainty [see Susman 1970b]).

2. One group member can seldom be assigned all the boundary-transaction activities required to maintain an entire mechanized or automated production process. Therefore, each member of a work group that deals with these advanced technologies is assigned a set of boundary-transaction activities that returns variances to predetermined specifications. This is the equivalent of partitioning and assigning conversion activities to work-group members who deal with conventional technologies.

3. Cell 2 conditions most closely approximate the task and boundary conditions facing work groups that deal with highly mechanized or automated equipment (see Figure 6.3, p. 138). As under cell 2 conditions, the three types of regulatory decisions are not separable from each other for reasons that are stated on page 138. Regulatory decisions are separable from the conversion activities regulated, of course. The latter are assigned to machines, while the former are assigned to humans.

4. Whether technically required cooperation is between conversion activities and uncertainty arises from the task (as in cell 3) or whether technically required cooperation is between boundary–transaction activities and uncertainty arises from the boundary (as in cell 2), the consequence for group members is the same; they are in reciprocal interdependence and coordinate their activities by mutual adjustment. No group member is likely to occupy a specialized role for making regulatory decisions when the group faces conversion and/or boundary-transaction activities that are reciprocally interdependent.

Cell 5 through 8 Conditions

Under cell conditions 5 through 8, the activities of the group members are in "pooled interdependence" (Thompson 1967); that is, each group member makes a discrete and independent contribution to total group output. The contribution is usually in the form of a complete product desired by a "customer" of the group; examples of such "customers" are higher management or a social entity external to the organization. If the group produces only one kind of product, each group member may make the same product. If the group produces more than one product, each group member or subgroups of members may make one of the group's different products. An example of a group whose members' activities are in pooled interdependence is a sales division in which each salesman is rewarded for his contribution to total division sales revenue. Another example is a group of migratory workers paid on a group basis for the number of tomatoes the group picks.

Group activities in pooled interdependence are coordinated by "standardization," which, according to Thompson (1967), "involves the establishment of routines or roles which constrain [the] action of each unit or position into paths consistent with those taken by others in the interdependent relationship." Standardization is the fundamental means for assuring that the performance of any system is consistent with the goals and objectives of its suprasystem(s). Whether an organizational unit regulates itself or is regulated by a higher-level unit, standards are required as a guide to achieving and maintaining steady-state conditions. In effect, work groups in each of the eight cells are coordinated by standardization, but only those groups in the last four cells are coordinated exclusively by standardization. There is a nested quality to these three types of coordination, as Thompson (1967) suggests. If mutual adjustment is required to regulate work-group activities, then a form of scheduling is also required. This is because mutual adjustment is a complex form of scheduling in "real time," since first one task is dealt with, then a second task, then, perhaps, back to the first. Furthermore, if scheduling is required, standardization is also required. This is because mutual adjustment and scheduling are performed to serve the standards a unit seeks to maintain. When work groups operate under cell conditions 5 through 8, there are no relationships between jobs, and, therefore, there is no need for coordination by scheduling or by mutual adjustment. Standardization stands out in such cases because it is the only form of coordination that is required.

Standardization is the form of regulation discussed in Chapter 5. March and Simon (1958), it will be recalled, established criteria by which to determine whether standards should contain specifications of quality and quantity of output or specifications of activities. Whichever set of specifications is used, its determination and achievement must be consistent with the goals and objectives of higher-level units, and, therefore, they must be set or accepted by them. If work-group members have sufficient power (by belonging to unions, having professional expertise) to have a say in what the standards are to be, then these may be negotiated between group members and higher-level-unit representatives.

Under cell conditions 5 and 6, conversion uncertainty is low. As conversion-activity patterns are easy to observe, standards will be based on activity specification—that is, programing. Both cell conditions are typical of job shops containing individual work stations, such as lathes, at which complete products are produced. Under cell conditions 7 and 8, conversion uncertainty is high. As conversion activities are difficult to program, standardization will be based on output specifications, such as quantity, quality, cost, delivery time, and so on. Standardization is affected by feedback of results to group members and by rewarding group members for their contribution to the larger organization's goals and objectives.

Although coordination by standardization is likely to be upwardly dispersed under cell conditions 5 through 8, there are circumstances under which allocation and/or boundary-maintenance decisions may be retained by work-group members. For example, under cell conditions 5 and 7, boundary-transaction uncertainty is low, so boundary-maintenance decisions may also be upwardly dispersed to higher-level units. But, if group members work on their own self-constrained jobs, as they would in cells 5 through 8, and have to share raw materials or other resources, they could, if they so desired, jointly make allocation decisions or elect a group member to make these decisions on behalf of the group. One of the most common allocation decisions made by work groups under these conditions involves the deployment of group members themselves to activity/resource sites. Maintenance or service crews frequently make decisions of this kind. Group members may convene for a short period, daily for example, to decide where each member is going to work for that day. They might then disperse themselves over a wide geographical area, not seeing each other for the remainder of the day.

Under cell conditions 6 and 8, boundary-transaction uncertainty is high, so questions of what, where, and when raw materials or resources will cross the group's boundary are relevant to group members. The sharing of such inputs among group members is one of the basic conditions under which the group would appoint someone to make allocation decisions on behalf of the group as a whole. If group members are attending to their own individual assignments and, perhaps are also deployed over a wide geographical area, someone may have to be assigned the role of looking after the "big picture" to assure that total group resources are properly utilized. This role is made easier if all group members are multiskilled in all activities required to maintain group standards. In such a case, discretion to handle "localized variances" can be downwardly dispersed to each group member.

FIGURE 6.5

Distribution of Regulatory Decisions Under Varying Conditions Faced by Groups Within Cells 5 through 8

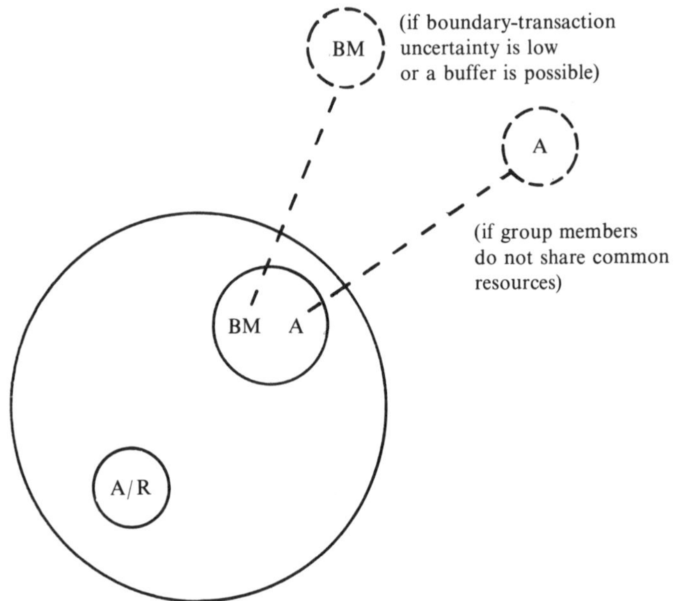

CELL 5: Conversion uncertainty low, boundary-transaction uncertainty low, technical cooperation not required.

CELL 6: Conversion uncertainty low, boundary-transaction uncertainty high, technical cooperation not required.

CELL 7: Conversion uncertainty high, boundary-transaction uncertainty low, technical cooperation not required.

CELL 8: Conversion uncertainty high, boundary-transaction uncertainty high, technical cooperation not required.

Source: Compiled by the author.

Otherwise, a group member performing a specialized allocation role would be burdened with the responsibility of deciding who was the best person to send where to do what.

Figure 6.5 summarizes the discussion of distribution of regulatory decisions under varying conditions faced by groups within cells 5 through 8.

PART III

SOCIOTECHNICAL SYSTEMS

INTRODUCTION TO PART III

Sociotechnical design is based on principles from two different worlds between which a fundamental schism exists. The technical world is organized around rational principles of efficiency, while the phenomenal world within which humans live their daily lives is organized around psychological principles based on cognition and emotion. The principles by which one world is organized are not necessarily or even likely to be the same as those by which the other world is organized.

The objective of sociotechnical design is to bridge the two worlds through a "best match" between a social system organized around phenomenal-world principles and a technical system organized around technical-world principles. As discussed in Chapter 7, the achievement of a best match makes optimal use of the resources of both systems. The resources of the two systems are optimally used when the two systems are "directively correlated" to coproduce an outcome that is desired by the members of the sociotechnical system.

A work group is self-regulating to the degree that group members define themselves as system contributors rather than job-holders. Chapter 8 discusses how the supervisor can facilitate definitions among work-group members that are consistent with their role as contributors to a self-regulating work group.

Chapter 9 summarizes the approach to design developed in this book.

CHAPTER

7

DESIGN OF SOCIOTECHNICAL SYSTEMS

THE SCHISM BETWEEN THE PHENOMENAL AND TECHNICAL WORLDS

Part II provided the conceptual tools to represent the task and boundary conditions that work groups face and recommended structural alternatives that are consistent with efficient and effective work-group performance. However, we have not yet asked why work-group members would be motivated to organize themselves in any of the recommended ways or to perform any of the prescribed activities. If it were simply assumed that work-group members would carry out such recommendations, then no advance would have been made beyond scientific management. One explanation for why work-group members may not perform so "rationally" is that instruction or learning has been inadequate. However, if work-group members are simply not motivated to take actions that are consistent with effective and efficient work-group performance, this has yet to be fully explained.

It is fundamental to a sociotechnical analysis to recognize that a schism exists between the technical "world" organized around rational principles of efficiency and the phenomenal world within which humans live their daily lives. The principles by which one world is organized are not necessarily or even likely to be the same as those by which the other is organized. The organization of the phenomenal world, consisting of values, beliefs, expectations, emotions, and so on, has consequences for behavior that may not always be consistent with effective work-group performance. Whether consistent or not, behavior must be understood in terms of the phenomenal world, the dynamics of which have led to the behavior, not by remodeling such behavior by the logic of efficiency demanded by the technical world. To do the latter is to be guilty of a basic criticism against scientific management, which is to understand man and how he functions in terms of the mechanical world, to remold man in the machine's image.

Goods and services will not be produced unless tools, machines, materials, and information are rationally organized according to the laws of physics, chemistry, and so on. However, even if a significant portion of the production process is automated, sooner or later human beings will enter the process and play a significant role in maintaining it. Unless they perceive and comprehend their world in a manner consistent with the requisites of production, less than effective and efficient production will result. The fundamental difference between humans and their tools, machines, and materials is that when the latter are arranged to produce rationally goods and services, that arrangement "exists" for no other purpose. Humans, however, exist for themselves, not solely for the part they might play in a production system. Human actions based on the perspective of the phenomenal world serve human ends that may or may not be consistent with the ends that production systems are designed to serve. The phenomenal world consists of conscious and unconscious fantasies, myths, values, emotions. Actions that serve these aspects of the phenomenal world just might also, but by no means necessarily, lead to actions that produce goods and services. Actions leading to one are not inherently incompatible with the other; indeed, the main objective of sociotechnical analysis is to design systems that minimize or eliminate such incompatibility. Our analysis begins, however, with acceptance of the fundamental schism discussed above between the technical and phenomenal worlds. Failure to accept this schism results in production systems designed with humans conceived solely as means to production-system ends. The phenomenal world of the system's human components would appear fantastic to the designer, so he chooses to ignore this world's existence. However, actions performed that serve no ends of a system's human components are equally fantastic to the latter, who come to experience what Jean-Paul Sartre defines as "fantastic," "the revolt of the means against the ends" (see Boguslaw 1965).

PERSPECTIVES FOR VIEWING TASK-ENVIRONMENT/ WORK-GROUP RELATIONSHIPS

In Chapters 5 and 6 we explored the nature of the task environments that work groups face. It might seem that the elements of such environments are mostly physical things, since so much attention in this book has been devoted to work groups that produce tangible products. More generally, however, task environments consist of a mix of physical, conceptual, or social elements the proportion of which depends on the task the work group is assigned. For example, a work group facing a predominantly conceptual task environment is one that is solving a mathematical problem or solving a riddle. Examples of a work group facing a predominantly social task environment is a negotiating team engaging in collective bargaining or a group producing services such as entertainment. Finally, an example of a work group facing a predominantly physical task environment is a group producing manufactured or processed goods. Moreover, even in cases like the latter, on which so much of our discussion has focused, the elements of a work group's task environment shift as the nature or phase of the group's task shifts. For example, work groups producing physical products face conceptual task environments when they have (or should have, as will be discussed shortly) planning and design tasks to perform. Also, members of such work groups face social task environments when they procure raw materials and resources from and dispatch finished products to persons within their own or other organizations.

As already discussed in the chapters of Part II, the elements of task environments are generally interdependent and form systems in and of themselves. From a technical perspective, the interdependence between such elements may be understood independently of any actions that work-group members may contemplate. For example, the concepts of a mathematical problem whose solution may yield a higher product output (such as chemicals or oil processing), may form a system based on the principles of logic. Persons who make up a work group's social task environment, particularly if such persons are members of a formal organization, form a system based on the policies, procedures, and instructions that they have mutually agreed will guide their activities. The elements of a work group's physical task environment form concrete systems whose parts are located and related to each other spatiotemporally. In the latter case, the relationships between system parts are a function of physicochemical laws as well as the rational, economic decisions characteristic of production or operations management. Most of the recommendations in Chapter 6 concerning the distribution of self-regulatory decisions within work groups were based on this perspective.

There is also a transactive perspective from which to view the mutual interpenetration between work-group members and the work group's task environment. The discussion in Chapter 5 assumed that the elements of placid-randomized and placid-clustered internal task environments were predominantly physical and spatiotemporally related and suggested what effects knowledge or ignorance of the interrelationships between such elements might have on work-group dynamics. Similarly, the discussion of disturbed-reactive and turbulent external task environments assumed that elements were persons with whom work-group members were interrelated socially and suggested what some of the consequences of competitive or incongruent goals and values might be.

Group-member anxieties and subsequent defenses may arise from the way machines, tools, conveyances, and so on, are arranged over a geographical area as well as how they are joined together by the timing and movement of raw material and information. For example, the isolation and dependency on others experienced by coal fillers mining by the longwall method led to various types of group defense mechanisms such as absenteeism and scapegoating (Trist and Bamforth 1951). Also both pulp workers and furniture assemblers experienced anxiety and anger at being blamed for product quality deficiencies over which they had no control but that were caused by the actions of groups preceding them in the work flow (Emery and Thorsrud 1975).

There is also a predominantly phenomenal perspective from which to understand work-group dynamics. For example, work-group members may have strong feelings toward some task-environment elements. Following the psychoanalytic theory of Melanie Klein (1959), such elements become "good" objects or "bad" objects depending on how closely they match internalized images held by group members of objects toward which they had previously associated strong feelings, generally in childhood. Adults retain internalized images of important persons, things, and events from their childhood toward whom (which) they have had aggressive or erotic thoughts. To the small child, thought is not distinct from deed and anxiety is aroused by the possibility that the objects of such thoughts will retaliate by punishing the child or by withdrawing affection; to a child, living or inanimate things may do this. Strong feelings such as guilt, jealousy, and envy are generated by such possibilities, and the child defends himself against them by the primitive mechanisms of projective identification and introjection. Projective identification is the process of attributing parts of oneself (such as unacceptable thoughts) to an external object—for example, "He, (or she or it) thinks or does bad things, not I." Introjection is the process of taking in an external object so that it becomes part of oneself: "I am the admired (or hurt) object." At an unconscious level, adults continue to use the same defenses as they did as children. When feelings similar to those of childhood are rearoused by persons, events, or things having some association to the internalized images retained as an adult, projective identification and introjection are used to defend against such feelings.

Menzies (1960) provides several illustrations of how ward nurses defended themselves against feelings of compassion, pity, and disgust that were aroused in them by the patients they cared for—for example, by ritual task performances, detachment of feelings, and unwillingness to take responsibilities. Defenses such as these had a negative impact on the effectiveness of ward operations and turnover of staff personnel. Similarly, in our coal-mining project, the initial reaction of several of the men on the first autonomous section to a safety program stressing, among other things, safer roof-control techniques was that the program was quite useless; a safety program is, essentially an aggressive act toward conditions (objects) that are inherently dangerous and, as it were, capable of retaliation. The men said they considered it all a matter of fate whether or not a man was injured or killed: "There's a rock out there with your name on it."

Work-group members may also have strong unconscious as well as conscious feelings toward the group as an object and toward some of the group's members, especially those who exercise leadership. Like an element of the work group's task environment, the group itself or any of its members can potentially be good or bad objects for other members. In fact, whenever people come together to form any kind of face-to-face group, a "social field" is created of conscious and unconscious assumptions about others as well as about their purpose for being together (Bion 1961). A number of conscious and unconscious conflicts must be resolved before individuals can successfully work together as a group. These conflicts revolve around the distribution of attention, power and prestige, tangible and intangible goods, and love and affection. Again, projective identification and introjection are important mechanisms for dealing with the feelings evoked by the assumptions and conflicts to be dealt with in forming a group.

Dunphy (1972) considers projective identification and introjection central to the development of cohesion in groups. The construction of a "shared group fantasy" from similar internalized objects is the affective basis of group life.

> Group integration occurs through the matching of similar internalized objects so that a delineated range of modes of relating is established, i.e., the group arrives at a consensus about the class of internal objects to which links will be made and the range of appropriate responses which will be brought into play. Through this sharing of fantasies, the group constructs a common mythology which, when attained, gives the members a satisfying sense of meaningfulness to group life (p. 48).

Not all objects have clear-cut attributes, and sometimes an object produces both good and bad feelings simultaneously. Group members may have great difficulty in cooperating in joint undertakings if one or both members have ambivalent feelings toward the other, especially if one of them is a formal leader. Jaques (1953) describes a psychic process through which ambivalence is reduced by identifying with the "good" attributes of a desired object and projecting its "bad" attributes into other objects. The process is illustrated by the case of a first officer on a ship who, in addition to his normal duty, is held responsible for many things that go wrong but for which he is not responsible.

> Everyone's bad objects and impulses may unconsciously be put into the first officer, who is consciously regarded by common consent as the source of the trouble. By this mechanism the members of the crew can unconsciously find relief from their own internal persecutors and the ship's captain can thereby be more readily idealized and identified with as a good protective figure (p. 283).

The preceding illustrations of the strong, often mixed, feelings aroused by membership in a group reinforced by equally strong feelings arising from dealing with the work group's task environment suggest the strength of investment that group members have in a group structure and culture supportive of mechanisms that allow them to defend themselves against such emotions. Reliance on such mechanisms explains a great deal of the resistance shown by groups when requested or otherwise required to give up their present group structure and adopt a new one. An important task of sociotechnical design is to provide a forum within which group members can explore and discover the most effective way to make such a transition. Procedures such as those Clark (1970a, 1970b) develops in "task group therapy" may be used to help groups to work through and accept a group structure more compatible with the task environment the group faces.

THE FUNDAMENTAL PROBLEM OF DESIGN

Enough examples have been provided of the interpenetration of task environment and work group as well as of the properties that each exhibits as systems in their own right to suggest the complexity of the problem the sociotechnical designer faces. He must search for a link through which the resources of both systems can be optimally used without destroying or otherwise undermining the integrity of the other. The members of a work group who are instructed by higher-level units to be an appendage of a physical production system will react against such instructions in a manner unanticipated by the latter. On the other hand, a work group that allows the unconscious fantasies of its members to take priority over engagement with the group's task environment will not likely produce a product that meets the demands of higher-level units.

The foregoing problem will not be solved without recognizing the schism between the technical and phenomenal worlds discussed in the first section of this chapter. The work group is a social system the structure and dynamics of which may be best explained from the phenomenal world perspective of those who make it up. The explanatory concepts are thoughts and feelings; the designer's questions are guided by psychological theories. However, the task-environment elements the work group faces constitute a technical system the structure and dynamics of which may be best explained by the logic of efficiency applied to elements obeying physicochemical laws. Perhaps the only clear exception to the last statement is when work groups face a task environment consisting primarily of social elements—for example a psychiatric team dealing with one or more patients. Even in this case, the therapeutic bias held by some of the team's members may predispose them to treat patients more from a technical than a phenomenal world perspective—for example, behavior modification versus existential therapy.

The technical and phenomenal world perspectives are not always irreconcilable. One may find that members of primitive cultures merge the unconscious with the conscious in taking skilled actions to produce cultural artifacts such as houses and tools (see Alexander 1964). However, the "rationalization" of modern production creates pressures for conscious knowledge to supersede unconscious skills and the functional requisites of the logic of efficiency are not conducive to artistic sublimation. The question the sociotechnical designer must ask is whether the demands for efficient and effective production can be met without at the same time reopening the gap between action and affect that traditional methods of work design produce.

The remainder of this chapter is organized around two mutually reinforcing concepts, the *primary task* of a work group and the *best match* between a work group and its task environment. Each when manifested in concrete organizational forms provides the means by which work-group members may unite affect and action in pursuit of desired outcomes. Each concept is a guide toward establishing conditions for elements of a work group's task environment to become objects of directed action for its members. The problem is to establish conditions that encourage a distribution of group emotions and defenses that is consistent with the group taking actions that ultimately lead members to experience self-enhancement. Combining the language of this chapter with that of Chapter 3, the problem is to establish conditions encouraging group members to take actions toward "good" objects and away from "bad" objects, actions that are also consistent with the pursuit of goals and objectives acceptable to higher-level units.

THE PRIMARY TASK

The primary task of the work group is the task the work group accepts to pursue at a particular time—for example, to produce a product with particular qualities within given cost and time constraints (see Rice 1958). Acceptance of a primary task permits group members to focus their emotional and intellectual efforts toward a future outcome they deem desirable.

Work groups differ from other social entities in that their reason for being from a phenomenal perspective must come to terms with the requisites for producing a product by rational means. Primary groups such as families, voluntary social groups, and so on, may, however, exist for their own sake, that is, for the conscious and unconscious needs they satisfy for their members.* Work-group members must satisfy such needs also but do so in such a way as to perform a "sophisticated task" in a reality-based manner. As Bion (1961) has pointed out, doing this means to give up functioning predominantly upon unconscious assumptions and to behave as an "adult," an unconsciously "hated" obligation.

As discussed in the last section, the nature of the task environment may induce emotions in group members that are inconsistent with accepting a primary task compatible with the goals and objectives of higher-level units. This is particularly so if the achievement of the primary task offers no opportunities to experience feelings of self-enhancement or if higher-level-unit members withhold information useful to achieving the task or if they act in a demeaning way toward work-group members. Such circumstances are less likely to face work groups consisting of master craftsmen; they will more readily accept a primary task requiring them to produce a product because they and others are likely to admire the product produced and the skill required to produce it.

The sociotechnical designer would have to devote a great deal of thought to providing conditions that would encourage group members producing a highly standardized product to accept a primary task compatible with the goals and objectives of higher-level units. Part of the solution is to encourage group members to perceive as good objectives those task-environment elements whose conversion (as this is defined in Chapter 5) contributes to producing the group's product. Even when work groups

---

*Emery (1959) calls groups of this type "sociopsychological systems" to distinguish them from work groups, which, as will be seen shortly, are sociotechnical systems.

produce standardized products, their task environments contain many elements with the potential of becoming objects of this kind. The following examples illustrate how such routine circumstances may be transformed to offer opportunities for personal engagement.

Producing

It is not necessary that attributes of the product itself or the physical act of producing it be the sole source of good objects. The production process itself may be quite routine and the product itself uninteresting; however, having the opportunity to produce the product at increasing levels of quantity or quality and at decreasing costs may provide the basis for a great deal of personal satisfaction. Some of the objects of directed action in such cases may be physical, such as dials or gauges, but genuine opportunities to improve performance by problem-solving will take group members into the realm of conceptual objects, such as chemical equations, theory of mechanics, and hydraulics. Success of actions toward conceptual objects is judged by performance data fed back to group members directly or at short intervals. By such data, group members can evaluate their progress toward ever more efficient performance goals. The achievement of such goals will be more self-enhancing (1) the greater the problem solving required and (2) the greater the organizational rewards provided for effective solutions.

The preceding appears to describe the dynamics in operation among members of the experimental departments at the Hunsfos Pulp and Paper Mill and the Norsk Hydro Fertilizer Plant described by Emery and Thorsrud (1975). Performance in both departments, which utilized continuous-process technologies, was measured in quality, costs, downtime, and so on, and provided the basis for a bonus paid above the employee's normal wages. Even though production in either department was highly automated and the product itself "unglamorous," the problem solving required to improve performance was complex and challenging and receiving a bonus was a symbol of accomplishing a difficult task.

It might be worthwhile to point out at this time that financial gain-sharing between management and work-group members may be desirable and even ethically imperative for an undertaking in which work-group members make the kinds of contributions just mentioned; however, it may not be the critical factor in producing feelings of self-enhancement. Whyte (1955) cites several unsuccessful implementations of the Scanlon Plan that concentrated on the plan's financial aspects and ignored the critical role of participative decision making in devising and implementing the bonus plan. Money, in addition to what it can buy, is also a symbol to which significant affect may be attached. If management has made all the important decisions in setting up the means for workers to be financially rewarded, then workers may feel manipulated. In such a case, workers may, at best, feel ambivalent toward the money by projecting good and bad qualities into it or, worse, only bad ones ("I lost my self-respect by pursuing a carrot that management dangled before me").

Planning

Returning to the problem of providing self-enhancing conditions to work-group members who produce standardized products, it is important to point out that desired relations with objects need not be achieved within any specifiable time period to be the focus of emotional investment. Again, our perspective shifts from producing the product itself toward problem-solving to produce a product more efficiently and effectively. In the conceptual realm of problem solving, good objects may be achieved within time periods of any specifiable length (minutes, hours, days). According to Ackoff and Emery (1972), outcomes that group members achieve within any specifiable time period would be referred to as the "goals" of group action. However, group actions may also bring group members closer to the achievement of outcomes without actually achieving them within the time period specified. In the latter case, Ackoff and Emery would refer to such desired outcomes as the "objectives" of group action.

An attempt to organize group actions so that goals are embedded in objectives was described in Chapter 3, although there the language referred to the creation of larger action-wholes. Coal miners were encouraged to organize their daily action to pursue a goal measured in linear feet per day. These daily actions are tactics that move the group closer to its objective of efficient and effective production per belt move (occurring approximately every ten days after production has advanced the coal face by 180 linear feet).

The planning required by the section as a whole to achieve efficient and effective production for ten-day periods constitutes a shared strategy within which day-to-day shift tactics are embedded. Continuous communication is required between shifts so that their respective members can update their tactics to assure that the ten-day objective is effectively met.

Tactics are distinguished from strategy on the basis of what Schultzenberger (1954) calls the "span of foresight." The size of the span of foresight is determined by the distance (in time or space) to which one can see the consequences of action. If the actor believes he knows the best or at least a satisfactory set of actions to achieve his desired outcome, he selects a *strategy*. If the actor does not know enough about the consequences of his actions to choose the best set of actions to achieve his desired outcome, he will proceed according to the criterion that seems best from his present perspective and revise it at each step. The choice of action he takes at each step is a *tactic*. If the actor can determine all the consequences that follow from his actions to his outcome, then his tactic and strategy are one and the same.

Designing

A third way in which self-enhancing conditions may be provided to work-group members who produce standardized products is by focusing efforts on the redesign of the task, technological, boundary, or structural conditions faced by the work group. Redesign efforts such as these require problem solving that is difficult to carry out at the work place, although ideas for redesign may evolve here. Such efforts require a forum created for this purpose such as the participative design workshops discussed by Emery and Emery (1974) or the section conferences used in our coal-mining project.

The desired outcome in the case of work-group design is an imagined set of future work-group conditions that all members of the problem solving forum, including work-group members as well as relevant members of higher-level units, believe will lead to more efficient and effective performance and personal self-enhancement. Designing a new set of work-group conditions is a much more complex process than planning how to produce a product. In the former case, the designer is altering a social as well as a technical system. The effect of any redesign decision altering the structure of the group itself or the conditions it faces is a permanent disturbance of the way the group has accommodated itself to the conflicts and emotions generated by seeking to reestablish the old equilibrium or establish a new one. When either is achieved, the set of conditions will constitute a "steady state." Any organizational unit is an open dynamic system, and there are any one of a number of different conditions and "paths" to such conditions by which an open system may achieve a new steady state.

The last-mentioned characteristic of open systems, referred to by Von Bertalanffy (1950) as "equifinality," increases a system's potential for adaptation, but to members of any design forum it opens up a new dimension of complexity and uncertainty that the traditional designer does not see or, if he does, doesn't always recognize as important. The uncertainty and complexity result from the fact that the designer(s) cannot predict beyond a relatively short period, and then even within this period sometimes not too well, what the consequences of a design decision will be for the work group or immediate (even distant) organizational levels. Any design action taken is likely to set off emergent processes within any of an organization's relevant subsystems, as each seeks to accommodate to the disturbance.

The Labor/Management Steering Committee that guided the coal-mining project learned only too well that a planned intervention into a social system may produce unintended consequences. Nine months after the first autonomous section was formed, the initial results in terms of reduced accidents, number of safety violations, costs, and so on were encouraging (see the last section of this chapter for details). When mine management made a decision to expand production by adding a fourth operating face section, it seemed to the Steering Committee to be an opportune time to begin this new section as an autonomous one. The Steering Committee saw no reason at this time to discontinue the policy of paying all who volunteered to work in an autonomous section the top rate in the mine. This was believed justified because all members of the first autonomous section were requested to perform or to learn to perform all the jobs on the section, some of which normally paid the top rate. It had been believed that the common top rate for all would weaken the present one-man/one-job thinking that was prevalent and strengthen each member's identity with the primary task of the group as a whole. It was anticipated that senior, well-experienced miners would be the ones to bid into the new autonomous section, as had been the case with the first section. However, very few such miners did so because they had already established personal relationships on their present crews and didn't wish to sacrifice this for the uncertainties of working with new men under unfamiliar conditions. The unanticipated result was that many jobs on the new section were filled by apprentices with little more than 90 days of mining experience. The inequity created by "green" miners receiving higher pay than men with many years of experience outraged the sense of distributive justice of the latter. This inbalanced state was tolerated for five months only because production was halted by a month-long national strike coinciding with expiration and negotiation of a three-year contract as well as by the year-end holidays.

Prior to and during this time, performance on the two autonomous sections continued to improve, and management as well as the 54 men on the two autonomous sections became more deeply committed to the project's continuation and expressed the wish that autonomy spread to the mine as a whole. Many of the men in the rest of the mine, partly from anger over past inequities and partly because of misinformation fueled by the rumor mill, tried to prevent this from happening, and, together with some union officers, who were dismayed by the internal

FIGURE 7.1

Strategic and Tactical Decisions in Sociotechnical Design

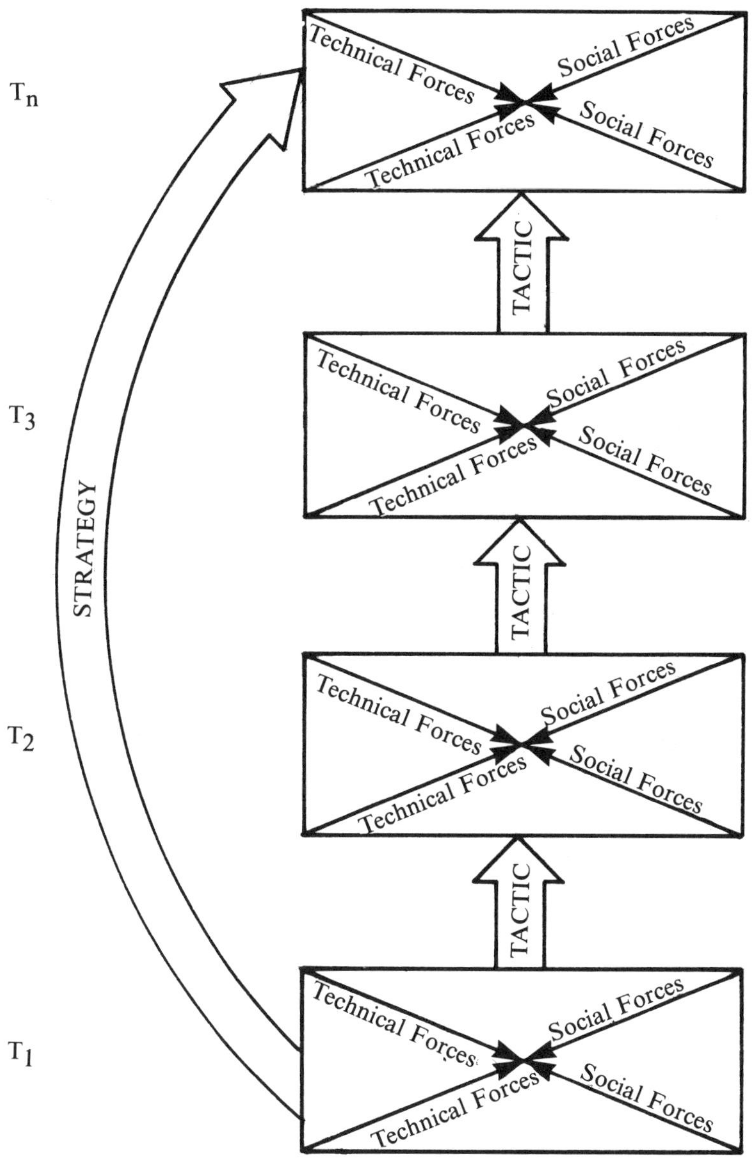

Source: Compiled by the author.

dissension the current circumstances had created, sought to terminate the project by a vote at the local union hall. In order to ensure the project's survival, the mine management agreed that if the local union voted to extend autonomous working to the mine as a whole, all miners not presently autonomous or not regularly earning top rate under contract would receive top rate within their respective sections for 90 working days (surface jobs had a lower top rate than underground jobs). At the end of this period, each miner would have to demonstrate to a management committee that he was qualified to perform jobs beyond his regular job. If a man qualified, he would retain the top rate. If he did not, he would return to his regular contract rate. The men on the present autonomous sections would have much less time to qualify than the others.

The degree of uncertainty involved in efforts to redesign a sociotechnical system can be illustrated by a diagram that is analogous to what Lewin was trying to describe in Figure 3.1. Within any one of the series of slices shown in Figure 7.1 is a set of social and technical "forces" in equilibrium (to use Lewin's terminology). At the end of the series of time slices (top right) is shown an imagined set of social and technical forces under which the designer(s) believe a work group will function more effectively than it does presently. For example, the designer(s) may believe as in the coal-mining project that the present work-group reward structure based on one-man/one-job should be changed to a structure rewarding group members for knowledge possessed and a willingness to use it as required. Achieving this or any other set of future conditions at T_n is an objective toward which a strategy may be devised. Suppose, for example, the designer(s) believe they can predict what an action at T_1 will produce at T_2—for example, the positive consequences thought to follow from initially paying all group members the same rate. The action at T_1 is a tactic embedded in the strategy to achieve the desired set of future conditions at T_n. The tactic may set off "emergent" events leading to a new set of conditions at T_2—for example, the unanticipated reluctance of more senior men to bid for higher-paying jobs and the disturbance to distributive justice that resulted. It is not until conditions at T_2 have been reached that the new situation can be assessed and new tactics devised to take the next step, which, again, may set off emergent events leading to a new equilibrium at T_3. For example, the tactic at T_2 might be offering to pay all employees the top rate for 90 days in order to head off the attempt by some union members to terminate the project (and reestablish the old equilibrium at T_1). If the employees accept the pay offer, a new equilibrium may be established at T_3. Each successful tactic moves the group closer to the set of future conditions that will eventually be reached at T_n.

What all of the preceding means for any effort undertaken to redesign the social and technical conditions facing work groups is that the participants in any design effort cannot plan at the start how their design efforts will turn out. Any contemplated action can only be based on the contemporaneous set of forces then operating. The strength, direction, and combination of such forces will change with each action taken. Sociotechnical system-designing is then really a learning process to which all affected by contemplated actions must be committed. Initiation of such a learning process at least requires an intuitive if not explicit understanding of how social-system change occurs but also requires a commitment to values that are congruent with and facilitate a learning process. Such values were briefly explored at the end of Chapter 5. It is the task of an effective facilitator of group processes, whether an occupant of a staff position within the organization or an outside consultant, to help the participants in any design setting to explore or discover whether they can commit themselves to such values.

Directively Correlated Systems

The importance of the primary task is that through its acceptance by group members the work group's social system will be joined with its technical system to coproduce the group's products. A sociotechnical system is a conjunction of a social system and technical system, each of which operates according to different principles. Although these two systems are different from each other, they operate in parallel in any concrete work setting. The objective of sociotechnical design is to establish conditions allowing these two systems to operate in complementary fashion. The technical and social systems of a work group will be directively correlated (Sommerhoff 1969) when work-group members can effectively use elements of the technical system as objects toward which directed actions are taken to produce desired outcomes—notably, acceptable products and member self-enhancement.

Sommerhoff's formulation of directive correlation is a formal mathematical statement that is conceptually very similar to Chein's (1972) formulation of directed action. The reader will remember the apple-eating example described in Chapter 3. One doesn't complete the directed action "to eat an apple" by walking over and standing next to an apple. Rather, a series of relationships is established between the subject and the apple that terminates when the apple has been eaten. These subject-object relationships change as different subject and object attributes become relevant to the outcome of eating the apple. This conceptualization of subject-object relationships suggests a much more complex interpretation of causality than implied when the subject or object is conceived as the sole "cause" of

FIGURE 7.2

Directive Correlation Between a Social and Technical System

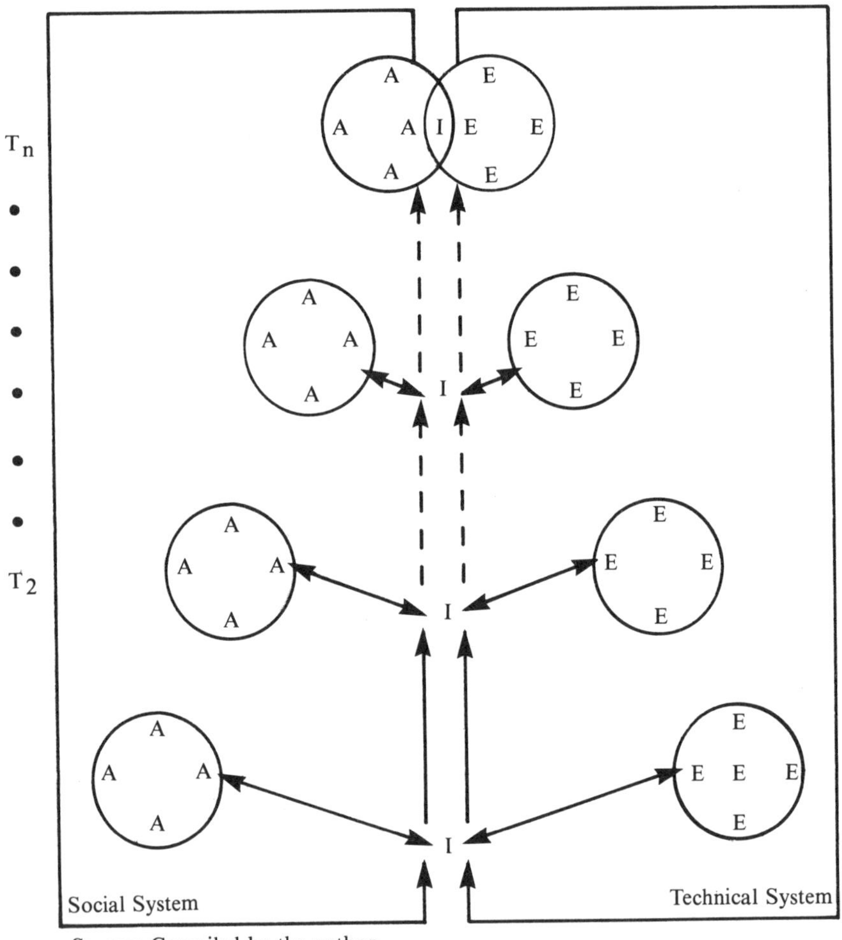

Source: Compiled by the author.

outcomes. Lewin (1935) considered the latter conceptualization an error of Aristotelian thinking. In the former case, the person and the apple are both "prompting forces" for the other. But the "reality principle" has taught him that wishing alone doesn't make things happen automatically. He has learned to behave in congruence with physical, chemical, and biological laws so as to facilitate actions that will "set off" events that will result in his desired outcome. He has also learned that his own actions are insufficient to set off such events. Certain physical, social, and conceptual elements are required as coproducers (Ackoff and Emery 1972). When such elements are recognized as such, they will become objects of directed action.

Figure 7.2 is another perspective on the model depicted in Figure 7.1. In describing the latter, reference was made only to social and technical forces within each of the time slices. However, at any given time, the social forces make up significant aspects of a work group's dynamics, and the technical forces are significant elements of the work group's task environment. These two interacting systems become directively correlated when parts of both systems are used by work-group members to pursue a desired outcome at T_n. Achieving the desired outcome at T_n could be the group's primary task—for example, one of the objectives sought through producing, planning, or designing, as these processes have been described.

The two directively correlated social and technical systems form a new system, a sociotechnical system. The technical system at the lower-right of the figure consists of a set of physical, social, and conceptual elements (E) that are interrelated or potentially interrelated. "Potentially interrelated" means that the relationship between elements may be "dormant" until such elements are seen by members of the social system as coproducers of a desired outcome.

The social system in the lower left of the figure consists of work-group members whose actions (A) are organized on the basis of the values, beliefs, expectations, and fantasies they share, the assumptions they hold about the technical system they face, and the directives they have accepted from higher-level units.

The social system becomes directively correlated with the technical system at time T_1, when either system becomes a "starting condition" for the other. The social system becomes a starting condition for the technical system when members of the former devise and share an image (I) of a desired outcome that is achievable when the two systems are related in a particular manner at time T_n—that is, at a time when social system members will have established a particular set of object-relationships with technical system elements. The image that exists through T_1, T_2, and so on, guides action to the desired future outcome at T_n. An image of the desired future may rally the social system's resources whether the desired outcome is clear cut and achievable in a finite time period—for example, a product of acceptable quality in two weeks—or is abstract and unachievable within any specifiable time period—for example, to create a group structure that provides greater learning opportunities to group members. As discussed in the previous section, social-system members seldom possess sufficient knowledge to anticipate all the relationships that will exist between themselves and their technical system at times $T_1 \ldots T_n$. If, however, the members possess knowledge to anticipate a relationship that will exist at T_2, then they will take action to achieve that relationship, assess the consequences of their action, and devise a plan to achieve the next anticipated relationship at T_3. This process will be repeated until the outcome desired at T_n is achieved.

Above, it was said that when two systems are directively correlated, either system may be a starting condition for the other. In actual practice it may be difficult at times to decide which system initiates the interaction. Take, for example, the case of a work group facing a predominantly social task environment—for example, a psychiatric team dealing with disturbed family members; both systems will change as a result of the interaction. However, it is possible for a technical system to monopolize initiations for a social system if the components and interactions of both have been prescribed by a superordinate system. Such is the case when the technical system faced by a work group has been designed by superordinate levels to minimize the decisions the work group can make. The superordinate level accomplishes this by specifying in advance of required actions all decisions that work-group members would be required to make. Such a feat requires some simplifying assumptions about the operating principles of the work group as a social system as well as of the technical system it faces. The simplest assumption is that the social system is an extension of the technical system, and so the former is modeled in the latter's image. If the technical system consists mainly of machines and the relationships between machines, the model of man that emerges is obvious. The consequence of designs based on this assumption is that work-group members will experience the technical system as an alien force. No objects are likely to emerge from its elements toward which group action will be directed, and, assuming the group does not choose sabotage, members, at best, will perform actions to satisfy minimally demands from higher-level units.

THE BEST MATCH

The second major concept around which this chapter is organized is the best match between a work group and its task environment. A best match occurs when the work group can produce its product in a manner most compatible with the organization of task-environment elements and the sociopsychological dynamics of its members. In this way, the concept of best match complements that of the group's primary task—that is, when the outcome the group desires can be produced under conditions allowing the joint optimization of the resources of the work group and its task environment.*

Chapter 6 summarized eight possible sets of task and boundary conditions that work groups can face as a consequence of decisions made by higher-level units. From the technical-world perspective of rational efficiency, recommendations were also made of what were believed to be the most effective and efficient distribution of regulatory decisions between work-group members under each of these eight sets of conditions. As already suggested, any array and relationship between technical-system elements creates a field of demands with which a work group must deal. The work group itself as a social system also creates a field of demands for its members based on the emotions and conflicts aroused by group membership, the history of the group and larger organization, the values that group members bring with them as representative of their culture, and so on. The demands arising from a work group's technical system as well as from its social system may or may not be suitably matched to produce a product acceptable to the larger organization. The larger organization represents a third system also creating a field of demands, which are economic in nature. It sets the critical standards that the work group must meet and issues directives that it deems necessary for work groups to follow. The demands of this system along with those of the technical system significantly influence the nature of the task environment the work group faces.

If the match between the demands of these three systems is not a good one, each will set up interference to satisfaction of the others, "leading to a state of disequilibrium, so that achievement of the overall goal will be endangered and in the limit made impossible" (Trist et al. 1963, p. 7). The best match between these demands is an optimization of the sociotechnical system as a whole, which tends to require less than optimum satisfaction of the demands of any of its component systems.

---

*Since the mid-1960s, Emery and Trist have in their writings generally used the term "joint optimization" in place of "best match." Prior to the time Emery came up with the joint-optimization formulation, the best-match concept was used in all the Tavistock work. However, caution should be exercised before totally excluding the latter in favor of the former, as joint optimization connotes a level of metric sophistication that it is doubtful the sociotechnical designer will ever achieve.

It may be assumed that the larger organization will make few alterations in its standards or directives unless macroenvironmental changes suggest a reappraisal is in order of its present market, product, or pricing strategies. While some accommodation in a technical system is possible in the short run, once higher-level units have made decisions affecting a work group's task and boundary conditions, its technical system is relatively fixed. The ideal situation is for the sociotechnical designer to collaborate with higher-level units before such commitments are made. If this is not possible, only the social system offers sufficient flexibility in its sociopsychological structure to provide a best match to limiting conditions set by the technical system as well as by the larger organization.

The concept of best match doesn't imply that one and only one design permits the most effective utilization of task-environment and work-group resources. Both systems are open systems, and consequently, within the constraints imposed by their most critical requirements (such as task and boundary conditions), alternative arrangements exist that will yield the same level of sociotechnical system performance. This property of open systems —equifinality (Von Bertalanffy 1950)—makes the concept of "best" match seem self-contradictory, but, nevertheless, more than one design alternative can be a "best" match to the demands to be met.

On reflecting about the most appropriate social system for each of the eight cell conditions described in Chapter 6, one might conclude that when group members face both high uncertainty and interdependence, as they would under cell conditions 2, 3, and 4, the most appropriate social system must support a division of labor that allows flexible interchange between job holders as well as sanction the giving and receiving of mutual assistance. This applies also when referring to the relations between subgroups making up a larger group; for example, the fillers made up one of the task groups of a larger cycle group in the longwall method of coal mining (Trist and Bamforth 1951). As has already been suggested and will be further elaborated, a social structure is more likely to develop such attributes when there are minimal status and pay differences between its members and when forums exist for group members to explore and develop values supporting such a structure.

Under cell conditions 5 and 6, there is little or no need for coordination between relatively low-skilled job-holders, and a more rigid division of labor may be justifiable and, perhaps, superior to a more flexible one. This may be even more the case under cell conditions 7 and 8, where job-holders are not interdependent and may be highly skilled (see Table 6.1). Under such conditions, a value structure that supports substantial status and pay differences may be compatible with and supportive of effective work-group performance.

The above recommendations supporting a rigid division of labor apply only if gains in immediate production are not offset by the impediments this might create for training opportunities and career mobility. A rigid division of labor may also limit the contributions that group members can make to planning and designing because of the narrow perspective it encourages.

A continuous coal-mining face section faces task and boundary conditions like those of Cell 2 (see Table 6.1). The following brief sociotechnical analysis is part of the still ongoing coal-mining project of Trist, Susman, and Brown. A labor/management steering committee was formed at the project's inception to evaluate the research team's analysis and to decide which of its recommendations to implement. While no clear-cut division of effort existed among all the contributors, the research team viewed itself as a catalyst and facilitator for labor and management. The following analysis was presented to members of the union and management as the project evolved. As the reader might suspect, it was not presented in the "neat" format described here, and some of the present explanations have been provided for the reader's benefit.

Just as there is no single arrangement that will produce a best match, there is no specific formula that a designer can follow to achieve it. The design process is a search for the best solution to what appears to be a set of conflicting requirements between a social and a technical system. The best solution is necessarily an innovation as well as a work of art in the broadest sense of the term. If the solution were obvious, it would merely be calculated; there would be no design problem as such. As will be discussed in the next chapter, there is a nine-step model that can serve as a guide to the proper questions the designer should ask of the design problem he faces. However, there is no way for the designer to obtain an adequate understanding of social-system dynamics except overlapping his frame of reference with those of social-system members. Empathy and shared understanding are the most effective tools the designer can use for understanding social system behavior. The most effective means of learning how to facilitate a best match is practice and thoughtful analysis of the successes and failures of others.

The Technical System

In the continuous mining of coal by the room-and-pillar method (see Cassidy 1973), coal is cut at the face by a large machine with a continuously rotating drum studded with sharp bits. Below the drum, coal is gathered by large crablike arms and dumped onto one of two shuttle cars that are alternately filled and then are driven down an entry or crosscut* to a feeder where the coal is emptied onto a continuously moving belt conveying the coal to the surface. Each time the face is cut 20 feet wide and 16 feet deep, the mining machine (the continuous miner) is withdrawn to a new face, leaving space for the newly exposed roof to be timbered and bolted. This sequence of activities constitutes the basic conversion process in development of a section. What remains after a section has been developed gives a checkerboard appearance of alternating open rooms and solid pillars. Following section development, the coal is removed from the pillars causing a controlled collapse of the roof, which is preceded by retreat of the mining equipment to a new pillar further from the original working face. Against this "figure" of activities is the "ground" consisting of preparatory tasks such as hanging or moving ventilation curtains and power cables, as well as maintenance tasks, such as making repairs, and moving supplies. All preparatory-maintenance tasks are essential to continuance of the basic conversion process.

In essence, the coal-mining system is a transport system; the basic conversion process consists of transporting coal from the face to the surface. The primary task of this system consists of keeping the system running as smoothly and continuously as possible. However, at the present stage of technological development, a significant discontinuity exists between the system's basic components. The productive capacity of the continuous miner far exceeds the capacity of the rest of the transport system to move the cut coal to the surface. If the continuous miner were to run continuously, as its name implies, it would be capable of cutting up to 4,000 tons per shift; however, due to waiting time between shuttle cars, delays due to mechanical breakdowns, poor communication, unnecessary or poorly timed moves, and so on, the continuous miner cuts on the average only 350 tons per shift (see Faltenmeyer 1974).

Barring major innovations in haulage systems, productivity increases will result from more effective coordination between the 27 men and 3 foremen who operate a geographical section of the mine. The nine men on each shift of a section are as follows: the miner operator who runs the continuous miner; the miner helper who places timber at the freshly cut face, hangs ventilation curtains, moves power cables that energize the continuous miner and so on; two shuttle-car operators; two roof bolters; the mechanic; and two support men who maintain the conveyor belt, build permanent ventilation stoppings, lay tracks, and haul supplies to the face.

---

*A pathway in the coal seam perpendicular to an entry.

Psychosocial Consequences of the Technical System

As illustrations of the concept of best match between social and technical systems, three examples of psychosocial consequences of the technical system follow. None of these examples is independent of the other two, and additional examples could have been provided. A more thorough sociotechnical analysis of this method of continuous mining will be published at the completion of the project.

1. Isolation of men during work performance: During an eight-hour shift, effective operation of the mining system requires that the nine shift members and the foreman have a shared understanding of what is required to minimize delays and shutdowns. For example, communication between the two support men and the men at the face (miner operator, miner helper, roof-bolters, and shuttle-car operators) is essential to assure supplies being at the face when needed. Also, roof-bolters must know the mining sequence (in what order entries and crosscuts are "taken") in order to estimate the size of bolts and timbers they will need and when they will need them. Knowledge of the latter requires coordination between the miner operator and his helper as well as with the two support men. Due to the nature of underground mining, once work has begun, communication and coordination on a real-time basis is minimal and inhibited by the distance between the men (sometimes several hundred yards) as well as by darkness and noise. Therefore, effective coordination depends on establishing consensus concerning what is to be done before work on the shift begins; that is accomplished by a shared "mapping" of what is required and when it is required. In essence, what is required is effective planning and consensus-building at the lowest level of the organization, the work-group level. Middle- and upper-level managers are encouraged to learn planning and consensus-building skills early in their careers, but little or nothing of this is understood at the work-group level, where such skills are equally necessary.

2. Continuity between shifts: The manner in which each nine-man shift operates the mining system significantly influences how the next shift is able to perform its tasks. For example, how well the miner operator takes a crosscut (at 90 degrees to an entry under the mining plan used) influences how easily shuttle cars can travel the distances between the continuous miner and the feeder (sequential interdependence). Furthermore, whether or not support men shovel debris and fallen coal from crosscuts and entries determines whether the next shift can begin to cut coal immediately or must instead take time to clean up what the previous shift has neglected (sequential interdependence). Although it is not officially sanctioned by middle-management members, the emphasis they place on tonnage per shift

encourages the members of each shift to neglect any preparation or maintenance work that has no immediate consequence for increased shift tonnage. For example, each shift is encouraged to mine out of the intended cycle and take only crosscuts and entries that yield tonnage quickly and easily, skipping those having puddles, geological faults, a bad roof or bottom and so on. The result is a competitive game the winners of which get high tonnage; the losers are the shifts that are left with the worst conditions and, consequently, the lowest tonnage. Another variation of this game focuses on who must take the most crosscuts; taking crosscuts yields less coal for the same effort as taking entries. Being a good player at this game requires anticipation of conditions and maneuvering appropriately; these are the same skills that are required for constructive planning. However, instead of planning to set up the next shift so that it will mine maximum coal within the approved mining cycle (and total tonnage across the three shifts maximized) the members of each shift use their planning capabilities to thwart the "absent other" (disturbed-reactive task environment). As each shift alternately wins and loses, fantasies (taking the form of scapegoating, for example) about the other shift are reinforced, thus providing little encouragement for constructive coordination.

3. Uncertainty of conditions: About every ten days during section development, the mining system is literally picked up and moved 180 feet forward. The conveyor belt and track are extended, and the power supply is moved ahead. With every such move, members of the section must cope with new geological conditions (boundary-transaction uncertainty). As progress is made toward the next move, shuttle-car paths lengthen and the distance between the support men and face men increases. The changing location of men and equipment raises questions of where variances arise in the section and where corrective action is required. Contingencies such as these make it difficult to anticipate the conditions under which work and its coordination take place.

The traditional factory facing relatively constant conditions may be able to cope with its production system by assigning to each member of a group a set of tasks that only he is to perform. This method of job assignment, a carryover from the mechanical world-view of design (Chapter 2), is prevalent in the mining industry but inappropriate for the conditions of uncertainty with which groups of miners must cope (see Trist et al. 1963; also Susman 1970b). Under this method of job assignment, unanticipated or unspecified tasks "slip through" the spaces left between the sets of tasks that are assigned. Since they are unanticipated or unspecified, they are the tasks of "no one." In traditional design, first-line management is supposed to be responsible for coordinating between tasks; however, the foreman is as isolated by distance, darkness, and so on as his men, and, thus, he is unable to meet the responsibility adequately. Consequently, tasks and their coordination go unattended, resulting in shutdowns and delays that could be avoided.

Facilitating the Best Match

Having considered continuous mining under room-and-pillar methods as a transport system and some of its psychosocial consequences, we may proceed with the search for the social system that provides the best match to it. The dilemma of searching for the best match is that we will never know when we have achieved it. Both the technical system and social system are open systems, subject to influence by their respective environments. Thus we cannot achieve a consistent, singular, maximum joint product of the two systems without sealing off both systems from any external disturbances, which it is not possible to do. Thus, our only way of knowing if we have succeeded in achieving the best match between the two systems is if our performance data suggest we have moved the socio-technical system to a consistently higher steady-state level of functioning than previously. The following recommendations should facilitate the achievement of such a match.

1. Definition of the primary task: When the social-system members' definition of their primary task is congruent with what the technical system is best designed to do, both systems will be more effectively utilized. Acceptance by management and the work group of a definition of continuous mining as a transport system rather than as a production system per se will encourage both organizational levels to be alert to key variances that affect the performance of a transport system. For example, search is likely to intensify on how to maximize use of the miner per miner-move, as well as to minimize delays and shutdowns.

2. Performance measurement of the primary task: Increasing the sizes of action-wholes was discussed in Chapter 3. The primary task will have a natural "pull" of its own if its performance and evaluation are organized into the units that are intrinsic to the work that is required. Completion of a belt move is one such natural unit. In the language introduced earlier in this chapter, taking as many daily cuts as possible (each is 20 feet wide and 16 feet deep) is a tactic embedded in a strategy of moving the group closer to its objective of achieving a belt move (after cutting 180 linear feet) in the shortest time possible. If performance data are fed back to work-group members in units such as time and costs per belt move rather than by units that are accounting or calendar conveniences, the units will "stand by themselves" as bases around which directed actions are organized.

Performance data should be evaluated according to social units containing those members whose contributions are most interdependent in pursuit of the primary task. In continuous mining, the shift is not a natural social unit for evaluating performance. The section consisting of 27 men and 3 foremen working in the same geographical territory is a natural unit containing those men whose tasks are most intensely interdependent in operating and maintaining the transport system. As we discussed above, evaluation of performance by shifts encourages competition rather than cooperation toward common goals and objectives.

Performance data should be evaluated in terms that are consistent with and reinforce the definition of continuous mining as a transport system. As mentioned above, performance of a transport system is improved by discovering ways to maximize use of the continuous miner and minimize moves, delays, shutdowns, and so on. Improvements of this sort require application of analytic skills to data representing key variances in the operation of a transport system. Data such as number and lengths of delays, tonnage per minute of operating time, costs of supplies, and so on, if made available to work-group members and their foremen, will provide the vehicle they need for problem solving and the setting of performance objectives. Data representing such key variances will become objects of directed action—that is, of problem solving—if such action, in turn, helps produce outcomes that improve system performance and if such action may be taken by the group members themselves. In addition to manipulating these objects for their intrinsic satisfaction, they will have the "in order to" quality of improving system performance. Consistent with Kleinian psychoanalytic theory, pursuit of maximum production (good objects) through actions that minimize delays (bad objects) is a distribution of psychic resources that minimizes ambivalences toward a goal or objective and encourages a fuller utilization of the members' problem-solving skills.

3. Dealing with uncertainty: Variances occurring under conditions of high uncertainty and task interdependence are most effectively controlled if several or all group members possess the necessary skills to reduce variances. In this case, the group as a whole possesses a reservoir of skills to be deployed as unanticipated variance arises. Delays will be minimized if corrective action can be taken by those located nearest (in space or time) the source of this variance rather than by those who hold a particular job title. It is not necessary for the group to follow any rigid scheme of rotation to achieve sufficient skill redundancy. What is required is that values exist in the group that encourage members to learn all group tasks. Minimal pay and status differences between members will facilitate the occurrence of such learning.

4. The shift foreman's role should facilitate the implementation of all the above recommendations. He can do this by making boundary-maintenance decisions for the work group rather than making decisions

that group members can and should make for themselves. One boundary activity is to assure the efficiency and adequacy of all communication with other groups whose contributions influence the performance of the transport system—such as maintenance and supplies, personnel. Additionally, the foreman's role in safety should be strengthened; he is the one who may be criminally liable if work on his shift is performed under unsafe conditions. His retreat from day-to-day coordination of work-group members will allow him more time to study state and federal mining regulations, to enforce them, and to train his men to work safely. By functioning as a trainer, the foreman can also aid the group to become multiskilled. He need not possess all the requisite skills himself to do this, but he must know where such training resources are available in the larger organization so that they can be made available to his men. Finally, the foreman can encourage the group to plan ahead by using problem-solving techniques and helping the group to achieve consensus. These kinds of skills are rarely taught to first-line management, although their practice may make a significant improvement in performance.

5. Numerous "enabling conditions" exist in the mining of coal underground that facilitates the creation of self-regulating work groups. It is easy, for instance, for coal miners on a section to experience themselves as a group because they are physically isolated from other members of the organization and the tasks of each man are highly interdependent with those of another. The four preceding recommendations are also enabling conditions encouraging the group to be self-regulating. They encourage a conceptual redefinition among group members concerning what the group is and what they believe they can accomplish. New action and new action possibilities follow conceptual redefinition of the task and what is required to achieve it.

Implementation

This section reports briefly on some of the methods used to implement the recommendations of the preceding sociotechnical analysis.

Orientation Period

A six-session orientation period began in December 1973. The entire section of 27 men and 3 foremen met every Monday and Friday for all-day meetings for three weeks in an aboveground classroom. Tuesdays, Wednesdays, and Thursdays were regular working days on the new section underground. During orientation meetings, autonomous work-group concepts were explained—for example, mining as a transport system, type of data needed to improve system performance and so on. All job tasks were reviewed, and the men received a job safety program and a review of the state and federal safety laws. In addition, experiential exercises in group problem-solving were given, generally within the context of issues that the Steering Committee had not foreseen and that required resolution.

Initial Learning

A period of several weeks then followed during which the men worked at the jobs they initially bid on but were encouraged to begin learning other jobs. They were to familiarize themselves with the concrete application of state and federal laws and begin to learn to coordinate the activities of their section. As the primary focus during this period was on learning, management agreed to an eight-week moratorium on pressure for production.

Throughout the next 12 months, the research team concentrated on the building of several mechanisms for training and development as well as for conflict resolution. Some of these are listed below.

Section Conferences

At approximately six-week intervals, all 27 members of the section and the 3 foremen met in the aboveground classroom, where events of the last six weeks were reviewed and the next six weeks planned, usually with members of the Steering Committee attending. During these meetings the men were paid their regular daily rate. Such time for review and planning was considered by the men and by management as of no less importance than time on the job. Each believed it would pay off in more effective performance in the long run. Between each six-week interval, the research team systematically gathered data on absenteeism, productivity, delays, costs, and so on for feedback and discussion at section conferences.

Underground Visits

Two graduate student assistants hired to work with the research team made underground visits two days a week.* They were instructed to reinforce the concepts discussed in the classroom meetings, to follow up on ambiguities,

---

*The research team was very ably assisted in this regard by the efforts of Melvin Blumberg and James B. Thurman.

and to collect information on section behavior and evolving mining practices to be discussed at the next section conference.

Joint Commitee

A joint committee was formed consisting of an elected representative from each of three shifts, plus one member each from the mine-wide union Safety and Mine Committees, plus an equal number of management including one of the three foremen from the section. This committee met at irregular intervals to settle disputes that arose on the section, deal with operational issues requiring cross-shift planning, and otherwise contribute to the development of a section-wide social unit.

Foremen Meetings

Approximately twice each month, the three foremen, often with other members of management present, met with the research team to discuss issues related to development and training in their new role. A four-point agenda was developed for these meetings: (1) *Safety:* What unsafe acts were the men stopped from doing since the last meeting; what violations were observed and what corrective actions were taken? (2) *Training:* Who in the section has learned a new job or task? (3) *Inside/Outside Relations:* Issues related to supply ordering, preventive maintenance, and development decisions were discussed with appropriate members of management who were asked to attend these meetings. (4) *Planning and Consensus Building Skills:* Experiential exercises were given concerning problem-solving skills, manner of communication, conflict resolution, and so on.

Performance Results

The performance data collected reflect the objectives that the management and union hoped would be achieved as a result of the introduction of autonomous working in the underground section. The major, but not exclusive, goal expressed by the union was increased underground safety. Management was also concerned with safety but gave equal emphasis to reduction of mine absenteeism, productivity, and costs.

The research team presented an analysis of preliminary performance data to the Steering Committee after the first autonomous section had been operating for a year (see Trist, Brown, and Susman 1975). At this time, a second autonomous section had been operating for only four months, a period that included a month-long strike and several holidays. Therefore, only data for one autonomous section and two nonautonomous sections were analyzed. As part of the guidelines specified by the research team's sponsors, the National Quality of Work Center and the Economic Development Administration of the United States Department of Commerce, there was to be an independent evaluation performed by a separately funded team. This team, headed by Professor Paul Goodman of Carnegie-Mellon University, was to collect attitudinal and production-related data at the beginning of the experiment, after 18 months, and after three years. These data were to be published for the general scientific public, which might more readily accept results done by an independent group with little vested interest in the program's outcome. Such data were not available to the research team or the Steering Committee in time to influence the course of development of the project.

Comparisons

Neither of the two nonautonomous sections operating at the beginning of the experimental year is particularly suitable for comparison with the autonomous section. One nonautonomous section had better conditions for most of the year than did the autonomous section as well as an equipment advantage. The other nonautonomous section had worse conditions and some different equipment. Data for 1973 are presented for suggestive purposes only, as any comparisons with 1974 must be interpreted very cautiously as compositions of the crews on each section changed when the autonomous section was created. Furthermore, as the mine is small in number of operating sections and employees, it was virtually impossible to "seal off" interaction between personnel of the various sections. For example, autonomous-section foremen told the other foremen of their activities and training experiences, which some of the latter began to adopt on their own.

The research team considered the mine as a whole as the proper unit of analysis, recognizing that "contamination" effects are important data in their own right. Progress on the autonomous section would ultimately have to be measured in a longitudinal record of the section against its own past performance. Comparisons with other sections would have restricted use, though they could be illuminating.

Table 7.1 shows federal violations assessed against each of the three sections for 1973 and 1974.

TABLE 7.1

Violations of the 1969 Coal Mine Health and Safety Act

	Autonomous	Nonautonomous A	Nonautonomous B	Total
1973	18	19	10	47
1974	7	37	17	61

Source: Compiled by the author.

The reduction in violations for the autonomous section is quite dramatic. This reduction to about half the number as in 1973 occurred in spite of an overall increase in violations for the mine as a whole. The increased number of violations on the other two sections can be attributed to the increased number of visits by federal inspectors to the mine, especially following a fatal accident on nonautonomous A in September 1974. The autonomous section had fewer violations in 1974 even with more visits by federal inspectors.

The figures in Table 7.2 are for all reported accidents and those of them that were lost-time accidents.

TABLE 7.2

Accidents

	Autonomous	Nonautonomous A	Nonautonomous B	Total
1973				
Reported	6	5	4	15
Lost time	2	3	2	7
1974				
Reported	7	14	11	32
Lost time	1	3	2	6

Source: Compiled by the author.

The reported and lost-time accident rate for the autonomous section is superior to the other two sections for 1974: The higher incidence of reported accidents for the mine as a whole in 1974 may have been due, in part, to more stringent reporting requirements requested during the year by governmental agencies. Minor accidents such as cut fingers and bruises were not reported in 1973. Furthermore, the research team also was informed that conditions in the mine were generally more difficult in 1974 than in 1973. If so, the overall incidence of reported accidents on the autonomous section is impressive, as this section maintained its overall 1973 record, while that on the other sections increased.

Table 7.3 shows the number of absences (excused and unexcused) for each section in 1973 and 1974. The overall figure for 1974 can be attributed to the fewer number of days worked due to the month-long strike in November and early December.

TABLE 7.3

Absences

	Autonomous	Nonautonomous A	Nonautonomous B	Total
1973	233	289	115	637
1974	135	187	112	434
	(2.5%)*	(4.8%)*	(2.5%)*	

*Absences per man-day worked.

Source: Compiled by the author.

The rates of absenteeism on all sections are exceptionally low for the mining industry. The national average is 12.5 percent of man-days worked. There is no obvious explanation why nonautonomous B has had a consistently low absentee rate. It might be that under certain types of bad conditions men don't want to let each other down; they share the bad as the way of enduring it.

On the experimental section, it was expected that a more positive attitude would mean that men would be less wasteful of supplies and take better care of equipment. Moreover, as learning proceeded, the costs of supplies and maintenance should decrease. Table 7.4 shows inside costs (production and maintenance) per ton per quarter of 1974 for each of the three sections.

TABLE 7.4

1974 Costs
(in dollars)

	Autonomous	Nonautonomous A	Nonautonomous B
First quarter	1.58*	0.836	1.56
Second quarter	1.40	1.12	1.73
Third quarter	1.24	1.05	1.38
Fourth quarter	1.13	3.56	1.41

*First-quarter figures on all sections exclude January. Costs not calculated by sections until February 1974.

Source: Compiled by the author.

A number of factors must be taken into consideration before a final determination of actual costs is made. There has been substantial inflation in the costs of some supplies, such as roof bolts, for which corrections must be calculated. Also, the type of mining that predominated throughout the year on each section must be controlled for; for example, the autonomous section did a great deal of pillar work in 1974 for which fewer supplies are generally required than for development. However, these corrections are unlikely to alter the basic differences in trends. The costs data for the autonomous section show a downward trend, while this is not the case for the other two sections.

The rate of production has not yet shown a significant increase, though it was the impression of management that it was beginning to increase in the fourth quarter of 1974. Evaluations can only be made by comparing production between dates comparable for the same type of production and equivalent geological conditions and over a significant period of time—for example, two to three years. At this time, the only statement that can be made with assurance is that production has not decreased as a consequence of the program's introduction nor as a cost of improving the safety level. It is a currently accepted belief in the coal industry that one of these goals—production or safety—must be sacrificed for the other.

CHAPTER

8

THE SUPERVISION OF SELF-REGULATING SYSTEMS

When individuals find themselves in situations that limit their ability to act, it is generally the case that a redefinition of the situation will lead to the emergence of new action possibilities. So it is when work-group members and supervisors come to perceive themselves as participants in "self-regulating systems"; they will behave differently than they did when they perceived themselves as job-holders in traditional organizations.* The theme of this chapter as well as of much of this book is that human action is guided by the definitions of the situations that the actors face. Consistent with this theme is the sociotechnical designer's responsibility to examine his own definitions of operatives and managers and the situations they face as well as his belief in the contributions each can and should make to organizational objectives. Several reconceptualizations of the role of operatives and managers are offered in the following pages as well as procedures for reinforcing these new conceptions. It is the writer's opinion that understanding of self-regulating systems will not come from drawing up a list of their supposed attributes. As the conditions for nurturing self-regulating systems are not congruent with traditional organizational forms, little will be understood of such systems until the designer has created and

---

*The expression "self-regulating system" might be used instead of "autonomous work group" when referring to the dynamic, adaptive, learning aspects of work-group functioning. Although the two expressions are somewhat interchangeable, "autonomous" has a structural rather than a process connotation and might be better used when referring to the distribution of decision-making between work groups and higher-level units.

maintained the conditions for their full-fledged operation. The responsibility of the designer is, therefore, to discover and reinforce conceptions and actions that are congruent with the realization and maintenance of self-regulating systems.

This chapter deals primarily with the supervision of self-regulating systems. The supervisor is assumed to be a member of the lowest level of management. However, in many cases, the function of supervision can be performed by an elected group leader. When this is so, the reader should, where appropriate, substitute the term "group leader" for that of "supervisor."

Consistent with the sociotechnical framework, supervision of self-regulating systems is conceived as supervision of two systems rather than one, the social and the technical. As each system displays different dynamics, different types of supervisory behavior are required for each. As the two systems are directively correlated, intervention in one system cannot be undertaken without considering its implications for the other system. However, for the purposes of analysis, primary consideration will be given in the beginning of this chapter to supervision of the technical system and secondary consideration to supervision of the social system. This emphasis will be reversed as the discussion proceeds.

CRITIQUE OF THE JOB AS A BASIC DESIGN UNIT

In Chapter 6, the work group's task environment was assessed to decide whether or not some work-group members should occupy specialized roles for making regulatory decisions on behalf of the group as a whole. Sets of conditions were outlined under which performance might improve by having one or more members occupy such specialized roles. However, the reasons for creating specialized regulatory roles are different from those that justify a rigid division of labor between jobs. One or more group members may occupy specialized regulatory roles regardless of whether there is also a rigid division of labor among those who actually perform the activities regulated. A one-man/one-job division of labor is seldom recommended for the actual performance of activities. The only clear exception might be when activity/resource sites are widely dispersed geographically and job-holders share no common resources.

Several times throughout this book it has been suggested that work-group members can most effectively perform their required activities if they are not hampered by a rigid division of labor. The rationale behind recommending flexible job boundaries was not that it will increase job variety for work-group members, although this may be a desirable byproduct. The recommendation was based on a design principle that differs fundamentally from principles that characterize traditional methods for designing work. The design principle is that analysis for partitioning and assigning activities begins at the level of the group; the work group is the basic building block of work design. In traditional work design, analysis begins at the level of the job; the individual job is the basic building block of work design. In the latter case, each activity or aggregate of activities (tasks) is identified as the responsibility of a particular individual. Each individual is then assigned to a particular geographical area where his tasks are located. The interactions between jobs are then determined by the manner in which their tasks are linked spatiotemporally.

Boundaries between jobs are drawn on the basis of one of two criteria: (1) the average variance arising from an individual's assigned tasks or (2) the peak variance with which an individual is able to cope. The criterion of average variance is used when jobs are sequentially interdependent—as on assembly lines. In such cases, the designer seeks to maximize production by minimizing delays due to one individual having to wait for another individual to finish his task before beginning his own, the designer balances the line. In devising algorithms for line balancing, traditional designers supplement the individual-job building-block assumption with the assumptions that on average different individuals work at the same pace, on average an individual works at the same pace throughout a shift, and on average variations in parts and equipment can be ignored (see Ingall 1965).

Emery (1975, p. 6) noted Ingall's review of assembly-line balancing and commented that an average "does not even tell us whether the exact average state has ever occurred.... At any one time on a line it is most improbable that all aspects are operating at their average value. Typically something is always non-average, wrong, or when one thing is wrong so are half a dozen other things." When tasks are sequentially interdependent, variances arising from one task are likely to increase variances in other tasks. Unless corrective action is quickly taken, the variance may spread to other tasks until the entire set of interdependent tasks is affected. If regulation of the "line" is external to a group assigned to a supervisor, all of the supervisor's time may be taken up in correcting variances between tasks by coordination and allocation, leaving him no time for the role he is best placed to perform, boundary maintenance.

The criterion of peak variance for establishing job boundaries is most often used when tasks are in simultaneous or pooled interdependence. Tasks in either type of interdependence are frequently required in the monitoring of automated or semiautomated equipment. In such cases, jobs have to be so bounded that the individuals assigned to them can cope with the peak variances arising from the tasks that make them up. The dilemma with using such a criterion is that it is seldom that all individuals working in the same area or sharing the same "work piece" simultaneously face peak levels of variance. A frequent occurrence is that most individuals have nothing to do but watch a great deal of the time, while their fellow workers might be experiencing a temporary overload.

The latter result occurred in the wire-drawing department at Christiana Spigerverk (Emery and Thorsrud 1974). Workers were to respond to unpredictable breakages in wire being run across their benches by shutting off the motor and welding the wire. The interdependence between benches was of the pooled type. Each man worked at his own bench and was paid for production on his own machine alone. When a worker at any particular bench ran into a great deal of difficulty in wire breakages, workers at neighboring benches ignored this and concerned themselves with their own bench even when they had nothing to do.

Both Rice (1958) and E.J. Miller (1975) have observed members of weaving groups form into separate task groups and fail to offer assistance to other task groups. The interdependence among subgroups was pooled for those who formed subgroups by number of looms worked; the interdependence among subgroups was simultaneous for those who formed subgroups by the particular tasks performed, replacing old bobbins with new ones. These patterns of subgroup formation occurred frequently even when group methods of working were introduced that encouraged sharing a common group task and operating with flexible job boundaries.

The explicit rationale for replacing individual methods of working with group methods of working is the proposition that a group can more effectively allocate its resources when and where required to deal with its total variance than can an aggregate of individuals each of whom is assigned part of the variance. In the latter case, it is assumed that the sum of individual efforts to correct variance will sum to the correction of the total balance. However, as has been shown, establishing job boundaries by the average or peak variance criterion can be very costly to performance. The evidence from several experiments in introducing autonomous, self-regulating methods of work (Rice 1958; Hill 1971; Emery and Thorsrud 1975) is that performance gains more than offset the costs of training all group members to become multiskilled to perform all of the group's required tasks.

HOLISTIC SYSTEMS

Attention now shifts to consideration of the social-system properties a work group must possess if it is to deploy its members flexibly to meet variances when and where they occur. This section will focus on the social-system properties required; later sections will focus on how such properties may be obtained.

Work-group members who flexibly deploy themselves as required would not define their contributions to the group's products in terms of any particular job they might perform. In place of the job, members would define themselves relative to their value as a contributor to the primary task of the group as a whole. This shift of identification from the job to the group transforms an aggregate of individuals into what Angyal (1941) calls a holistic system. A holistic system has one and only one construction or governing principle. It cannot be discovered by summing the direct relationships between members but by finding the superordinate system in which the members are connected or by defining "the positional value of members relative to the superordinate system" (p. 254). In our discussion, members of a work group would define themselves by their positional value to the work group. The primary task of the group is the construction principle that guides group members to distribute themselves as needed.

When work-group members define themselves by their positional value to the group, each member embodies in his own behavior, the construction principle of the group as a whole. This means that each group member internalizes the primary task of the group and allows it to guide any action he takes. In this way the work group has resources for using and adapting to its task environment that traditional groups do not have. In traditional work groups only the supervisor is presumed to guide his actions by the outcome the group is to achieve. When he decides on the actions to be taken he instructs group members on what they should do. The members of a traditional work group can only guide their behavior by their individual job requirements.

In contrast, when every group member's behavior is guided by an accepted primary task, each knows or is capable of learning what actions to take to achieve the common outcome. If he lacks knowledge about how to convert raw materials or correct variances, he need not wait for instruction by a supervisor nor wait for any other group member to take action for him. No matter where in the group he is located or when an action is required, the primary task of the group will be his guide for deciding what action to take. The more frequently group members use the primary task in this way, the more they learn about the task environment their group faces. The more knowledge that becomes available to the group as a whole, the greater the group's capacity to adapt to its environment.

A system may increase its adaptive capacity by choosing one of two different strategies. The strategy of increasing a system's adaptability by increasing the shared knowledge available to the system as a whole embodies a design principle that Emery and Trist (1973) have called "redundancy of functions." It is the design principle of groups whose members learn about their task environment by reference to a shared primary task. The other strategy of increasing a system's adaptability is to increase the number of parts that do the same thing. This assures that if one part fails or wears out, another will be there to do what is required. When the latter principle, redundancy of parts, is applied to work design, a number of low-skilled, easily replaceable workers are instructed on what to do. Once such instruction has occurred, no further learning takes place or is presumed required. A coordinator performs the specialized function of overseeing the task of the group as a whole.

The latter strategy for increasing system adaptiveness is effective when work groups face task environments that are static so that all required action can be planned. The task environment should also contain elements that are largely unrelated to each other so as not to overwhelm the adaptive capacity of the coordinator. Task environments are seldom as static and loosely connected as this, and if they were they would be experienced as placid-randomized by work-group members, with all the consequences this implies for apathy and rebellion (Chapter 5). The coordinator may then simultaneously face two negative consequences of traditional work design. He will face more complexity than he can handle and receive no assistance in handling it from work-group members. The frequent result is that the coordinator "exports" the variance he can't handle to other organizational units. A new hierarchical level will likely emerge to coordinate what the coordinator can't coordinate, thus contributing to further bureaucratic growth.

The members of work groups that adapt by using the strategy of redundant functions need no external coordinator, as the coordinative function is redundantly performed by all group members as it is required. Furthermore, as more members of such groups become multiskilled through learning, the likelihood increases that appropriate action will take place as required and that less variance will be exported beyond the group.

ADAPTING TO DYNAMIC TASK ENVIRONMENTS

Continuous learning among work-group members increases the capacity of the group to adapt to dynamic, richly connected task environments. The task environments facing work groups may be dynamic for several reasons:

1. Actions on raw materials with unknown or unstable properties may produce unintended consequences in the work group's internal task environment. The likelihood that this will occur is greater, the richer the connectedness between task-environment elements.
2. Competitive or uncoordinated actions toward members of other organizational units may produce disturbed-reactive or turbulent external task environments.

3. Changes may occur in the quantity, quality, or flow of raw materials—for example, the quality of fir and spruce inputs to the chemical pulp department at the Hunsfos Mill (Emery and Thorsrud 1975)—or supplies—for example, the restricted availability of loom spare parts and shuttles to weaving groups (E. J. Miller 1975).

4. Higher-level units may alter their performance standards—for example, the weaving mills increased their quality standards as they sought to be more competitive in their growing markets for exported cloth.

5. If a work group accepts its primary task to be improving the efficiency with which it produces its present products, group members will be searching for and discovering new task-environment elements and relationships between elements through problem solving. The latter will also be the case when the group accepts planning or designing as its primary task. In general, the longer the projected time horizon to achieve a desired outcome, the less likely that group members can predict what the consequences of their actions will be. Furthermore, the wider the scope of elements affected in achieving the desired outcome, including social-system as well as technical-system changes, the more likely that the task environment will take on emergent properties.

It is very unlikely that a work group will possess at any one time a sufficient reservoir of knowledge and skills to deal with a dynamic task environment. The knowledge and skills required are not only technical—for example, how to convert raw materials—but social—for example, how to achieve consensus or compromise within and between organizational units. Adaptability to dynamic environments cannot be judged by what group members now know or what they can do, but by their potential to increase this reservoir of knowledge and skills through continuous learning. In general systems language, work groups whose members are capable of continuous learning are "variety-increasing systems" (Ackoff and Emery 1972). Such systems are called variety-increasing because their members continuously learn to increase the variety of responses they are capable of making toward a dynamic task environment. Social-system members thus adapt to increasing variety in their task environment by learning an equal variety of responses to it (see Ashby 1956). Such learning is not strictly limited to increasing the number of tasks its members can perform. It extends to their making better coordination and allocation decisions or to learning any other way to restructure the group so as to achieve their desired outcomes more effectively. In a variety-increasing system, the structure of the group is a means or an instrument to achieving the group's desired outcome; the structure of the group is never an end in itself. Within limits set by the values and defenses that their present structure supports, group members will change their structure if an alternative is judged to better achieve a desired outcome.

In contrast to work groups that are variety increasing, traditionally designed work groups are generally "variety-decreasing systems" (Ackoff and Emery 1972). The members of such systems are encouraged by the manner in which higher-level units reward them to perform a smaller variety of actions than they are capable of spontaneously producing or learning. The members of variety-decreasing systems are prescribed means or instruments to a structure that higher-level units have designed for achieving predetermined ends. Such systems may adapt to their environments if all elements and their relationships are known so that an appropriate number of responses can be planned to deal with them. However, if the environment is dynamic in any of the ways suggested above, the system will have no capacity to learn new responses to deal with the unanticipated elements. Variety-decreasing systems cannot cope with unanticipated environmental variety by learning new responses to it. The members of such systems cease to learn once the variety of their actions is assumed equal to the variety contained in their task environment. Typically, any learning that took place was devoted to eliminating irrelevant responses rather than acquiring new capabilities.

GROUP MEMBERS AS SYSTEM CONTRIBUTORS

Several examples have been provided of the negative consequences of designing work groups as aggregates of individual job-holders coordinated by an external agent. Self-regulation is inhibited by the traditional conception of work-group members as individual job-holders. The concept of "job" limits each member to the performance of a limited number of circumscribed tasks. What is beyond the job is not the responsibility of the job-holder; he is taught to ignore information and required actions that fall outside his job domain. In the language of Chapter 3, the job becomes the center from which action originates and to which action is done. The boundaries between the "I" and the "not I" become coincident to the boundaries of the job. If all group members were to behave this way, any unanticipated required action (to correct a variance) is the responsibility of "no one"; it falls between the designated jobs. In traditional job design, coordination between jobs, like unanticipated action, is the responsibility of no one within the work group; it is the sole responsibility of the group's supervisor.

Figure 8.1A illustrates the work group conceived by its members as an aggregate of individual job-holders coordinated by an external agent. Each job is shown with solid boundaries around it and with no overlap between jobs. Such a conception has its most deleterious influence on work-group performance when technical cooperation is required between group members

FIGURE 8.1

The Work Group Composed of Job-Holders or System Contributors

Figure 8.1A

The Work Group Conceived as an Aggregation of Individual Job-Holders

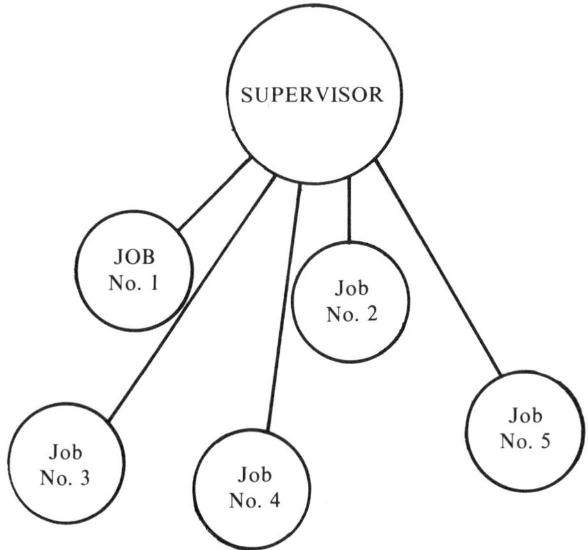

Figure 8.1B

The Work Group Conceived as a System of Contributors

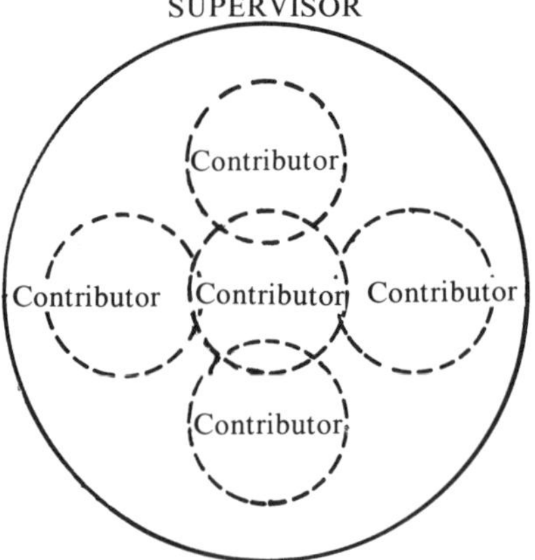

Source: Compiled by the author.

and conversion or boundary-transaction uncertainty is high or the task environment is otherwise dynamic. Under these conditions, effective work-group performance requires continuous mutual feedback of information between work-group members. Even when members face less uncertain and less interdependent conditions, there are rare exceptions under which performance would not benefit from spontaneous cooperation among group members.

The formation of self-regulating work groups is achievable by teaching group members to conceive themselves as system contributors rather than job-holders (see Figure 8.1B). In such a conception, job boundaries are permeable and overlap each other. As a system contributor, the group member performs specific tasks but is also responsible for the success of the group as a whole. Meeting this latter responsibility doesn't require that he perform every task in the group's domain as often as every other member. But it does require that he give up exclusive right to perform a particular subset of tasks. He can, however, if he desires or if it is necessary, perform any of the other tasks in the group's domain.

Psychoanalytically speaking, as a system contributor rather than a job-holder, the member projects the boundaries of self to the group as a whole yet simultaneously retains an individual identity through his own distinctive contributions. This psychic distribution allows a balance between the two forces postulated by Angyal (1941) to be diametrical, but complementary trends in human motivation. According to Angyal (pp. 173-74):

> The trend [toward autonomy] is distinctively individualistic. It is a self-association of the organism, it tends to master and govern the environmental happenings, it aims at achievement and conquest. In the trend toward homonomy the emphasis is displaced from the individual to the collective, to superindividual wholes in which the person tends to submerge himself. The goals of the homonomous trends are sharing, participation, union.
>
> The antagonism between the two principles is probably only apparent. While the organism in its autonomous trend extends its influence over increasingly large fields of events, in its homonomous trend, although submerging itself in superindividual wholes, it does not destroy itself. On the contrary, by identifying oneself with and experiencing oneself as part of superindividual wholes, one expands beyond the narrow individual self....

NURTURING THE EVOLUTION OF SYSTEM CONTRIBUTORS

A group of system contributors is a design innovation that is radically different from a design that produces an aggregate of job-holders. The values and practices of the larger organization must correspondingly change if the design innovation is to succeed. An aggregate of job-holders may be created by design fiat, but a group of system contributors evolves through proper care and nourishment. The larger organization must support this evolution by protecting an "infant" group from undue trauma. The development of supportive working relationships between group members will be impaired unless special care is taken to prevent turnover of work-group personnel, as occurred at the Teesport Refinery of Shell U.K., Ltd. (Hill 1971) or intraorganizational shifting of personnel between weaving groups at Calico and Jubilee Mills (E.J. Miller 1975). Development of supportive working relationships was also impaired at Calico and Jubilee by a shortage of spare workers and neglect of training.

Disturbances to steady-state functioning tend to inhibit the latent homonomous forces within the work group causing system contributors to regress toward individualistic modes of working. Phenomenologically, there is a contraction of the boundaries that the individual has extended toward the group as a whole. The inability of technical staff to achieve steady-state conditions at Teesport Refinery was a contributing factor to a regression of this sort. A similar regression occurred in weaving groups when their members encountered production difficulties. Group members limited their activities to specific subsets of looms or to specific tasks—such as filling bobbins—when their groups experienced difficulties in procuring spare parts and supplies.

The evolution of group members into system contributors will also be impaired unless specific measures are taken to counteract practices generally associated with traditional work design. For example, individual piece-rate systems tend to foster restrictive work practices and other devices to protect employee interests. For example, employees of the wire drawing department of Christiana Spigerverk strongly resisted any movement away from the rule of one-man/one-machine toward a group method of working. The men feared that any such movement would permanently increase manning standards and reduce the work force. Resistance such as this can be overcome by binding agreements between management and worker's representatives that no reductions in wage or employment will result from experimenting with new methods of working.

The larger organization may also take measures to (1) provide group members with performance data on a group, rather than an individual, basis, (2) develop a reward structure that pays workers for what they know rather than what they do, and (3) encourage self-selection of work-group members. Each measure has been associated with successful attempts to establish self-regulating work groups.

A change program to faciliate group members to see themselves as system contributors can begin with efforts by all members to learn all the tasks for which the group is responsible. The supervisor of the work group can arrange a schedule that allows each group member to rotate to a different job and to be taught that job by the group member who is currently most proficient at it. The supervisor's responsibilities might then include the appraisal of training and learning undertaken within the group and evaluation of the progress made by each group member.

SUPERVISION AS BOUNDARY MAINTENANCE

Self-regulation by work-group members does not mean that supervision is a redundant function, although it might appear so to those who conceive the supervisor's main responsibility to be coordination of work-group members. Instead, when the latter is the work group's responsibility, the role of supervision that emerges is mediation between the work group and its environment. This role is multifaceted and requires that the supervisor understand and intervene in both the technical and phenomenal worlds that he and work-group members inhabit.

In traditionally designed work groups, the supervisor makes nearly all the decisions occurring within the work group's domain. His decisions concern coordination, allocation, and boundary maintenance. The supervisor's area of decision-making remains broad, relative to that of the work group.

The work group's area of decision-making widens relative to that of the supervisor when work-group members learn to make their own coordination and allocation decisions or any other responses that may be required to produce the group's product. The function remaining to the supervisor is boundary-maintenance. The decisions which make up this function include communication across the group's boundary to other groups to alter the quantity, quality, or flow rate of raw materials or resources. Those decisions make up the technical-world aspects of the boundary-maintenance function and will be discussed below.

The size of the total decision-making area that contains both the supervisor's as well as the work group's decisions has increased. This results from the fact that the release of the supervisor's time from making decisions that work-group members can make frees him to engage in more long-term planning as well as in other managerial functions to be discussed later. Thus, the increase in work-group decision making relative to that of the supervisor in no way implies a distribution of the supervisor's boundary maintenance function. Indeed, it is a critical function and the supervisor who performs it may retain a great deal of power over group members. For example, decisions retained by supervisors might include the decision to promote or terminate the employment of a work-group member, to authorize capital expenditures for tools and machines, and so on. The degree of power the supervisor retains may be influenced by (1) whether self-regulating work groups are inaugurated by unilateral management action, (2) whether concessions to a union seeking to share power with management are made, or (3) whether such groups are initially self-regulating and related to an "autonomous work group" for groups that negotiate and operate under contracts that impose obligations on both parties for a certain period of time. All other groups may be called "relatively autonomous."

TECHNICAL-WORLD ASPECTS OF BOUNDARY MAINTENANCE

Boundary Transactions

Boundary maintenance in the technical world is a Janus-faced function for the supervisor to perform. One of the two faces of this function deals with raw materials and other inputs before they cross the group's boundary as well as the removal of outputs from the group. As the primary means for reducing boundary-transaction uncertainty are not located within the work group, but in the work group's external task environment, the supervisor looks from the boundary outward into the work group's environment. His function is to reduce uncertainty concerning boundary transactions by buffering, leveling, forecasting, or rationing activities (see Thompson 1967). Some of his activities include negotiating delivery dates, coordinating inventories, combining work-group outputs with outputs from other groups —for example, as in assembly plants. If the supervisor's decisions result in a more predictable flow of acceptable inputs and outputs, then work-group members can plan more effectively for production.

Internal Regulation

The other face of the supervisor's Janus-faced function looks from the boundary inward toward conversion and maintenance activities. His function requires him to take actions on internal task-environment elements that are beyond the control of work-group members. Due to limits in technology, information processing, and the nature of raw materials, boundaries can seldom be drawn so that work-group members can make all regulatory decisions. Self-regulation of the work group is not impaired, however, if work-group members retain control of decisions requiring the shortest reaction time and/or have the most direct impact of those aspects of performance for which group members are held responsible. Frequently, the consequences of activities are "exported" across time (shifts) or territory (areas) boundaries. The responsibility of the supervisor is to see that he or other groups in the organization regulate consequences such as these.

The supervisor regulates variances arising from conversion activities that are beyond the capacities of work-group members to regulate by looking inward from his boundary role to the work group's internal task environment. As discussed in Chapter 6, limits in technology, information-processing capacity, and so on influence the distribution of regulatory decisions between work-group members and supervisors. If neither the supervisor nor work-group members can effectively make these decisions, the consequences of group actions will be exported beyond the group into other parts of the organization. They will produce variances of increasing amplification as a greater number of systems and system levels are affected.

Variance Exportation

Work groups frequently export the consequences of their decisions and activities across a time boundary. A time boundary exists when a group cannot produce its product within a standard (eight-hour) shift and "store" it in a nondeteriorating state until the group can return to work on it. A second shift that follows will have to continue production where the first shift left off. However, for the second shift to perform satisfactorily, information regarding the state of the product has to be properly communicated to it. E. J. Miller (1959) provides an example from a textile mill in which yarn is dyed as one of several steps leading to the completion of the cloth-weaving process. The dyeing process itself takes more than one shift to complete and the quality of the dyed yarn deteriorates rapidly unless each step of the dyeing process—for example, soaking, dyeing, drying, spinning is completed according to a tight time schedule. To assure that the schedule is properly maintained, the supervisor's boundary role requires that he communicate to the next shift supervisor any exigencies that have occurred on the previous shift that might affect the time schedule and thus the dyeing process. Performance of the boundary-maintenance function requires that the supervisor view the totality of the work group's tasks and responsibilities and communicate adequate information to the whole group or to individual members when appropriate.

A similar exportation across a time boundary occurs if two or more work groups share the same "set-up" for producing a product and if set-up conditions left by one group significantly affect the ability of the other group to perform its activities. In the mining of coal, the condition in which the work section is left by one shift influences how well the next shift that shares the section is able to mine coal. If the ability of a second shift to mine coal is impaired by the actions of the first, the second-shift supervisor can communicate the problem to the first and outline some corrective steps to be taken. Supervisors can communicate the outcome of their discussion to their respective groups and, if deemed appropriate, recommend that representatives be elected from each to develop solutions. As discussed in Chapter 7, these efforts at problem solving may not succeed unless performance is measured by a section-wide criterion that encourages cooperation rather than competition between shifts.

Work-group members and supervisors draw upon their available repertoire of knowledge and skills when they repair their own equipment. The likelihood is greater that a problem will be noticed and repaired sooner, if some or all group members have learned to diagnose and repair equipment. Such an outcome is consistent with increasing system adaptability by the strategy of redundancy of functions. Such a strategy applied to maintenance functions has been implemented with considerable success at the Norsk Hydro Fertilizer Plant (Emery and Thorsrud 1975) and at Shell U.K. (Hill 1971).

Production and maintenance activities are frequently assigned to different work groups because (1) production-group members lack appropriate maintenance skills, (2) craft unions restrict the distribution of maintenance skills, and (3) higher management believes that maintenance skills will be better utilized if they are grouped into service centers. Under such circumstances, variances arising from equipment breakdowns cross a technology or skill boundary (see E.J. Miller 1959). Correction of such variances requires the supervisor to perform the boundary-maintenance function of calling on other groups within the organization to repair or adjust his group's equipment. The speed and reliability with which supervisors are able to make such services available to their group depend on how well group members and the supervisor can anticipate maintenance problems through proper diagnosis of equipment operations as well as on the kinds of bargains, negotiations, or other relationships that supervisors establish with maintenance groups and other service centers (see Dalton 1959, Sayles 1964).

In each of the above examples, performance of the boundary-maintenance function requires work-group supervisors to be alert to any activities having consequences or to any variances that cross a time, territory, or skill boundary. The effectiveness with which variances are corrected depends on the supervisor's ability to recognize when deviations from standards occur and to take appropriate action. They may take such actions themselves or communicate the need for action to those groups with relevant skills. Emery (1967) has developed a nine-step analytical model for sociotechnical inquiry that work-group members and their supervisors can use for planning or designing. Within a proper design forum, such as a section conference, all organizational members whose responsibilities are related to the production of a particular product can explore how best to distribute decision making to increase product quality and quantity as well as to reduce operating and social costs.

Emery's nine-step model was formulated from experiences gained with advanced continuous-process technologies and is summarized below (adapted from Trist 1973):

1. An initial scanning is made of all the main aspects—technical and social—of the *selected target system*—that is, department or plant to be studied.

2. The *unit operations* are then identified—that is, the transformations (changes of state) of the material or product that take place in the target system—whether carried out by men or machines.

3. An attempt is made to discover the *key variances* and their interrelations. A variance is key if it significantly affects (1) either the quantity or quality of production, and (2) either the operating or social costs of production.

4. A table of variance control is then drawn up to ascertain *how far the key variances are controlled by the social system*—the workers, supervisors, and managers concerned. Investigation is made of what variances are imported or exported across the social-system boundary.

5. A separate inquiry is made into social-system members' perception of their role and role possibilities as well as constraining factors.

6. Attention then shifts to *neighboring systems,* beginning with the support or maintenance systems.

7. Attention continues on the boundary-crossing systems on the input and output side—that is, supplier and user systems.

8. The target system and its immediate neighbors are then considered in the context of the general management system of the organization as regards the effects of general policies or development plans of either a technical or social nature.

9. Recycling occurs at any stage, eventually culminating in design proposals for the target and/or neighboring systems.

THE PHENOMENAL-WORLD ASPECTS OF BOUNDARY MAINTENANCE

The function of boundary maintenance in technical-world terms is to balance demands that simultaneously arise from the work group's internal and external task environments. External-wise, the supervisor performs this function by regulating the flows of inputs and outputs across the work group's boundary. Internal-wise, this function is performed by monitoring the consequences of group conversion activities and regulating variances that are beyond the members' regulatory capacities, especially those that are frequently exported beyond the work group's boundary.

As discussed in Chapter 7, membership in a group arouses thoughts and feelings among group members about themselves, about task-environment elements, and about those who make decisions on their behalf—that is, supervisors. The manner in which supervisors exercise their boundary-maintenance function may lead group members to feel appreciation, admiration, resentment, or envy toward them. The manner in which the supervisor performs the boundary-maintenance function in phenomenal-world terms is no less important than how it is performed in technical-world terms. Appropriate actions from the phenomenal-world perspective assumes that group members will deal with thoughts and feelings in a manner that facilitates achieving outcomes that higher-level units can accept.

The Psychological Contract Between the Work Group and the Organization

The personnel policies and attitudes of managers at the highest levels of the organization influence how the work-group supervisor is to perform his boundary-maintenance function. For example, the manner in which higher-level units deal with work-group members affects the degree of commitment that the latter will give to the pursuit of the goals and objectives of higher-level units. This commitment is the outcome of an implied psychological contract between the organization and its members that influences how limited or extended identification with the organization will be. For example, if the organization treats workers as if they were costs of production to be minimized, workers, in turn, will offer only minimal contributions toward the organization's goals and objectives—a fair day's work for a fair day's pay. However, if the organization treats workers as valuable organizational members capable of quality work and creative efforts, workers are more likely to offer spontaneous contributions to the organization. Furthermore, regardless of whether or not a reward structure is designed to allow group members to share in the gains of increased group performance, self-regulation will not be encouraged unless work-group members have reason to believe that their efforts will be acknowledged and appreciated by the organization.

Generally speaking, from the perspective of work-group members, the supervisor is the singular individual who represents the organization and its management to the work group. As a result, he is the recipient and source of the sentiments that work-group members hold toward the organization as a whole. They may see their supervisor as holding the same assumptions about them as they perceive higher levels of management to hold. If group members perceive higher management to hold assumptions that are consistent with the members committing themselves to the organization, the supervisor will have a reservoir of good-will upon which to draw. Contrariwise, it will be difficult for the supervisor to harness group efforts toward a common objective if group members believe that higher management considers them unable to make worthwhile contributions to it. If the latter is the case, the supervisor may try to ensure an organizational commitment among work-group members through their commitment to him personally. He, rather than the organization, is trying to establish the terms of a psychological contract by demonstrating his belief in their capabilities and through his ability to demonstrate that he will "stick up for" and "fight for" his group members by representing their interests to higher management. This is a precarious role for the supervisor to play, however, because the possibility exists that he will lose his boundary-maintenance perspective and promote group interests at the expense of the larger organization. However, even if the supervisor is able to establish an organizational commitment among work-group members, it is still an undifferentiated or unspecified commitment, which the supervisor and group members must translate into meaningful and achievable outcomes before concerted group action can be taken.

Definition of the Primary Task

Supervisors may also perform another social aspect of their boundary-maintenance function by assisting group members to define and accept a primary task. He may, for example, assist group members to formulate producing, planning, or design tasks as they are required. In the case of planning and design tasks the supervisor may furnish the group with technical resources and establish a forum within which such tasks can take place. Helping the group to define a primary task more congruent with the demands of the work group's technical system may lead to producing outputs more efficiently and effectively—for example, defining continuous methods of mining coal as a transport system (Chapter 7).

Definition and acceptance by the group of a primary task that is also acceptable to the larger organization is only the cognitive or intellectual part of this aspect of the boundary-maintenance function. As Bion (1961) has pointed out, regardless of whether membership in the work group was voluntary or involuntary, members may unconsciously assume that the group has been convened for purposes other than the production of a product or a service. Bion has suggested that any group behaves simultaneously at two levels. At the manifest level the group meets to perform a specific "sophisticated" task. At the same time it behaves as if it had made one of three discrete assumptions: to reproduce itself, called "pairing"; to obtain security from one individual upon whom the members can depend, called "dependence"; or to preserve itself by attacking someone or something or by running away, called "fight-flight."

Bion calls a group behaving according to one of these unconscious assumptions a "basic group," to distinguish it from the "work group" operating on a "sophisticated" task. It is his hypothesis that to maintain a sophisticated level of behavior, the work group must use the emotions associated with one basic assumption to suppress and control the other two. Specifically, one might hypothesize that group members might combine the basic assumption of fight-flight with a task that requires full utilization of the group's physical and intellectual resources—for example, to overcome forces of nature threatening them. Similarly, group members might combine the basic assumption of pairing with a task to redesign the work-group structure. Rice (1965, p. 13) illustrates how group members may use a basic assumption in pursuit of a sophisticated task.

> Thus for a group involved in a fight the appropriate assumption that should be mobilized is "fight-flight" and the group uses this assumption to suppress and control "pairing" and "dependence." But if casualties mount, the group may no longer be able to suppress the emotions associated with reproduction or security, and its members lose their stomach for fight and the basic assumption may change.

Coal miners may use the basic assumption of dependence when carrying out the phase of the mining cycle they call "pulling pillars." This phase is extremely anxiety-producing—as the writer knows from firsthand experience—as it requires the systematic collapse of large sections of roof. Thick supporting timbers snap like matchsticks as the roof heaves and rolls toward a thunderous collapse. The section crews have developed an elaborate mythology about the face supervisor's uncanny ability to predict the exact second that a roof will collapse. One story that was frequently told to the research team concerned a face supervisor who announced to his crew that the roof would collapse at the precise second he said it would. To prove his point, he walked under a rather active piece of roof, counted to a preannounced number and returned to his crew. The roof collapsed as predicted as soon as he had walked away from under it. This story was told several times to different members of the research team. It was told with so many variations in where it took place and who the supervisor was to suggest that the crews used this story to reduce the anxiety associated with planned or unplanned roof collapse. Their anxiety was relieved by projecting omniscience onto the supervisor. Inexperienced coal miners were frequently observed to stay very close to their supervisor when pillars were pulled—almost following his very footsteps as if to stay within his magic, safe circle.

Ward nurses may also use the basic assumption of dependence to avoid taking responsibility for attending to critically ill patients (Menzies 1960). The nurses tended to shift this responsibility toward more senior nurses, idealizing the latters' mature and responsible behavior, while underestimating such behavior in themselves and their peers. Similarly, coal fillers were a noninterdependent aggregate performing tasks that were affected by the conditions that a previous shift left for them. One of the defenses that fillers manifested under these circumstances utilized the basic assumption of pairing. Several fillers would form informal subgroups that engaged in antisocial or competitive behavior (Trist and Bamforth 1951).

The affective component of the boundary-maintenance function is difficult to perform when the work-group functions at two levels simultaneously. Conflict may exist between the basic group and the individuals who compose it, between the work group and the basic group—for example, as appears to be the case with ward nurses—and between the work group suffused with the emotions associated with one basic assumption and the other basic assumptions that are repressed or denied. Conflicts of these types may interfere with the most effective mobilization of the affective energies of group members as they pursue their tasks. The function of leadership is to express on behalf of the group the emotions associated with the prevailing basic assumption. If the task of the group is to be effectively accomplished, the supervisor must express on behalf of the group a basic assumption that minimizes interference with the task to be achieved. Leadership training exercises may help him to perform this function more effectively.

The function of supervision in defining the work group's primary task may be likened to the function of the ego to the individual. It is the "executive" function that assures that intellectual and emotional resources are marshaled to achieve an outcome requiring transaction with the concrete, technical world. However, it should be pointed out that group members frequently feel ambivalent toward the one who exercises task leadership, making it difficult for a task leader to meet the members' socioemotional needs and perform his primary leadership function (see Bales and Slater 1955). According to Etzioni (1964), the capacity of a supervisor to be a socioemotional leader is greatly reduced by the predominantly instrumental initiations that he must make in a utilitarian organization such as a business organization. Etzioni considers the task and socioemotional-role requirements to be fundamentally incompatible with each other. Socioemotional leadership consists of tension reduction, conflict resolution, anxiety reduction, and so on. If the supervisor cannot simultaneously be a task and a socioemotional leader, he may have to share one of his roles with a group member so that both the technical and phenomenal aspects of the boundary-maintenance function will be performed.

Definition and Acceptance of Desired Outcomes

When a work group defines and accepts a primary task, cognition and affect are united in pursuit of a "reality-based" outcome. The desired outcomes of work groups producing goods and services are generally definable in terms of output measures such as quantity and quality of production and delivery dates. If possible, such outcomes should be measured in time units the completion of which create psychological closure—for example, production of a complete product or service. If such completion requires the contributions of more than one work group—for instance, across three shifts in the mining of coal—serious thought should be given to broadening the time horizon or the measures by which the outcomes are defined and evaluated so that cooperation between groups is encouraged—for example, measuring performance by belt moves in coal mining.

Another social aspect of the supervisory boundary-maintenance function is the definition and setting of goals and objectives. In performing this function, the supervisor does not dictate goals to group members but helps them to achieve consensus concerning what these should be. He should direct his activities toward clarifying issues, asking members what information they require, making sure all who have relevant input to the decision have contributed, and determining whether the group is ready to make a decision. The supervisor can help group members to build a quick consensus on solutions to short-term problems by providing them with information from other parts of the organization. However, chronic problems are better dealt with if all who have relevant inputs to the problem or are affected by the solution meet in a problem-solving forum, such as day-long conferences.

Once goals and objectives are accepted, the actions of group members will have the "in order to" quality of action directed toward achievement of desired outcomes. It is fundamental to realization of self-regulating work groups that supervisors conceive human behavior to be purposeful. When group members are allowed to be purposeful, they will use group structure to achieve goals and objectives. Otherwise, group members will be used by the group structure to do simply what designers have prescribed for them to do. The goals and objectives that group members pursue must be realistic, however, and it is the supervisor's responsibility to assess the resources available to the group and to inform group members of his assessment of the group's probability of success. As a result of his action, group members might either reset their level of aspiration or ask for resources that will make the goal's achievement more likely (see Hughes 1965; Zander 1971).

Purposeful behavior is fundamental to self-regulation of a work group. When their behavior is purposeful, group members perform a boundary-maintenance function of their own that complements the one performed by the supervisor. Two processes contribute to the group member's boundary-maintenance function. First, a goal or object sets up a "force field," in Lewin's terminology, by which group members determine what actions, events, things, and relationships are valued or not valued—that is, which are to become objects of directed action in Chein's (1972) language, or coproducers in the language of Ackoff and Emery (1972). Secondly, Herbst (1962) hypothesizes that, in seeking a desired outcome, group members take actions to achieve and maintain a preferred level of functioning (steady-state) as well as take actions to avoid or move away from less preferred levels of functioning. To quote Herbst (p. 162):

> The group, in other words, will operate so as to incorporate one set of activities, maintain its activity rate within a certain range and create certain types of interlinkages between activities and to eject other activities, resist changes in the activity rate and avoid the formation of other types of activity structure. We get in this way the operation of an introjection-rejection process which is the equivalent to the maintenance of a boundary.

Planning for Goal Achievement

The supervisor's consensus-building skills may also be used to help group members to plan for the outcomes it desires. Such planning may be for the short term or for a longer time horizon depending on whether the group's primary task at a particular time is producing, planning, or designing. If the time duration is long or the steps to be taken are complex, it may be impossible for the supervisor or group members to anticipate all the steps necessary to achieve a desired outcome. Under such circumstances, the supervisor may help the group to plan for achievement of an initial goal. When this goal has been achieved, the supervisor may help group members evaluate whether such achievement has moved the group closer to achievement of its objective and, finally, to plan for achievement of the next goal.

An important aspect of the supervisory boundary-maintenance function is to assure that the group remains focused on achievement of future outcomes. The value of focusing on the future was discussed in Chapters 3 and 7 in terms of "embedding" current action into larger action-wholes. Such embedding gives meaning to current actions that otherwise would be isolated in an undifferentiated eight-hour day. An illustration of this principle was offered in evaluating the performance of groups of coal miners at the completion of belt moves occurring at five-to-ten-day intervals.

An orientation to the future is required at nearly all managerial levels, but its relevance at the operative level is denied or at least unacknowledged by traditional designers. In addition to its value in giving meaning to current action, a future orientation provides group members with experience in dealing with the abstract. The traditional conception of operatives as "task-doers" rather than "planners" encourages operatives to think only in the concrete "here and now" and leads to work design that denies operatives any practice in dealing with the abstract. Responsibility for planning encourages group members to deal with an abstract future. Also, assessment of the consequences of action encourages abstract thinking, since assessment requires data that symbolize and "stand for" actions and outcomes (see Goldstein 1939). Consistent with the reconceptualization of operatives as planners is the supervisor's responsibility for seeing that appropriate planning data are generated and that sufficient time is made available for work-group members to discuss and evaluate such data.

Problem-Solving

A final social aspect of the supervisory boundary-maintenance function is to encourage group members to solve their own problems. A reconceptualization of group members as "problem-solvers" rather than "task-doers" is consistent with the supervisor's performance of this function. As the successful implementation of several Scanlon plans makes clear (Whyte 1955), increased production and reduced costs are not the result of workers doing prescribed activities faster, as though workers were like an electric motor supplied more electricity. Improvements resulted from workers who under the new system felt they had more to gain by sharing their problem solutions with management rather than by keeping these solutions to themselves.

Reconceptualization of group members as problem-solvers doesn't automatically produce improvements in work-group performance. It is romantic to assume an untapped resource will be instantly released only by the retreat of an "oppressive" management structure. Instead, the creation of autonomous work groups offers an opportunity that may be seized or lost depending on how the supervisor performs his boundary-maintenance function. If new action does indeed follow reconceptualization, then supervisors who conceive work-group members as problem-solvers will take action that encourages group members to diagnose and offer solutions to work-related problems

The actions that supervisors must learn to take are like those of a process consultant (see Schein 1972) who teaches group members the values and skills of problem-solving. Schein's illustrations of the practice of process consultation are exclusively at the upper- and middle-management level. But, as has been suggested before, the learning of process consultation skills is no less important for supervisors and operatives. Partly by emulation and partly by observing and feeding back process observations to group members, the supervisor can encourage a climate in which solutions to problems are freely expressed. The supervisor can accomplish this if, by his actions, he treats errors by group members as learning opportunities and encourages group members to teach each other how to avoid such errors in the future.

CHAPTER 9
EPILOGUE

This book has outlined a set of design concepts that is congruent with the structure and cultural patterns we can now anticipate will make up a significant part of our postindustrial future. As Emery and Trist (1973) point out, these patterns have been in the making for decades, and their future form can already be discerned in the present. Chapter 1 outlined the continuing trend toward an economy dominated by the production of services rather than goods. Also outlined were the sociocultural and educational changes accompanying this trend. Not only are trends and changes such as these mutually reinforcing, they are also inducing changes in the nature of the field in which a society's organizations, groups, and individuals interact. They are inducing what in Chapter 5 was referred to as a turbulent environment that is characterized by increasing instability and uncertainty. As the environment made up of national and transnational institutions becomes increasingly turbulent, it is also increasingly unregulable by the methods of planning and control we have utilized in the past. Evidence accumulates daily reminding us how important it is that new methods of societal regulation be devised and implemented before the rush of events exceeds our capacity for learning how to deal with it.

Terreberry (1968) traces the properties of open systems as they evolve from less complex to more complex states of organization. These system states evolve as a function of changes in the number of other systems with which a focal system has transactions as well as in the character of these transactions—that is, from placid-randomized to disturbed-reactive environments. Systems evolve to their most advanced state under conditions in which the environment itself takes on dynamic properties of its own—that is, when the environment is turbulent.

Terreberry surmises correctly that the rate of evolution of environments exceeds the rate of evolution of component systems. Furthermore, she presents an outline of types of system adaptation to increasingly complex and uncertain environments that corresponds generally to the outline shown in Table 5.2. However, turbulence between an environment's component systems also signifies that a response is required that comes not from further evolution of component systems but from evolution of a higher-level system that will regulate their interactions.

Turbulence between the components of any system level signifies that the components at that level can no longer be regulated by principles that successfully maintained the system in the past and promoted its present state of development. Turbulence at any system level signifies that a higher-level system is required to regulate the lower system according to new principles. Higher-level regulatory principles are derived from what Pattee (1973) calls an "alternative description" or a reclassification of the details of the lower level. Accordingly, societal turbulence can be reduced by development in the next highest system level, which is a system of values at the level of culture.

System components are reclassified when they are to perform new functions for their own level. This book has offered clues as to how a turbulent environment might be regulated through strategies introduced for the design of work groups. Open systems at any level are assumed to share properties that make cross-level generalizations possible. One strategy incorporates the principle of redundancy of functions. The greater the number of system components that can regulate themselves, the less variance a higher-level system need regulate. Utilizing this strategy, the burden on a higher-level system for regulating variance is much less than it would be if only a few of the lower system's components were specialized to reduce variance for the rest. In the latter case, variance at the lower system level that exceeds the regulatory capacity of a few specified components will be exported to a higher system level for regulation. At the societal level, a strategy based on the principle of redundancy of functions would relieve government of some of its operational planning responsibilities, providing it more time for normative planning and establishing the enabling conditions within which society's organizations, groups, and individuals can plan for themselves.

Complementary to the strategy of regulation by redundant functions is the strategy of facilitating the emergence of values that may be shared among a system's components. These values will serve as a common ground upon which the components may interact. Common ground increases the ability of each component to predict the consequences of its actions. Work places and organizations designed by scientific management and bureaucratic principles, respectively, contribute to turbulence at the societal level by the individual alienation and social anomie they induce. These contributions to turbulence are minimized to the extent that the next highest system level, the cultural level, develops new values consistent with personal engagement and social cohesion. Table 9.1 lists four values that are evolving from their industrial predecessors but that are more congruent with the affluence and complexity of postindustrialism. More recently, Emery et al. (1974) have proposed an alternative set of values or ideals that they believe to be more effectively adaptive to turbulent environments; these are nurturance, humanization, homonomy*, and beauty. Ultimately, individuals, not society or its organizations, create new values (see Ackoff and Emery 1972). However, society's organizations can facilitate the dissemination of new values. Science-based enterprises and universities have been the most consistent proponents of the new values discussed here. These institutions

TABLE 9.1

Changing Cultural Values in the Transition to Postindustrialism

From	Toward
1. Achievement	Self-actualization
2. Self-control	Self-expression
3. Independence	Interdependence
4. Endurance of distress	Capacity for joy

Source: Emery and Trist (1973), p. 174.

are "leading parts" in the transition to postindustrialism (Emery and Trist 1973). Planned use of the mass media to purvey these values will reinforce what has begun in the leading parts, thus hastening the development of a common ground.

Neither strategy will contribute to increasing society's capacity to regulate itself unless both are pursued on multiple fronts and at all societal levels. This book has pursued these strategies at the level where work is

---

*Emery et al. (1974, p. 61) borrow the term "homonomy" from Angyal and define it as the "wish to be in harmony with a unit one regards as extending beyond this individual self; not independence.

performed because work increasingly has become more than the means for producing goods and services. It is also a means for preparing citizens for more active and effective involvement in societal decision making. A work experience that artificially divides action from purpose, as traditionally designed work does, binds the energies required for social learning and inhibits the contributions that individuals can make to social collectivities. An objective of this book has been to demonstrate through argument and example that divisions between managers and operatives, between planners, problem solvers, objective seekers, and doers are artificial and have been fostered by the practices, assumptions, and values of traditional work design. These divisions dissolve when the nature of work is conceptualized to encourage purposeful behavior at all organizational levels. This book has offered such a reconceptualization of work.

Design principles are not additions to culture; they are representatives of the culture itself. They are artifacts that emerge from the images, language, and concepts that characterize the prevailing world-view. Intimately associated with a world-view, but conceptually distinct, nevertheless, are world hypotheses (Pepper 1942). A world hypothesis originates in an analogy or "root metaphor," which provides a wide-ranging comprehension of the world. Pepper originally developed four world hypotheses: formism, mechanism, contextualism, and organicism. The root metaphor underlying mechanism is the machine, which also underlies the design principles of scientific management. The root metaphor underlying organicism is the organism, most clearly exemplified by the biological cell, an open, dynamic system. This latter metaphor underlies many of the design principles discussed in this book. The reader may do more to realize the objectives of this book by internalizing the organic root metaphor than by remembering any detailed procedures for designing work systems. The nine-step model for sociotechnical analysis presented in Chapter 8 has probably contributed most by encouraging its users to "think organically" when designing in a particular concrete setting. In effect, this type of thinking prepares the ground upon which traditional social science tools as well as techniques of operations research can find new meaning and value.

Pepper (1966), in *Concept and Quality,* extended his earlier work by formulating a fifth world hypothesis called "selectivism," the root metaphor of which was the purposive act.* Design principles based on this root

---

*Purposive behavior can be considered to be a lower order than purposeful behavior. Pepper defined purposive behavior as goal seeking behavior. Ackoff and Emery (1972) make a conceptual advancement by defining purposeful behavior as, at least, objective seeking, if not value

metaphor build upon organic design principles but go considerably beyond them by placing the purposeful human being at the center of the design process. From the latter perspective, the frontiers of design exploration are reversed. Design will advance at the frontiers of the mind of man, through exploration in language, myths, and imagery. The frontiers of design reachable through "outer world" logic will advance no further without exploring the "psycho-logic" of man's inner world.

The following points covered in this book summarize the approach to design developed in it.

1. Design begins from the perspective of a whole unit because the unit of design is more than the sum of its parts. Units are selected that allow a unit's members to perform meaningful primary tasks. A meaningful primary task performed by a unit's members decreases the degree of external regulation that the unit requires because the task itself directs action toward desired outcomes.

2. Design is not the exclusive province of the physical, biological, or social sciences. Design questions are not discipline-based. They arise from a nexus of problems that only manifests itself in a particular concrete setting.

3. The design process proceeds on the assumption that chemico-physical events and human action are best understood when appreciated from a technical and phenomenal viewpoint, respectively. In the first instance, the relationship between the designer and the object designed is nonreflexive; it is, in Jantsch's (1975) words, an "I-it" relationship. In the second instance, the relationship between the designer and the subject "designed" is reflexive; it is, in Jantsch's usage, an "I-thou" relationship in which the designer understands the subject by "taking the role of the other." The two systems, the social and the technical, organized around different principles are then directively correlated when desired outcomes are pursued.

4. A cultural system functions at a higher system level than either a social or technical system and is no less essential in the design process. A cultural system articulates the values that individual members seek and serves as a guide for selecting the constraints for social and technical systems. While the latter two systems are understood from technical and phenomenal

---

(or ideal) seeking behavior. The relationship between goals, objectives, and values has been clarified several times in this book (see p. 114). According to Ackoff and Emery, (pp. 240-41), only a purposeful system "may change its goal in order to better pursue the same objective."

viewpoints, respectively, a cultural system is understood by adopting what Jantsch (1975) describes as an "essential attitude." An essential attitude goes beyond the "I-thou" relationship in which two or more entities communicate but maintain separate identities. An essential attitude establishes union between observer and the observed and focuses on the "we," on the identity of forces acting in the observer and observed. Quoting Jantsch (p. 88): "It is the sense of participation, together with the whole world, in the great order of process called evolution which makes it possible to learn about the universe by inquiring into our inner world." Jantsch considers the essential attitude necessary for the discovery of new values and the conscious design of culture.

5. The language, concepts, and images used in designing work groups or organizations can stifle or liberate human action. Scientific management described the human contribution to the production process in a language that was too restrictive for describing the contributions that humans can make. It used the language of anatomy and physiology, describing activity at the skeleton-muscular level. With such a language, control can be achieved only by further specification of activities, and the greater the specification, the greater the control, reaching a limit in the complete specification of activities. More efficient and effective control can be achieved by an alternative description of activities in a richer language, a metalanguage. Thus, the language of organic systems is a conceptual advancement over scientific management in describing human action in terms of functions rather than activities. The language of purposeful systems is richer yet by describing human action at a higher level of abstraction in terms of goals, objectives, and values, and allowing each unit at the same time more discretion in the way it makes its contributions to the larger whole.

Following a principle of hierarchical control established by Pattee (1973), the designer should seek to optimize the number of constraints on lower-level units and optimize the "loss of detail" in higher-level units. The designer achieves this with a language that provides an alternative description of the same unit; in the first case, a language internal to the unit (structure); in the second case, a language external to the unit for use at a higher system level (function). This is a more complete statement of the principle of minimum specification formulated by Herbst (1974). As Pattee (1973, p. 93) observes, "too much constraint on too many details leads to what we might call bureaucratic 'freezing up' of the system, whereas too few constraints lead to ineffective function, and ultimately to anarchy." A meaningful primary task defines a unit's function. Detailed specification for an organizational unit can be provided by the unit's members if they are provided an appropriate forum to do so.

6. The design process does not end when a fixed set of conditions has been met. Design is an evolutionary process with the focus of contributions shifting between members of higher and parallel organizational levels and the members of the units being designed. In addition to performing the function of boundary maintenance, supervision sets the enabling conditions within which a system may grow to meet its internal and external requirements.

As discussed in Chapter 2, an organic world-view has been evolving for some time. It is unlikely that it will emerge full-blown as the result of a major social upheaval. Rather it will likely show itself strongly in some organizations, while not at all in others, and it will emerge as relevant to the solution of some problems rather than others. Interconnections between organizations and problems will become more frequently apparent as parts of the social environment become increasingly interdependent. As the relevance of the organic world-view is recognized across organizations and problems, its presence will be found with increasing intensity, frequency, and duration. Eventually, a critical mass is reached when the images, language, and concepts of the organic world-view will take on self-generating and mutually reinforcing properties of their own and will rapidly replace those of the mechanical world-view that preceded them.

Complementary to the organic world-view, but beyond it, evolution-wise, is a "telic" world-view guided at its center by man, the purposeful being. A world directed toward an end or *telos*, from the Greek, is a world directed by awareness that actions are taken in the hope of bringing about a consciously desired future. Should a telic world-view emerge, man will realize a potential that has been his since he was first capable of self-reflection, that is, of being able to supersede the forces of physical and biological evolution and become the arrow pointing the way to the future (see Teilhard de Chardin 1959). If such a world-view is accepted, the images, language, and concepts of a culture will become themselves legitimate objects of design to be explored by adopting an "essential attitude." In adopting such an attitude, the design process returns full circle to being more like the "unselfconscious process" by which primitive cultures produce artifacts (Alexander 1964) than to the highly rational design process characteristic of Western society for the last three centuries. This book has addressed the problem of work design in symbols that convey organic and telic metaphors in the hope of hastening the emergence of a world-view that places proper confidence in human possibilities.

BIBLIOGRAPHY

Ackoff, R.L. 1960. "Systems, Organizations, and Interdisciplinary Research." *General Systems Yearbook* 5:1-8.

———. 1969. *A Concept of Corporate Planning.* New York: Wiley-Interscience.

———. and F.E. Emery. 1972. *On Purposeful Systems.* Chicago: Aldine, Atherton.

Alexander, C. 1964. *Notes on the Synthesis of Form.* Cambridge: Harvard University Press.

Allport, G. 1937. *Personality: A Psychological Interpretation.* New York: Henry Holt and Company.

Angyal, A. 1941. *Foundations for a Science of Personality.* New York: Viking Press.

Argyris, C. 1964. *Integrating the Individual and the Organization.* New York: John Wiley and Sons.

Ashby, W.R. 1956. *An Introduction to Cybernetics.* New York: John Wiley and Sons.

Atkinson, J.W. and N.T. Feather. 1966. *A Theory of Achievement Motivation.* New York: John Wiley and Sons.

Baldamus, W. 1961. *Efficiency and Effort.* London: Tavistock Publications.

Bales, R.F. and P.E. Slater. 1955. "Role Differentiation in Small Decision-Making Groups." In *Family, Socialization and Interaction Process,* ed. T. Parsons et al., pp. 259-306. New York: Free Press.

Barnard, C. 1938. *The Functions of the Executive.* Cambridge: Harvard University Press.

Bartlett, F.C. 1932. *Remembering: A Study in Experimental and Social Psychology.* Cambridge: Cambridge University Press.

Bell, D. 1961. *The End of Ideology.* New York: Free Press.

———. 1972. "Labor in the Post-Industrial Society." *Dissent,* Winter: 164-89.

Bendix, R. 1956. *Work and Authority in Industry.* New York: Harper and Row.

Berg, I. 1971. *Education and Jobs: The Great Training Robbery.* New York: Praeger Publishers.

Biganne, J.F., and P.A. Stewart. 1963. *Job Enlargement: A Case Study.* Ames: State University of Iowa, Bureau of Labor and Management, Research Series no. 25, July.

Bion, W.R. 1947-51. Various papers in *Human Relations.* Collected in *Experiences in Groups,* 1961. London: Tavistock Publications.

Blauner, R. 1964. *Alienation and Freedom.* Chicago: University of Chicago Press.

Blumberg, P. 1969. *Industrial Democracy: The Sociology of Participation.* New York: Schocken Books.

Boguslaw, R. 1965. *The New Utopians.* Englewood Cliffs, N.J.: Prentice-Hall.

Boulding, K.E. 1956. *The Image: Knowledge in Life and Society.* Ann Arbor, Mich.: University of Michigan Press.

Braverman, H. 1974. *Labor and Monopoly Capital: The Degradation of Work in the Twentieth Century.* New York: Monthly Review Press.

Browne, A.A. 1965. "Artifacts, Automation, and Human Abilities." In *Operations Research and the Social Sciences,* ed. J. Lawrence. London: Tavistock Publications.

Burden, D.W.E. 1975. "Participative Management as a Basis for Improved Quality of Jobs: The Case of Microwax Department," Shell U.K., Ltd. In L.E. Davis and A.B. Cherns (eds.) *The Quality of Working Life,* Vol. 2. New York: The Free Press.

Butera, F. 1975. "Environmental Factors in Job and Organizational Design: The Case of Olivetti." In L.E. Davis and A.B. Cherns (eds.) *The Quality of Working Life,* Vol. 2. New York: The Free Press.

Cassidy, S.M., ed. 1973. *Elements of Practical Coal Mining.* New York: American Institute of Mining, Metallurgical, and Petroleum Engineers.

Chandler, A.D. 1962. *Strategy and Structure: Chapters in the History of the American Industrial Enterprise.* Cambridge: MIT Press.

Chase, R.B., and N.J. Aquilano. 1973. *Production and Operations Management.* Homewood, Ill.: Richard D. Irwin.

Chein, I. 1972. *The Science of Behavior and the Image of Man.* New York: Basic Books.

Clark, J.V. 1970a. "Task Group Therapy (I): Goals and the Client System" 23: 273-77.

———. 1970b. "Task Group Therapy (II) Intervention and Problems of Practice" 23: 383-403.

Cobb, S., and S. Kasl, 1970. "Blood Pressure Changes in Men Undergoing Job Loss: A Preliminary Report." *Psychosomatic Medicine* 32: 19-38.

Conant, E.H., and M.P. Kilbridge, 1965. "An Interdisciplinary Analysis of Job Enlargement: Technology, Costs, and Behavioral Implications." *Industrial and Labor Relations Review* 18: 377-95.

Dalton, M. 1959. *Men Who Manage.* New York: John Wiley and Sons.

Davis, L.E. 1957. "Toward a Theory of Job Design." *Journal of Industrial Engineering,* 8, 305-9.

Davis, L.E., R.R. Canter, and J. Hoffman. 1955. "Current Job Design Criteria." *Journal of Industrial Engineering* 6: 5-11.

Davis, L.E., and E.S. Valfer. 1965. "Intervening Responses to Change in Supervisor Job Designs." *Occupational Psychology* 39: 171-89.

Davis, L.E., and R. Werling. 1960. "Job Design Factors." *Occupational Psychology* 34: 109.

Derber, M. 1970. *The American Idea of Industrial Democracy, 1865-1965.* Urbana: University of Illinois Press.

Dill, W.R. 1958. "Environment as an Influence on Managerial Autonomy." *Administrative Science Quarterly* 2: 409-43.

Dunphy, D.C. 1972. *The Primary Group: A Handbook for Analysis and Field Research.* New York: Appleton-Century-Crofts.

Ellul, J. 1964. *The Technological Society.* New York: Vintage Books.

Emery, F.E. 1959. *Characteristics of Socio-technical Systems.* Document no. 527. London: Tavistock Institute of Human Relations.

———. 1963. *Some Hypothesis About the Ways in Which Tasks May be More Effectively Put Together to Make Jobs.* London: Tavistock Institute Document T176.

———. 1967. "The Next Thirty Years: Concepts, Methods, and Anticipations." *Human Relations* 20: 199-237.

———. 1972. "*Statement on Socio-Technical Analysis,*" unpublished paper presented to the International Conference on Socio-Technical Systems, Lincoln, England. See also Appendix 5 in P. Hill, *Towards a New Philosophy of Management.* New York: Barnes and Noble Books.

———. 1975. *The Assembly Line: Its Logic and Our Future.* Occasional papers in Continuing Education no. 7. Canberra: Australian National University.

——— et al. 1974. *Futures We're In.* Canberra: Centre for Continuing Education, Australian National University.

Emery, F.E., and M. Emery. 1974. *Participative Design: Work and Community Life,* Canberra: Centre for Continuing Education, Australian National University.

Emery, F.E., and E. Thorsrud., 1975. *Democracy at Work.* Canberra: Centre for Continuing Education, Australian National University.

Emery, F.E., and E.L. Trist. 1960. "Socio-Technical Systems." In *Management Science, Models, and Techniques,* eds. C.W. Churchman and M. Verhurst. London: Pergamon Press, pp. 83-97.

Emery, F.E., and E.L. Trist. 1965. "The Causal Texture of Organizational Environments." *Human Relations* 18: 21-32.

Emery, F.E., and E.L. Trist. 1969. "Sociotechnical Systems," in *Systems Thinking,* ed. F.E. Emery, Baltimore: Penguin Books.

Emery, F.E., and E.L. Trist. 1973. *Towards a Social Ecology: Contextual Appreciation of the Future in the Present.* London: Plenum Press.

Etzioni, A. 1964. *Modern Organizations.* Englewood Cliffs, N.J.: Prentice-Hall.

Evered, R.D. 1974. "Conceptualizing the 'Future': Implications for Strategic Management in a Turbulent Environment." *Dissertation Abstracts International* 34, no. 7.

———. 1976. "A Typology of Explicative Models," *Technological Forecasting and Social Change,* 9.

Fairbairn,W.R.D. 1952. *Psychoanalytic Studies of the Personality.* London: Tavistock Publications.

Faltenmeyer, E. 1974. "It's Back to the Pits for Coal's Future." *Fortune* 89 (June): 137-39, 244-52.

Faunce, W.A. 1958. "Automation in the Automobile Industry: Some Consequences for In-Plant Social Structure." *American Sociological Review* 23: 401-47.

Ford, R.N. 1969. *Motivation Through the Work Itself.* New York: American Management Association.

———. 1973. "Job Enrichment Lessons at A.T. & T." *Harvard Business Review,* January-February, pp. 96-106.

Frankl, V. 1959. *Man's Search for Meaning: An Introduction to Logotherapy.* Boston: Beacon Press.

French, J.R.P., J. Tupper, and E. Mueller. 1965. *Work Load of University Professors.* Cooperative Research Project No. 2171, U.S. Office of Education, University of Michigan, Ann Arbor.

Friedmann, J. 1973. *Retracking America: A Theory of Transactive Planning.* Garden City, N.Y.: Anchor Press/Doubleday.

Galbraith, J.K. 1967. *The New Industrial State.* Boston: Houghton Mifflin.

Giedion, S. 1948. *Mechanization Takes Command.* New York: Oxford University Press.

Gilbreth, F. 1911. *Motion Study.* New York: D. Van Nostrand.

Goldstein, K. 1939. *The Organism: A Holistic Approach to Biology Derived From Pathological Data in Man.* New York: American Book Company.

Gulowsen, J. 1972. "A Measure of Work-Group Autonomy." In *Design of Jobs,* ed. L.E. Davis and J.C. Taylor. Middlesex, England: Penguin Books.

Hackman, J.R., and E.E. Lawler, III. 1971. "Employee Reactions to Job Characteristics." *Journal of Applied Psychology* 55: 259-86.

Hatt, H. 1968. *Cybernetics and the Image of Man.* Nashville: Abington Press.

Hayek, F. 1969. "The Primacy of the Abstract." In *Beyond Reductionism,* ed. Arthur Koestler and J.R. Smythies. New York: Macmillan.

Heider, F. 1958. *The Psychology of Interpersonal Relations.* New York: Science Editions, John Wiley and Sons.

Herbst, P. 1962. *Autonomous Work Group Functioning.* London: Tavistock Publications.

———. 1970. *Behavioral Worlds: The Study of Single Cases.* London: Tavistock Publications.

———. 1974. *Socio-Technical Design: Strategies in Multidisciplinary Research.* London: Tavistock Publications.

Herrick, N.Q., and M. Maccoby. 1972. "Humanizing Work: A Priority Goal for the 1970s." In L.E. Davis and A.B. Cherns (eds). *The Quality of Working Life,* Vol. 1. New York: The Free Press.

Herzberg, F. 1968. "One More Time: How Do You Motivate Employees?" *Harvard Business Review* 46: 53-62.

Herzberg, F.W., B. Mausner, and B.B. Snyderman. 1959. *Motivation to Work.* 2d. ed. New York: John Wiley and Sons.

Hill, P. 1971. *Towards a New Philosophy of Management*. Epping, Essex: Gower Press.

Hill, R. 1972. "The Term Effort at Motorola." *International Management* 27: 43-45.

Hughes, C.L. 1965. *Goal Setting.* New York: American Managment Association.

Huse, E., and M. Beer. 1971. "Eclectic Approach to Organizational Development." *Harvard Business Review* 49 (September-October).

Ingall, E.J. 1965. "A Review of Assembly Line Balancing." *Journal of Industrial Engineering* 16, no. 4.

Israel, J. 1971. *Alienation: From Marx to Modern Sociology*. Boston: Allyn and Bacon.

Jantsch, E. 1975. *Design for Evolution: Self-Organization and Planning in the Life of Human Systems*. New York: George Braziller.

Jaques, E. 1953. "On the Dynamics of Social Structure." *Human Relations,* 6: 3-24. Reprinted as "Social Systems as a Defense Against Persecutory and Depressive Anxiety," In *New Directions in Psychoanalysis.* Eds. M. Klein, P. Heimann, and R.E. Money-Kyrle. London: Tavistock Publications, 1955, 478-98.

Jenkins, C. D. 1971. "Psychologic and Social Precursors of Coronary Disease. *New England Journal of Medicine* 284: 244-55.

———. 1973. *Job Power: Blue and White Collar Democracy*. Garden City: Doubleday.

Katz, D., and R.L. Kahn. 1966. *The Social Psychology of Organizations*. New York: John Wiley and Sons.

Kelman, H.C. 1961. "Processes of Opinion Change." In *The Planning of Change,* ed. W. G. Bennis, K.D. Benne, and P. Chin. New York: Holt, Rinehart, and Winston.

Ketchum, L. 1975. "A Case Study of Diffusion." In L.E. Davis and A.B. Cherns (eds.) *The Quality of Working Life,* Vol. 2. New York: The Free Press.

Kilbridge, M.D. 1960. "Reduced Costs Through Job Enlargement: A Case." *Journal of Business of the University of Chicago* 33: 357-62.

King, S.H., and S. Cobb. 1958. "Psychosocial Factors in the Epidemiology of Rheumatoid Arthritis." *Journal of Chronic Diseases* 7: 466-75.

Klein, M. 1932. *The Psycho-analysis of Children*. London: Hogarth Press.

———. 1948. *Contributions to Psychoanalysis 1921-1945*. London: Hogarth.

———. 1959. "Our Adult World and Its Roots in Infancy." *Human Relations* 12: 291-303.

Kluckholn, C. 1951. "Value and Value-Orientations in the Theory of Action." In T. Parsons and E.A. Shils (eds.) *Towards a General Theory of Action*. Cambridge: Harvard University Press.

Koestler, A. 1967. *The Ghost of the Machine*. Chicago: Henry Regnery.

Kohl, H.R. 1969. *The Open Classroom*. New York: Random House.

Kornhauser, A. 1965. *Mental Health of the Industrial Worker*. New York: John Wiley and Sons.

Lawler, E.E., and J. Suttle, 1972. "A Causal Correlational Test of the Need-Hierarchy Concept." *Organizational Behavior and Human Performance* 7: 265-87.

Lazlo, E. 1972. *Introduction to Systems Philosophy: Toward a New Paradigm of Contemporary Thought*. New York: Harper Torchbooks.

Lewin, K. 1935. *A Dynamic Theory of Personality*. New York: McGraw-Hill.

———. 1947. "Frontiers in Group Dynamics." *Human Relations* 1: 2-38.

———. 1951. "Vorsatz, Wille, and Bedurfnis." *Psychol. Forsch* 7 (1926): 330-85. English translation by D. Rapoport (ed.), in *Organization and Pathology of Thought*. New York: Columbia University Press.

Lewin, K., T. Dembo, L. Festinger, and P. Sears. 1944. "Level of Aspiration." In *Personality and Behavior Disorders*, ed. J. McV. Hunt, vol. 1. New York: Ronald Press.

Lewis, H. 1944. "An Experimental Study of the Role of the Ego in Work." *Journal of Experimental Psychology* 34: 113-26.

Maccoby, M. 1972. Introduction to H.L. Sheppard and N.Q. Herrick, *Where Have All the Robots Gone?* New York: Free Press.

March, J.G., and H.A. Simon. 1958. *Organizations.* New York: John Wiley and Sons.

Marglin, S.A. 1971. *What Do Bosses Do? The Origins and Functions of Hierarchy in Capitalist Production.* Cambridge: Harvard Institute of Economic Research, Discussion Paper, No. 222, November.

Margolis, B., and W. Kroes. 1974. "Work and the Health of Man." in *Work and the Quality of Life,* ed. James O'Toole, pp. 133-44. Cambridge: MIT Press.

Marrow, A.J., D.G. Bowers, and S.E. Seashore, 1967. *Management by Participation.* New York: Harper and Row.

Marx, K. 1961. "Economic and Philosophical Manuscripts." In *Marx's Concept of Man.* ed. E. Fromm. New York: Unger.

Maslow, A. 1943. "A Theory of Human Motivation." *Psychological Review* (July): 370-96.

McLuhan, M. 1964. *Understanding Media.* New York: McGraw-Hill.

McWhinney, W.H. 1960. "Organizational Form, Decision-Modalities, and the Environment." *Human Relations* 21: 269-81.

Meissner, M. 1969. *Technology and the Worker: Technical Demands and Social Processes in Industry.* San Francisco: Chandler Publishing.

———. 1971. "The Long Arm of the Job: A Study of Work and Leisure." *Industrial Relations* 10: 239-60.

Melman, S. 1958. *Decision-Making and Productivity.* Oxford: Basil Blackwell and Mott.

Menzies, I.E.P. 1960. "A Case-Study in the Functioning of Social Systems as a Defense Against Anxiety." *Human Relations,* 13: 95-121. Reprinted 1961 as Tavistock Pamphlet No. 3. London: Tavistock Publications.

Mesarovic, M.D., and D. Macko. 1969. "Scientific Theory of Hierarchical Systems." In *Hierarchical Structures,* ed. L.L. Whyte, A.G. Wilson, and D. Wilson. New York: American Elsevier Publishing.

Mill, J.S. 1963. *Essays on Politics and Culture.* New York: G. Himmelfarb.

Miller, E.J. 1959. "Technology, Territory, and Time: The Internal Differentiation of Complex Production Systems." *Human Relations* 22, no. 3

———. 1975. "Socio-Technical Systems in Weaving, 1953-1970: A Follow-up Study." *Human Relations* 28: 349-486.

Miller, E.J. and A.K. Rice. 1967. *Systems of Organization.* London: Tavistock Publications.

Miller, J.G. 1965. "Living Systems: Structure and Process." *Behavioral Science* 10: 337-39.

Mumford, L. 1970. *The Myth of the Machine: The Pentagon of Power.* New York: Harcourt, Brace, Jovanovich.

Ozbekhan, H. 1971. "Planning and Human Action." In *Hierarchically Organized Systems in Theory and Practice,* ed. P.A.. Weiss. New York: Hafner Publishing.

Palmore, E. 1969. "Predicting Longevity: A Follow-up Controlling for Age." *Gerontologist* 9: 247-50.

Parker, S. 1971. *The Future of Work and Leisure.* New York: Praeger Publishers.

Parsons, T. 1960. *Structure and Process in Modern Societies.* Glencoe, Ill.: Free Press.

Pattee, H.H. 1973. "The Physical Basis and Origin of Hierarchical Control." In *Hierarchy Theory: The Challenge of Complex Systems,* H.H. Pattee (ed.). New York: George Braziller.

Paul, W.J., Jr., K.B. Robertson, and F.W. Herzberg. 1969. "Job Enrichment Pays Off." *Harvard Business Review* 47: 61-78.

Pepitone, A. 1967. "Self, Social Environment, and Stress." In *Psychological Stress,* ed. M.H. Appley and D. Trumbull. New York: Appleton-Century-Crofts.

Pepper, S.C. 1942. *World Hypotheses.* Berkeley: University of California Press.

———. 1966. *Concept and Quality.* La Salle, Ill.: Open Court Publishing Company.

Perrow, C.B. 1965. "Hospitals: Technology, Structure and Goals." In *Handbook of Organizations,* ed. J.G. March, pp. 913-19. Chicago: Rand McNally

———. 1970. *Organizational Analysis: A Sociological View.* Belmont, Calif.: Brooks/Cole Publishing.

Peters, R.S. 1958. *The Concept of Motivation.* London: Routledge and Kegan Paul.

Polanyi, M. 1958. *Personal Knowledge: Towards a Post-Critical Philosophy.* New York: Harper and Row.

Pollack, A.B. 1954. *Forms of Retail Organization.* London: Working Press. Tavistock Institute.

Porter, L.W., 1962. "Job Attitudes in Management: I. Perceived Deficiencies in Need Fulfillment as a Function of Job Level." *Journal of Applied Psychology* 46: 375-84.

Porter, L.W., and E.E. Lawler, III. 1967. *Managerial Attitudes and Performance.* Homewood, Ill.: Richard D. Irwin.

Powers, W.T. 1973. *Behavior: The Control of Perception. 1973.* Chicago: Aldine Publishing.

Reeves, T.K., and B.A. Turner, 1972. "A Theory of Organization and Behavior in Batch Production Factories." *Administrative Science Quarterly* 17: 81-98.

Reich, C. 1970. *The Greening of America.* New York: Random House.

Rice, A.K. 1953. "Productivity and Social Organization in an Indian Weaving Shed: An Examination of the Socio-technical System of an Experimental Automatic Loom Shed." *Human Relations,* VI, 4, 297-329.

———. 1958. *Productivity and Social Organization.* London: Tavistock Publications.

———. 1965. *Learning for Leadership.* London: Tavistock Publications.

Riskin, C. 1974. "Incentive Systems and Work Motivations: The Experience in China." *Working Papers for a New Society* 1, no. 4, Winter.

Ritti, R.R. 1971. *The Engineer in the Industrial Corporation.* New York: Columbia University Press.

Roy, D. 1955. "Gains and Losses in Piecework." Chapter 5, in *Money and Motivation,* ed. William F. Whyte. New York: Harper Torchbooks.

Ryan, T.A. 1970. *Intentional Behavior.* New York: Ronald Press.

Sayles, L.R. 1964. *Managerial Behavior.* New York: McGraw-Hill.

Schacht, R. 1970. *Alienation.* New York: Doubleday.

Schein, E.H. 1972. *Process Consultation.* Reading, Mass.: Addison-Wesley.

Schultzenberger, M.P. 1954. "A Tentative Classification of Goal-Seeking Behaviors." *Journal of Mental Science* 100:97-102. Also in F.E. Emery, ed. 1969. *Systems Thinking.* Baltimore: Penguin Books.

Seeman, M. 1959. "On the Meaning of Alienation." *American Sociological Review.* 24: 783-91.

Selznick, P. 1957. *Leadership in Administration.* Evanston, Ill.: Row-Peterson.

Sennett, R., and J. Cobb, 1972. *The Hidden Injuries of Class.* New York: Alfred Knopf.

Shepard, J.M. 1971. *Automation and Alienation.* Cambridge: MIT Press.

Sheppard, H.L., and N.Q. Herrick. 1972. *Where Have All the Robots Gone?* New York: Free Press.

Simon, H. 1962. "The Architecture of Complexity." *Proceedings of the American Philosophical Society* 106.

Smith, A. 1937. *The Wealth of Nations,* ed. Edwin Cannon, Book I. New York: Modern Library.

Steers, R.M., and L.W. Porter. 1975. *Motivation and Work Behavior.* New York: McGraw-Hill.

Stinchecombe, A.L. 1959. "Bureaucratic and Craft Administration of Production: A Comparative Study." *Administrative Science Quarterly* 4: 168-87.

Sommerhoff, G. 1950. *Analytical Biology.* New York: Oxford University Press.

———. 1969. "The Abstract Characteristics of Living Systems." In *Systems Thinking,* ed. F.E. Emery. Baltimore: Penguin Books.

Susman, G.I. 1970a. "The Concept of Status Congruence as a Basis to Predict Task Allocations in Autonomous Work Groups." *Administrative Science Quarterly* 15: 161-75.

———. 1970b. "The Impact of Automation on Work Group Autonomy and Task Specialization." *Human Relations* 23: 507-77.

———. 1973. "Job Enlargement: Effects of Culture on Response." *Industrial Relations* 12: 1-15.

Susser, M. 1967. "Causes of Peptic Ulcer: A Selective Epidemiologic Review." *Journal of Chronic Diseases* 20: 435-56.

Tausky, C. 1973. "Meanings of Work: Marx, Maslow, and Steam Irons." Paper presented at American Sociological Association Meeting. August.

Taylor, F.W. 1911. *Principles of Scientific Management.* New York: Harper and Brothers.

Thompson, J.D. 1967. *Organizations in Action.* New York: McGraw-Hill.

Thorsrud, E., and F.E. Emery, 1964. *Industrielt Demokrati.* Oslo: Universitetsforlaget. Published in English: F.E. Emery and E. Thorsrud. 1969. *Form and Content in Industrial Democracy.* London: Tavistock Publications.

———. 1969. *Møt en ny Bedriftorganisasjon.* English Title: *New Forms of Work Organization.* Oslo: Tannum.

Toffler, A. 1970. *Future Shock*. New York: Random House.

Tolman, E.C. 1932. *Purposive Behavior in Animals and Men*. New York: Century.

Tolman, E.C., and E. Brunswick. 1935. "The Organism and the Causal Texture of the Environment." *Psychological Review* 42: 43-77.

Trist, E.L. 1973 "A Socio-Technical Critique of Scientific Managment." In *Meaning and Control: Essays in Social Aspects of Science and Technology*, ed. D.O. Edge and J.N. Wolfe. London: Tavistock Publications.

———. 1974. "Work Improvement and Industrial Democracy." Paper prepared for the Conference of the Commission of the European Communities on Work Organization, Technical Development and Motivation of the Individual. September.

Trist, E.L., and K.W. Bamforth. 1951. "Some Social and Psychological Consequences of the Longwall Method of Coal-Getting." *Human Relations* 4: 3-38.

Trist, E.L., G.W. Higgins, H. Murray, and A.B. Pollock. 1963. *Organizational Choice: Capabilities of Groups at the Coal Face Under Changing Technologies*. London: Tavistock Publications.

Trist, E.L., G.R. Brown, and G.I. Susman. 1975. "The Experiment in Autonomous Group Working at Rushton Mine," prepared for Labor/ Management Steering Committee of Rushton Mining Company, March.

United States Department of Commerce. 1952. *Consumer Population Reports: Consumer Income Series*, No. 9, p. 60.

———. 1971. *Consumer Population Reports: Consumer Income Series*, no. 80, p. 60.

van Beinum, A. 1963. *Work Reorganization in the Telecommunications Industry*. Doctoral Dissertation. Rotterdam: Erasmus University.

Vickers, G. 1965. *The Art of Judgment*. New York: Basic Books.

———. 1968. *Value Systems and Social Process*. London: Tavistock Publications.

Von Bertalanffy, L. 1950. "The Theory of Open Systems in Physics and Biology." *Science* 11: 23-29.

Vroom, V.H. 1964. *Work and Motivation.* New York: John Wiley and Sons.

Walker, C.R. 1957. *Toward the Automatic Factory: A Case Study of Men and Machines.* New Haven: Yale University Press.

Walton, R.E. 1972. "How to Counter Alienation at the Plant." *Harvard Business Review,* November-December, pp. 70-81.

Walton, R.E., J.M. Dutton, and H.G. Fitch. 1966. "A Study of Conflict in the Process, Structure, and Attitudes of Lateral Relationships." In *Some Theories of Organization,* ed. A.H. Rubenstein and C.J. Harberstroh, revised. Homewood, Ill.: Irwin.

Weed, E.D., Jr. 1971. "Job Enrichment 'Cleans up' at Texas Instruments." In *New Perspectives in Job Enrichment,* ed. John R. Maher. New York: Van Nostrand Reinhold.

Westerlund, Gunner. 1952. *Group Leadership.* Stockholm: Nordisk Rotogravyr.

White, R.W. 1959. "Motivation Reconsidered: The Concept of Competence." *Psychological Review* 66: 297-333.

Whyte, W.F. 1955. *Money and Motivation.* New York: Harper and Row.

Winnicott, D.W. 1958. *Collected Papers.* London: Tavistock Publications.

Wolfbein, S.L. 1971. *Work in American Society.* Glenview, Ill.: Scott, Foresman.

Work in America: Report of a Special Task Force to the Secretary of Health, Education and Welfare. Cambridge: MIT Press, 1972.

Zander, A. 1971. *Motives and Goals in Groups.* New York: Academic Press.

AUTHOR INDEX

SUBJECT INDEX

ABOUT THE AUTHOR

Gerald I. Susman is Associate Professor of Organizational Behavior at the College of Business Administration, The Pennsylvania State University.

Professor Susman's interest in work design and its economic and psychological consequences began in the mid-1960s when he commenced his doctoral studies at the Graduate School of Management, University of California, Los Angeles. It was there that he was introduced to the socio-technical systems approach for improving the quality of working life. The Graduate School of Management had recently inaugurated the first graduate program in socio-technical systems in the United States.

Professor Susman received his Ph.D. from the University of California, Los Angeles in 1968. His dissertation concerned the functioning of autonomous work groups in continuous process industries. Since joining The Pennsylvania State University faculty, Professor Susman has undertaken a survey study of the impact of automation on work quality sponsored by funds received from the National Science Foundation. More recently, he has been collaborating with union and management in exploring methods for improving the quality of work in the American coal mining industry.

Professor Susman is also the author of several book chapters as well as articles in such professional journals as *Administrative Science Quarterly, Human Relations,* and *Industrial Relations.*

RELATED TITLES
Published by
Praeger Special Studies

IMPROVING PRODUCTIVITY AND THE QUALITY OF WORK LIFE
Thomas G. Cummings
Edmond S. Molloy

THE SMALL FIRM OWNER-MANAGER: Entrepreneurial Behavior and Management Practice
John Deeks

STATE GOVERNMENT PRODUCTIVITY: The Environment for Improvement
Edgar G. Crane
Bernard F. Lentz
Jay M. Shafritz

WORKER MILITANCY AND ITS CONSEQUENCES, 1965-75: Directions in Western Industrial Relations
edited by Solomon Barkin